# Hard News

**Recent Titles in**
**Contributions in Women's Studies**

Women's Rights in France
*Dorothy McBride Stetson*

Charity, Challenge, and Change: Religious Dimensions of the Mid-Nineteenth
Century Women's Movement in Germany
*Catherine M. Prelinger*

Woman as Mediatrix: Essays on Nineteenth-Century European Women Writers
*Avriel H. Goldberger, editor*

Women and American Foreign Policy: Lobbyists, Critics, and Insiders
*Edward P. Crapol, editor*

From Ladies to Women: The Organized Struggle for Woman's Rights in the
Reconstruction Era
*Israel Kugler*

Unlikely Heroines: Nineteenth-Century American Women Writers and the
Woman Question
*Ann R. Shapiro*

Beyond the Public/Domestic Dichotomy: Contemporary Perspectives on
Women's Public Lives
*Janet Sharistanian, editor*

Speaking of Friendship: Middle-Class Women and Their Friends
*Helen Gouldner and Mary Symons Strong*

Sex and Pay in the Federal Government: Using Job Evaluation Systems to
Implement Comparable Worth
*Doris M. Werwie*

New Dimensions of Spirituality: A Biracial and Bicultural Reading of the Novels
of Toni Morrison
*Karla F. C. Holloway and Stephanie Demetrakopoulos*

Women and Music in Cross-Cultural Perspective
*Ellen Koskoff, editor*

Venomous Woman: Fear of the Female in Literature
*Margaret Hallissy*

# HARD NEWS
## Women in Broadcast Journalism

DAVID H. HOSLEY AND
GAYLE K. YAMADA

CONTRIBUTIONS IN WOMEN'S STUDIES,
NUMBER 85

Greenwood Press

NEW YORK
WESTPORT, CONNECTICUT
LONDON

**Library of Congress Cataloging-in-Publication Data**

Hosley, David H.
    Hard news.

    (Contributions in women's studies, ISSN 0147-104X ;
no. 85)
    Bibliography: p.
    Includes index.
    1. Broadcast journalism--United States.
2. Women in journalism--United States.   3. Women
in the broadcasting industry--United States.
I. Yamada, Gayle K.   II. Title.   III. Series.
PN4888.B74H67     1987       070.1 ′9 ′088042       87-10712
ISBN 0-313-25477-X (lib. bdg. : alk. paper)

British Library Cataloging in Publication Data is available.

Library of Congress Catalog Card Number: 87-10712
ISBN: 0-313-25477-X
ISSN: 0147-104X

First published in 1987

Greenwood Press, Inc.
88 Post Road West, Westport, Connecticut 06881

Printed in the United States of America

The paper used in this book complies with the
Permanent Paper Standard issued by the National
Information Standards Organization (Z39.48-1984).

10  9  8  7  6  5  4  3  2

For our parents
Tom and Virginia Hosley
Gordon and Kiyo Yamada

# Contents

# Preface

This book is an attempt to tell the story of women in broadcast news. It is an account that involves us all, for in the United States, where the media have such great impact, the evolution of women in news has both contributed to and reflected changes in our society.

Initially, women had a hard time even getting a chance to do news on radio. Most of those on the air in the early days of radio were men. The relatively small number of women heard were almost exclusively on entertainment broadcasts. A few women hosted programs targeted at homemakers. These shows were often a hybrid of entertainment and information. But then, as World War II broke out, more opportunities opened up for women. Abroad, a few women who were in the right places at the right times got the opportunity to broadcast when male reporters were not available or didn't want to go on the air.

The shortage of men at home during the war also forced broadcasting outlets to hire women. Local stations offered greater opportunities for women, not only because there were more of them, but because they were more likely to take whoever was available. The networks were slower to open their ranks to women. Many women got hired at the lower levels, but few were on the air regularly.

It was not until the civil rights movement and the women's movement of the 1960s and 1970s that large numbers of women began to gain equality in broadcast news. For the most part, radio and television news operations reacted to the changes in society, hiring and promoting women as they were required to by new laws. At a time when the broadcast media could have had a tremendous impact by leading the nation in their attitudes toward and treatment of women, they tended to follow.

Most opportunities for women in television news came in areas in which men were not interested. Often these women were on broadcasts shown in "fringe" times—early mornings or weekends. But from there, a few women integrated the remaining male bastions, substituting as anchors on the net-work weekday evening news programs and taking positions in board rooms. Still, few women have been able to crack the top network spots on the air or top executive jobs.

Our initial aim is to identify the newswomen who were pioneers in radio and television's developing years. A surprising number of women fought to expand their roles in broadcast news over the last half century. Though we have identified hundreds of women who participated in the development of radio and television news, no doubt there are omissions. The women whose stories we tell include those whose audiences were small as well as those who broadcast to millions, for they all contributed to what women in radio and television news are today. In later chapters, we focus on the women whose careers have had the most impact on radio and television and influenced American society. Most of those we profile were trailblazers—women like Sigrid Schultz, the first female radio foreign correspondent; Helen Sioussat, the first woman network news executive; Dorothy Fuldheim, the first woman to anchor a local television news program; and network correspondent Pauline Frederick, the dean of women electronic journalists. The careers of others are illustrative of their times and represent important aspects of the paths of women in broadcast news. Shirley Wershba, for example, got her start as a desk assistant at the CBS Radio Network during World War II, moved because of her husband's career, dropped out of the business to raise a family, then returned in television news. The challenges all these women faced in their struggle to do hard news might provide insight for journalists who see their circumstances today as unique. And perhaps from these earlier experiences, women broadcast journalists today can look beyond Barbara Walters in searching for role models.

Some of the issues that have faced American women in broadcast news are specific to their industry, but for the most part, women in this business have experienced the same problems as women in the workplace in general. For instance, newswomen on the air have faced discrimination because of their voices. From the beginning, those in charge usually felt women's voices did not carry authority and therefore women should not deliver the news. Today that notion has been largely discredited, but now women in television news are dealing with the question of aging. Many women fear they will not be allowed to gray on the air as their male counterparts do. The issues of equal pay, equal opportunity, and sexual harassment have faced women in most fields, including broadcast news. The women radio pioneers in the 1930s knew they were being paid less than men, for women in those days were not expected to support families. But that historical pattern has continued through modern times; a U.S. Census Bureau report, released in March 1987, found that although nearly 55 percent of adult American women work outside the home, they still tend to earn less than men.

Opportunities have always existed for women in broadcast news, but often only if men did not want them. It was not until affirmative action in the 1970s that large numbers of women were hired and promoted in a wide variety of jobs. Although many women were able to advance because of new legislation, they have not yet achieved equality because they still are not in the most powerful positions in broadcast news. At the local level, few women are news directors in major markets; at the networks, there are no female presidents. The swift advances by women in the 1970s no longer are being made, and particularly now, when the broadcast media are in a period of retrenchment, progress is likely to be slow.

Women in broadcast news have had to deal with problems in the home brought about by their profession. Broadcasting tends to attract ambitious and often insecure people. It is an extremely demanding business, with constant deadlines and competition. Understandably, the job puts a strain on personal relationships; there is an unusually high rate of alcoholism and divorce among broadcasters. The changing roles of women in broadcast news have meant changes in their traditional roles in society. Fifty years ago, a woman probably would have quit her job to follow her husband; today, that is no longer true. In examining the lives of women in radio and television news, we look at how they have juggled their careers and families, and at what cost. The early women were unusual in that they chose to pursue careers, often sacrificing personal happiness, while women today want professional success and personal satisfaction.

The number of women in broadcast news has exploded in the last twenty years. In writing about these more recent times, we shifted our focus from individuals to the challenges that face both women and men in the business today, for her story is his story, too. We hope that others will build on our initial account, and as the history expands, there will be greater opportunity for interpretation.

# Acknowledgments

Any project of this magnitude involves dozens of people who generously have given of their time and thoughts. We would especially like to thank Jules Dundes, director of the Mass Media Institute at Stanford University, whose invitation to teach there provided us with a marvelous setting in which to conduct our research. Adrian Arima, a true friend, literally went to the ends of the earth to provide us a place to live at Stanford. Janet Yamada Soto, friend and sister, also supplied shelter and support, and gave new meaning to the words, "in care of," when she patiently accepted delivery of ninety-nine boxes of our belongings as we moved back to California.

# Hard News

# 1 The Early Days

In the beginning of broadcasting, the medium itself was news. That voices hundreds of miles away could be heard on wireless radios in the early 1900s was considered a miracle. Some of the voices on experimental broadcasts by Ernst Alexanderson, Reginald Fessenden, and Lee de Forest were female, but no women gave the news. Singing and acting and, later, giving cleaning tips and recipes and reading commercials were a woman's place in radio's first decades. Changing that role took a war, an act of Congress, and a domestic revolution. And the evolution is not yet complete.

Women gave information on American radio in the 1920s as radio came into its own. But they almost exclusively were heard on "women's shows," like that of Marjorie Mills, a writer for the *Boston Herald*'s women's pages who broadcast on WEEI from a test kitchen at the *Herald*. For the next thirty years, most of the women who broadcast were on programs designed for homemakers. Nearly every station in America had at least one women's program daily, usually in mid-morning or early afternoon, when women were most likely to be listening. These radio programs "for the homemaker provided a vital element of companionship while at the same time they fulfilled some of her educational, informational and emotional needs."[1]

Most of the "homemaker" programs were talk shows, lasting from fifteen minutes to an hour. But along with the household tips and recipes came advice and sometimes news. Some women who started in this area of radio went on to become newscasters, and a few became known nationally. Those who were on the air during the thirties and forties were advised to have "a natural, clear voice that registers well," a college education or its equivalent, writing and public speaking experience, common sense, a pleasant personality, confidence; to be outgoing and able to "think on your feet."[2] Not many other qualifications seemed to be needed; being in the right place at the right time was just as important.

We're beginning our discussion of women in broadcast news with several of these women who spanned the "companion" category and the news area. For one thing, they show where women started as some of them moved into news jobs. They also show that "infotainment," the cross between information and entertainment, has a long history in broadcasting and that women's struggle for equality on the air today has its roots in radio a half century ago.

## WOMEN'S HOME COMPANIONS

### Ruth Crane: Modern Woman

Ruth Crane started a twenty-six-year career in broadcasting when she assumed the dual roles of women's editor and commercial editor of WJR, Detroit, in 1929. Born Ruth Franklin in Springfield, Missouri, she attended Northwestern University School of Journalism, teaching shorthand and typing at a nearby business college on the side. Crane's first job was in advertising at Hart Publishing Company. She married an advertising man and, after he died, got into radio.

Crane began at WJR as a commercial writer. The job soon evolved into her own program, a six-days-a-week broadcast called "Mrs. Page's Home Economies." It was common in those days for a broadcast to carry a fictitious name, such as "Mrs. Page." If the hostess left, her successor would use the same name; station management—and sponsors—hoped listeners would continue to be loyal to "Mrs. Page," not to the individual who portrayed her.

For all her duties at the station, Crane was paid $30 a week; by the time she left in 1944, she was earning $85 a week. She knew that "men on the air with far less responsibilities were paid much better, of course."[3] But as one of the few women in the field, at a time when women were not in the general work force in the numbers they are today, Crane had little standard of comparison for salaries. It was not uncommon in those early days for women to earn much less than men, for they were not thought of as having to support families. And though the role of women in the work force would change in the coming decades, the issue of pay parity—in broadcasting as well as in American society in general—would continue to be a point of discrimination.

Crane left WJR for WMAL, Washington, D.C., where she was women's activities director and hostess of the daily "Modern Woman" program. When television got started in Washington, a TV version of her radio show was broadcast on WMAL-TV, beginning in 1947. "I got into TV simply by being there—that's all. And naturally, they wanted to use the same people as long as they could. They didn't want to put on another staff to operate TV—we all doubled up."[4] Crane's duties included writing the skits, acting them out, and even modeling fashions. Along that line, a 1948 article in

*Broadcasting* magazine described her as having a "slim figure, sparkling eyes, and vivacious personality," with a "disarmingly frank habit of telling her age—she's forty-five."[5]

Crane lived her modern woman image with a commuter marriage, a notion practically unheard of in 1946 when she wed a manufacturer's representative, William H. Schaefer. He lived in Detroit, she in Washington. "We have a wonderful arrangement. . . . He has his work there and I have my work here. We see each other whenever we can and have a perfectly grand time together. Neither of us gets in the other's way, and we're both pleased with the setup."[6]

Crane was the founder and national president of the Association of Women Broadcasters, which was the predecessor of American Women in Radio and Television. She also headed the Women's Advertising Club of Washington and the American Newspaper Women's Club and was vice president of the Women's National Press Club.

### Mary Margaret McBride: Not a Grandmother

By far the most famous personality to blend entertainment and information successfully on a women's show was Mary Margaret McBride. She turned to radio after gaining recognition as a magazine and newspaper journalist. After the Depression caused a drop in fees for her print pieces, McBride won an audition in 1934 over fifty others to become "Martha Deane" on WOR, New York. For $25 a week, she portrayed a grandmotherly type who dispensed advice daily to listeners. It was a guise she could not keep up; after only a few broadcasts, she interrupted the program to tell her audience that, "I am not a grandmother at all, and I have no grandchildren, and from now on I intend to talk about myself," which she did to an adoring listenership.[7]

McBride was born in November of 1899 on a Missouri farm. She majored in journalism at the University of Missouri, earning her degree in two-and-a-half years while working part time on a local newspaper. She thought a career was more important than marriage and was hired by an editor of the *Cleveland Plain Dealer*, who told her she would be paid $35 a week. Again, the wage difference between men and women: The editor also told her that $35 was probably more than any woman reporter was worth, and if she wasn't, out the door she would be. McBride left the Cleveland paper of her own volition, taking a job as a publicist for the Interchurch World Movement so she could be in New York. Then she moved on to the *New York Evening Mail* as a feature writer, which led to magazine work and eventually to radio.

The forty-five-minute-long "Martha Deane Program" usually started out with interviews. McBride talked to everyone from midgets to the Dali Lama of Tibet, with a lot of authors and actors in between. She would talk about where she had been the day before and what she was reading, speaking with a bit of an Ozark accent. She conversed as though she were sitting with you in your living room or kitchen. McBride also was very interested in food and had the physique to show for it. Most importantly, she had the ability to mention her sponsors frequently and in such a way that most listeners couldn't tell where the show stopped and the commercial started.

CBS offered McBride a network show in 1940, and she took it. But it was only fifteen minutes each weekday, and she felt more at home in the longer format, so the following year she moved to WEAF and was heard for forty-five minutes at 1 P.M. weekdays. She was declared "Lady Number One of the Air" by *Radio-Movie Guide*, had the All-American rose named after her in 1943, and even was honored by the state of Missouri with her own day. By 1944 McBride was making $80,000 a year. Although her career declined as television emerged, she continued to broadcast until 1960.

## BEYOND WOMEN'S NEWS

### Fran Harris: From Advertising to News

Women's programs were just a starting point for several others. Frances Alvord Harris was working as an assistant in the advertising department of Himelhoch Brothers department store in 1929 when it was decided that a women's program on a Detroit radio station would boost store sales. She became "Julia Hayes," earning $150 a month for six half-hour shows a week and continued the program until 1934.[8]

Fran Alvord was born April 19, 1909, in Detroit and graduated from Grinnell College in 1929. She married Hugh Harris in 1932. After her stint as "Julia Hayes," she was out of broadcasting until she returned to another women's program in 1939, this time as "Nancy Dixon."

In 1943, Harris became the women's editor at WWJ, Detroit, where her duties included reading newscasts. She was the first female television broadcaster in Michigan in 1946, and was on both the radio and television stations until 1964, when she moved into management as special features coordinator. She retired from broadcasting in 1974 to become a businesswoman.

### Kathryn Cravens: "News through a Woman's Eyes"

Kathryn Cravens took an even more circuitous route to news. She was a radio actress at KWK in St. Louis in 1928, becoming woman's hour director in 1931, and then what she called "the first woman news commentator, coast to coast," for CBS in 1936.[9]

Cravens was born in Burkett, Texas, probably in 1900, the daughter of Dr. John and Rose Ann Cochran. She went to Hollywood to become an actress in 1919 and worked briefly for Fox Films before marrying Rutherford Cravens in 1922. She worked in stock theater companies through most of the next five years, appearing in such standards as "The Cherry Orchard" and "Berkeley Square."

Cravens's news career took off after she divorced her husband in 1937 and became "The Flying Reporter," logging more than a hundred thousand miles one year. She also gained some degree of recognition for her fashionable dress, consistently being named one of the best-dressed women in radio from 1938 to 1954.

In 1936, Cravens went to New York to begin a program on the CBS Radio Network for Pontiac Motor Company, "News through a Woman's Eyes." Her popularity was made evident by an offer Pontiac had her make on her broadcast: a free polishing cloth. Nearly a quarter million people sent in for one, doubling the previous record for a merchandise offer on a daytime network program.

By 1938 Cravens also was producing a syndicated newspaper column, "Thru [sic] a Woman's Eyes," and writing poetry and feature stories. She moved her fifteen-minute broadcast to WNEW in the early 1940s and became a commentator on WOL, Washington, D.C., in 1945. Cravens had wanted to become a foreign correspondent ever since the United States had entered the war and became WOL's reporter in Europe, sending shortwave reports back to Washington. They were called "Europe through a Woman's Eyes." Her reports included broadcasts from Berlin after American occupation, the Nuremberg trials, and post-war Balkans elections. WOL took out an ad in *Broadcasting* that showed Cravens in uniform and claimed she was the first woman radio correspondent accredited to any theater of war.[10] After the war, Cravens wrote a fictional account of her adventures, *Pursuit of Gentlemen*.

## NETWORK WAR CORRESPONDENTS

A half-dozen women had been heard from Europe before the United States had entered the war, and most of them had been close to the fighting. Like their counterparts at home, these first radio foreign correspondents were in the right places at the right times, but most of them also had special expertise that allowed them to report from abroad. Many had traveled or lived overseas; most spoke several languages.

The networks were willing to use women from overseas when a man was not available or when the bulk of reports was expected to be on "women's issues." However, war creates a lot of opportunities, and when a story breaks, you look for the person who can get the news on the fastest. In many instances during World War II, that person was a woman.

As developments in Europe intensified during the late 1930s, the networks no longer could rely on stringers who were newspapermen. They had to build their own staffs, and most of the hiring was done overseas by men like Edward R. Murrow, who did not necessarily share the prejudices against women of the corporate bosses back home.

Radio's ability to deliver news instantly helped it surpass newspapers as the number one source for war news. Women were a part of that success, and they often were surprised to learn their broadcasts from Europe were heard by hundreds of thousands of Americans.

Still, the women's reports were almost always at the end of the network European roundups, which would usually include four or five reports in a fifteen-minute broadcast. And they often were on weekend newscasts, when the male correspondents would have a day off.

### Sigrid Schultz: First Female Radio Foreign Correspondent

Sigrid Schultz was the first woman to broadcast regularly on an American network from Europe. She was the Mutual Radio Network's reporter in Berlin, although her main duties were as the *Chicago Tribune* correspondent-in-chief for Central Europe. It was in that role that Schultz made her first broadcast to America. William L. Shirer, CBS's European representative, had been covering the Munich crisis in September 1938. As part of one report, he interviewed a number of newspaper reporters, and Schultz, a leading correspondent for more than a decade, was one of them.

Schultz was born in Chicago but had seen much of Europe as a child. Her immigrant father was a portrait artist who frequently returned to paint and finally moved his family to Europe permanently in 1911. After graduating from the Sorbonne in 1916, Sigrid went to join her family in Berlin, where her father had established a studio. Her mother was in poor health, and the family stayed in Germany through World War I, registering as aliens. Schultz got a job as a tutor and translator—she spoke English, French, Dutch, German, and Polish. In late 1919, she went to work for Henry Little, the *Chicago Tribune*'s Berlin correspondent. As his secretary and assistant, Schultz sometimes wrote articles that were published in the *Tribune*. In 1925, she was named a correspondent.

Schultz was an acknowledged expert on the Nazis when Shirer put her on CBS, having interviewed Hitler as early as 1931. She was an acquaintance of Joseph Goebbels, and had him over to dinner more than once. Shirer wrote that Schultz was "the only woman correspondent in our ranks, buoyant, cheerful and always well informed."[11]

Mutual officials apparently heard the CBS interview and approached Schultz about reporting for them. Mutual was the newest network and tended to use part-time reporters, while NBC and CBS had several permanent representatives in Europe. By August 1939, Schultz was reporting frequently for Mutual. Her strength was her journalistic skill rather than her broadcasting ability. Schultz read her copy at a rapid pace with little pause for emphasis, and during some broadcasts, she would stumble badly or break into giggles. But her information was excellent, and as the print and broadcast media were not seen as competitors, she sometimes read the dispatches she had prepared for the paper. At the beginning of every broadcast, she identified herself as being from the *Tribune*.

Despite having two masters, Schultz was a dedicated reporter for Mutual and proved it through several harrowing experiences. She even was wounded in the line of duty; in August 1940, a bomb fragment hit her in the leg while she was on her way to a studio to report on the British bombing of Berlin. She managed to get there and record the broadcast—only to find out later that the report was never heard after all because of technical problems.

In early 1941, Schultz came down with typhus and was forced to return to America. Although she continued her distinguished career as a print reporter for many years, Schultz never again was a broadcast correspondent.

### Janet Murrow: Holidays and Hospitals

Janet Murrow doesn't consider herself to have been much more than a "greeting card" to American listeners from England, but she might have played a larger role in radio foreign correspondence had plans for her to be part of D-Day coverage been carried out. The wife of Edward R. Murrow, CBS's European director, Janet Murrow first broadcast from London on Thanksgiving Day, 1939. Her reports were almost always preceded by those of a man, usually her husband, discussing the "hard" news of the day. Her broadcasts included a description of Christmas shopping in London in 1939 and one telling about gifts Americans had sent to British citizens left homeless by bombings.

Janet Murrow had a good voice and was prepared to take a greater role in CBS's coverage as the allied invasion of France drew near. She had been covering hospitals in Britain and was scheduled to accompany a field hospital to France after the invasion. But the American ambassador to Britain talked her out of going, saying that she was needed to assist relief efforts in England. That virtually ended her short stint as a broadcaster.

### Mary Marvin Breckinridge: The Best Bet

Mary Marvin Breckinridge was the woman with the best chance for a successful career in broadcast news during World War II. A well-bred, well-educated woman, she had the journalistic skills and broadcasting delivery to make it. She also had timing, for she was in Europe when war broke out and she knew CBS's man in London, Ed Murrow.

That friendship with Murrow led to Breckinridge's brief career as a radio reporter from Europe. She had known Ed Murrow during their student days when both had been active in the National Student Federation. When Ed and Janet Murrow were heading to his new post as European director in April 1937, Breckinridge was on the same ship going to see the coronation of George VI. She had been a frequent visitor to Europe, and, in the tradition of the upper class of the times, she had been presented at court in England in addition to making a social debut in New York.

Breckinridge majored in history and languages at Vassar College and considered a career in foreign service before becoming interested in photography. She also learned how to shoot motion pictures and directed, produced, and shot *The Forgotten Frontier* during 1929-1930, which was about rural nursing care in Kentucky.

Breckinridge started shooting magazine photo layouts in the mid-1930s. In the summer of 1939 she had commitments for photo stories on the Lucerne Music Festival and a Nazi rally at Nuremberg. When Hitler's army marched into Poland in September, Breckinridge headed for London, arriving the night before war was declared. She went to the American Express office in central London to obtain a ticket home but found Picadilly Circus and the Haymarket crammed with Americans trying to return home. Thinking there might be an opportunity for a photojournalist in England, she went to the London office of Black Star, an international photo agency whose New York office already represented her. Photographers were in short supply because the British ones—almost all men—were being mobilized, so Breckinridge received several assignments right away. One was to photograph slum children being evacuated from London to the countryside; another was to show an English village preparing for war.

The Murrows invited Breckinridge over to dinner one night in November 1939. After hearing about the work she was doing, Ed Murrow asked Breckinridge to be on his upcoming Saturday night broadcast to America. Murrow had been tied to the city doing several broadcasts a day and welcomed an eyewitness report from someone who had been able to see war preparations going on outside London. He wanted to give his listeners back home the feeling of what it was like in a country going to a war that one day could—and would—involve the United States. To do that, Murrow sought people who had seen it for themselves and could tell their stories.

Before Breckinridge went on the air, Murrow gave her some advice: to use her full name—she was known by her middle name at home because a prominent relative was named Mary Breckinridge as well—and to keep her voice pitched low.

Within a few days, Murrow asked Breckinridge to do additional work for him. She agreed to spend the night with some women who had become part of the city of London fire department and do a broadcast about them. Another report followed, this time from Ireland, and after it, Murrow offered her a position with the network. She took a few days to pack and went to

Holland, making her first broadcast December 10, 1939, from Hilversum, east of Amsterdam, where the government radio facilities were located. In this particular broadcast of "The World This Week," Breckinridge followed William L. Shirer in Berlin, Warren Sweeney in New York, Eric Sevareid in Paris, and Murrow in London. Breckinridge gave her report on Dutch preparations for war in a clear, confident voice with an upper-crust accent. She talked about the "little man," which was probably on the advice of Murrow, who made concern for the common man a trademark of CBS war reporting. In general, the women correspondents tended to broadcast on weekends, and they virtually never led off the roundups.

Breckinridge broadcast again on December 16, and then on December 21, telling about the increasing numbers of journalists arriving in Holland, most of them staying at the Carlton Hotel. She also reported on frontier defenses that she had seen while on a bicycle tour of the countryside.

*Subs for Shirer.*    In January 1940, Murrow came to Holland, partially to give Breckinridge some advice about broadcasting, but mostly because he wanted to meet with Shirer in neutral territory.

The two men did a joint broadcast with Breckinridge, and on the way back from Hilversum, they enjoyed a snowball fight. While in Holland, Shirer asked Murrow for some time off, so Murrow asked Breckinridge if she would fill in for Shirer in Berlin. After a broadcast at the end of January about the severe winter and its impact on Holland's defenses, Breckinridge headed for Berlin, where Shirer introduced her around.

> The first night I arrived he took me out with him when he went out to broadcast [at the Rundfunk studios on the Kaiserdamm]. We stayed at the Adlon Hotel, which the Germans very kindly let be heated. They wanted to keep the journalists happy, and it was terribly cold that winter, like twelve degrees below zero. And you'd walk, I think, eight steps and feel to the right, and that was the entrance to the subway. There was a little glimmer [of light] there. You'd ride the subway a long way to the Rundfunk office building where the censors were, and get off at Adolf Hitlerplatz, in deep snow with high piles everywhere. Then you turned sharp right to get across the street and go in again. A German soldier and his police dog were there and he'd say, "*Ausweis Bitte*—Your pass please." And then, once inside, Shirer introduced me to everybody and I shook hands with censors and all different kinds of people. He introduced me around beautifully and then we went back at one or two in the morning; the underground trains were still running.[12]

Shirer originally had expected to be gone about a month, but he got sick in Switzerland and didn't return for six weeks. While he was away, Breckinridge did eighteen broadcasts and was able to score several exclusives. She also renewed an acquaintance with Jefferson Patterson, who was in charge of the prisoner-of-war section of the American Embassy. Following a brief courtship, he proposed and Breckinridge accepted. She returned to her post in

Mary Marvin Breckinridge prepares to take a picture of William L. Shirer and Edward R. Murrow with a little Dutch girl they met ice skating on a canal in January 1940. Courtesy Mrs. Marvin Patterson.

Holland and did nine more broadcasts before leaving for France May 8, 1940, on one of the last trains to get through to Paris before the Nazis invaded Holland.

*Marriage Ends Broadcasting Career.*    Breckinridge reported from Paris on May 10 about how things had been in Amsterdam when she left. She helped Eric Sevareid and Thomas B. Grandin, who had been working around the clock for CBS. On May 12 an official from the American embassy in Paris informed her that marriage to Patterson would signal an end to her broadcasting career. As the wife of a diplomat for the officially "neutral" United States, she could not have a job that might cause political difficulties for the American government. Breckinridge reported on May 17 on civil defense preparations in Paris and then went shopping for wedding items. She did eight more broadcasts from Paris before leaving on June 8, taking a circuitous route to Berlin. From Geneva, she cabled CBS her resignation: "Farewell Columbia. Have enjoyed working with you. Now leave gladly to marry Jefferson Patterson, first secretary of the American embassy in Berlin. Announcement publishable June 12. Columbia gets credit for engagement for making winter meeting Berlin."[13] On June 20, she became Mrs. Jefferson Patterson and had a three-day honeymoon before turning to the duties of a diplomat's wife that would occupy her for the rest of her married life.

Breckinridge might well have become the most prominent broadcast newswoman of the 1940s if she had continued her career in broadcasting. She had the strongest delivery of the women who reported from overseas to American radio listeners. And she had good connections, both with the elite of the East Coast and with Murrow. Most of the reporters Murrow hired in the early years of the war went on to become prominent radio and television newsmen and, without Breckinridge, came to be known as "Murrow's Boys."

## Margaret Rupli: The Sounds of War

When Murrow visited Breckinridge in Holland, he also gave some advice to NBC's reporter in Amsterdam, Margaret Rupli. She was married to British newspaperman David Woodward. While looking for a job, Rupli called the American legation and was told about an inquiry from Max Jordan, NBC's European representative. As the networks built their staffs, they took most of their new reporters from newspapers or wire services. They also got some by just asking around. Rupli contacted Jordan and recorded a voice test, which she passed. Rupli says her husband used to joke that if the shortwave facilities failed, she could just yell across the Atlantic. Her delivery was actually quite good, and she certainly sounded like an American, which was an important factor in being hired by the networks, who wanted the story of war in Europe told to America by Americans whenever possible.

Rupli knew Europe and European politics. She had spent her junior year studying at the University of Paris before returning to Goucher College, from which she graduated Phi Beta Kappa in 1931. She got a job paying $100 a month at the Geneva Research Center, then returned to the United States in 1934, where she worked for three years at the Department of Labor's Bureau of Labor Statistics. Her duties included some translation.

Rupli started a Ph.D. program at the University of Chicago in 1937, but she interrupted that to return to Europe in 1939, where she married Woodward, whom she had first met in Geneva six years before. They went to Berlin, but as war appeared inevitable, Woodward was transferred to Amsterdam.

It was from Amsterdam that Rupli did her first broadcasts for NBC. Once hired, she decided to broadcast under her maiden name since that was the one by which she was known in America.

NBC paid Rupli $25 for "short pieces"—ones under seven minutes—and $50 for longer ones. Payment for foreign correspondents varied. Each network had its core staff members who were on salary and were paid expenses and who got extra fees if their newscasts were sponsored. Rupli and most of the women reporters overseas were paid on a per broadcast basis. Many of these women also got expenses for living or travel. Because they were paid for each report, they probably had parity with men who were in the same arrangement. But the fee system also shows women were in a second echelon of the networks' overseas reporters, for the male reporters usually were on staff.

*Advice from Murrow.* Murrow gave Rupli his advice before she ever made a broadcast. He told her that if Holland was invaded, she should understate the situation. This was in keeping with the official policy of both networks, to be as impartial as possible, and to be calm and dispassionate. In the first three months of 1940, Rupli did few broadcasts, but starting in April she broadcast twice a week, almost always on weekends. One of her most elaborate broadcasts was done with the use of a Dutch broadcasting mobile truck, which relayed the program from the Dutch defense perimeter to the studios at Hilversum. The broadcast included soldiers singing and an interview with a military engineer explaining how water from the Rhine River might be used to halt an invasion. The interview was completely scripted in advance so Dutch censors could review it.

Although rumors persisted that the Nazis were going to invade the Low Countries, Rupli reported on May 9, 1940, the day before the invasion, that all was calm in Amsterdam, adding: "I feel quite sure that the group of soldiers that marches by my window tomorrow morning will be engaged in maneuvers and in nothing more serious."[14] The soldiers the next day were actually marching to defend their country, which was under Nazi attack. As the invasion began, Rupli was preparing a broadcast at Hilversum, trying to get her script approved. Max Jordan recalled that NBC news director Abe Schechter was on the talk-back channel to Rupli, and kept asking her what was happening. Air raid sirens could be heard and then bombs. When Rupli told Schechter she could not broadcast and had to leave, he pleaded with her to stay and go on the air so the bombs could be heard in America. But the censors never cleared her report, and the bombs were not heard.

*Escape to England.*    Rupli wanted to stay in Holland, and NBC offered her a staff position if she would. But her husband wouldn't leave the country without her and, because he was a British citizen and subject to arrest by the Nazis, they decided to go. With a stream of refugees leaving Holland, most conventional transportation was taken. But the British diplomats were resourceful and helped the couple get on an odd escape vessel.

> It was a little British coal barge that had been overlooked. They came up to the British Embassy in The Hague and said "Have you got anybody you want to put on?" It was a very motley crew: mixed marriages, British aviators who had been shot down for violating Dutch neutrality and now were freed, and the Sadler's Wells Ballet. There was straw in the hold, and I remember I had David on one side of me. He had picked up a bottle of whiskey and I had picked up toothbrushes and things like that. I remember it was the only time I got deliberately tight because I thought, "If I'm going down in the North Sea, there's no point in being sober." I had a banana, a piece of chocolate, and about a cup full of whiskey, and then I snuggled up and went to sleep. And when I woke up in the morning there was a shaft of light coming down into the hold, and I clambered up the ladder, and here were the Sadler's Wells people doing exercises on this narrow little walkway. And overhead there was this absolutely gorgeous British plane circling around.[15]

The coal barge had arrived at Harwich at the same time as the queen of the Netherlands came into port aboard a British destroyer. The airplane was for the queen, although Rupli had enough jewelry on to consider herself royalty. She had been given a number of diamonds by a Jewish refugee who had a sister in England and also was wearing her own jewelry. She just wore them as though it were an everyday thing, and the officials didn't say a word.

Rupli made one broadcast from London. In late May, she returned to the United States on the *President Roosevelt*, making a final broadcast for NBC as the ship was entering New York harbor. Rupli wanted to continue broadcasting, but NBC offered her only a late morning time slot once a week, which she did not think worth taking. So she returned to the Department of Labor, her six months in radio at an end.

## Helen Hiett: Headliners Award Winner

Just as Rupli was ending her work for NBC, Helen Hiett was beginning hers. Hiett joined the Paris bureau in the middle of May, having been hired in New York by Schechter and Jordan, who was in the United States to confer with Schechter on future coverage of the war. Hiett had been born in Chenoa, Illinois, September 23, 1913. As a high school student, she was a protege of F. F. McNaughton, the publisher of the *Pekin* (Illinois) *Daily Times.*

Hiett first went to Europe the day after she graduated from the University of Chicago in 1934. She took three years to get through college rather than the usual four. After graduating, Hiett continued her studies at the League of Nations in Geneva on a summer scholarship. She also hoped to string some articles to her hometown paper and applied for a press pass as soon as she arrived. When her scholarship ran out, Hiett got a job as a secretary at the Geneva Research Center, which paid $67 a month.

Because of the illness of other staff members, Hiett became the editor of the center's monthly newsletter. She took some classes at the Graduate Institute of International Studies and, in the summer of 1936, left to travel around Europe. Among other things, she studied how the Italian government was undermining the League of Nation's sanctions. She returned home to America in 1937, but went back to Europe as a Ph.D. candidate at the London School of Economics on scholarship from the Federation of American Women's Clubs Overseas. When the war began, Hiett left school and moved to France. She contacted French radio authorities about program ideas she had but received only an invitation to read an English translation of a Victor Hugo short story on the Radio Mondial channel.

In January 1940, Hiett and some friends started a publication, *Paris Letter*, which was an attempt to galvanize Americans to support the French. It offered letters from French soldiers at the front and stories about life in Paris during war. Hiett contributed an article to the newsletter giving an account of life at the front. She had been invited to spend Easter with a family living near Metz, and although the front was off limits to most journalists, she went as a private citizen and toured the French defenses as a guest.

The newsletter had gained a following in America, and Hiett returned to the United States in April to begin a lecture tour. She was intent on convincing Americans to enter the war. Just before her last speech on the tour, Hiett learned that the Low Countries had been invaded. Her impassioned talk before an advertising club in Rochester, New York, also was broadcast on a local radio station. When it was cut off before it ended because of other program commitments, a number of listeners called to complain. One of the people listening to the speech at the club encouraged Hiett to apply for a job with the networks and she went directly to New York. A meeting with CBS was not promising, but Jordan and Schechter were impressed by Hiett's background, including her ability to speak four foreign languages. She wanted to be sent to Paris, while the NBC news executives were thinking of Berlin. But Hiett said she couldn't stand to be that close to Nazis, so they said they'd call her if something else opened up.

*Reports on the Fall of France.*    Hiett waited a week, then decided to go home to Illinois. She dropped by Schechter's office on a Saturday to give him her home address, only to find that he and Jordan had decided to hire her for the Paris bureau. They already had obtained a plane ticket and visas for travel through Portugal and Spain. But there were problems with the French visa, and it seemed that it would take at least a month to obtain one. Hiett went across the street to the French Consulate and managed to wrangle the necessary papers. She took Jordan's place on the Pan American Clipper flight to Lisbon and was in Paris by May 21, 1940.

NBC had only one man there, Paul Archinard, who was glad to have some help. Hiett started broadcasting right away and got some immediate feedback on her work from New York. After reporting that some refugee children had blistered feet so severe that their outer layers of skin came off when health workers removed their shoes and socks, one of the New York producers reminded her that Americans were eating breakfast during some of her broadcasts. She was also advised never to use the word "blood."

Paris was bombed June 3, and Hiett, who had been at the French broadcast center when the attack began, rushed over to the NBC office to find Archinard and a secretary digging through the wreckage. Just then, the undamaged phone started ringing. The New York producers wanted Archinard, still reeling from the first attack, to go out into the streets with a microphone if the bombing resumed.

On June 10, Hiett and Archinard left Paris, following the French government to Tours, where a shortwave station was still in operation. They reported the fall of the French government, and on June 14 headed south again, this time to Bordeaux, where the last functioning transmitter available to them was located. It was a rough trip. They sometimes slept in fields, and Hiett didn't have a bath for ten days. When they finally arrived, they reported on the new Vichy government. Archinard left after several days to try and find his family outside Paris. The CBS men left by boat for England. Hiett stayed on, reporting the names of the men who would negotiate the French surrender. Her last report from France was on June 22.

In Bordeaux, Hiett had run into some friends from the *Paris Letter*. German troops were moving closer, and with them, danger, so the friends decided to try to reach a house in southern France where they thought they would be safe.

Trains had stopped running. Roads were blocked by people trying to get boats to England. Hundreds of automobiles were abandoned or given away like peanuts. An American girl I knew had a brand new Chrysler thrust upon her, but she didn't know where to go with it. I offered her hospitality with friends who

wanted to go to Nice if we could all go there in her car. She agreed. The diffi-
culty was that the car had Polish license plates and we had heard the Germans
were confiscating all the Polish and Belgian cars. We had to chance it. By way
of precaution we put black paint over the license plates to make them look like
French ones, hoping at the same time to beat the Germans out of town. We
met them at the first crossroads. A whole armored division was coming in
from a side road to take the main highway in the direction we were going.
After waiting two hours for it to pass, we started, at a snail's pace, behind it.
That was hard with the throttle of such a fast car underfoot. On a mad im-
pulse, I pulled out to the left and tried to pass the column which was several
miles long. Bedlam broke loose. German officers' cars behind began honking;
men began whistling and shouting things I unfortunately understood. They
wanted me to get out of their way. Since there was only a ditch on my left, I
shouted to a blond youngster driving an armored car on the right to slow down
and let me get in front of him. He did, and we spent the next two hours moving in the midst of the Army of Occupation.[16]

The car and occupants reached Nice safely. By now, though, Hiett was
eager to broadcast again and decided to go to Geneva where she could use
Swiss facilities. After doing a broadcast, Hiett discussed her next assignment with network officials. They decided on Spain. But Hiett's luck was
not good there. Spanish censorship was severe, and she was frustrated in
most of her attempts to broadcast. On top of that, Hiett contracted bron-
chitis. But she also got one sensational scoop.

*The Bombing of Gibraltar.*    Hiett had made friends with a group of
chorus girls passing through Spain on the way to entertain British troops in
Gibraltar. They invited her to go along and, since she wasn't getting much
reporting done, she said yes. They arrived in Gibraltar in late September
1940, just in time to witness three days of bombings. Unable to broadcast to
America because of a weak transmitter, Hiett apparently had to convince
British authorities that she was not an entertainer, but a reporter, before she
could leave British territory. She returned to Madrid, was initially blocked
by censorship, and then had two transmissions ruined by sunspots. Finally,
her report got through, and it received a good deal of newspaper coverage.
It also earned Hiett the National Headliners Club Award; she was the first
woman to win it.

When it continued to be difficult to broadcast from Spain, Hiett returned
to the United States via France. The day she docked in New York, March
31, 1941, NBC preempted its regularly scheduled program at 10 P.M. for a
special broadcast by the "first American girl radio reporter on the scene
when the big German push started against France." In a clear voice that
sounded young, Hiett described her "extraordinary" experience covering
the bombing of Gibraltar. You can hear her turning the pages of her script,
and as the broadcast goes on, her delivery slows down and her voice gets a

little deeper. Hiett's writing conjures up images as she tells what she saw and how she felt on the boat to Gibraltar: "It was an uncanny night that held no promise of morning."[17]

Once home, Hiett continued her broadcast career as a commentator for NBC. After eighteen months she left the network to become a guest lecturer at Stephens College in Missouri and wrote a book about her experiences. In 1944 she rejoined NBC as editor of network publications and research assistant for "University of the Air." But Hiett soon left again, this time to become a print correspondent, reporting from Italy, Austria, and Germany at the end of the war. She was able to reach Milan two days before U.S. troops, and she covered events in Italy after Mussolini's execution.

After the war, Hiett became the director of the *New York Herald Tribune* forum, which brought world leaders together once a year to discuss international problems. Later, a forum for high schools was added. Some of the forum events were broadcast, and at times, Hiett served as the moderator. But she never returned full time to broadcasting.

Hiett married publishing executive Theodore Waller March 28, 1948, and they had three children. She died August 22, 1961, in Chamonix, France, several weeks after a rock fell on her while she and her husband were climbing Mount Perseverance.

### Betty Wason: "Find a Man"

Perhaps the most interesting female radio foreign correspondent during World War II was Betty Wason, for she experienced problems that illustrate many of the prejudices against women broadcasting news.

Elizabeth Wason was born in 1912, and grew up in Delphi, Indiana. She attended Oberlin College, then transferred to Purdue, receiving a B.A. in home economics in 1933. She held a number of jobs during the Depression, including a position with the Kentucky Utilities Company as a home economist. Wason used that background to gain a program on WLAP, Lexington, Kentucky, which was a variation of the women's programs heard across the country. She organized a weekly luncheon for members of women's clubs. For an admission price of twenty-five cents, each club member got a complete lunch, and the club got fifteen cents per person back in a refund. So for a dime a head, Wason had to feed and entertain the women, which she did with a running commentary that was broadcast live on WLAP. She also did most of the cooking in advance, getting college girls to serve the meals for a dollar in wages and a free lunch.

Wason used that experience to gain a position at a Cincinnati station. But she was fired within a week because she could neither write nor read a script very well; nearly all of her broadcasting in Lexington had been ad-libbed. Her next job was at *McCall's* in New York, and then she joined the Raymond C.

Mayer public relations firm in 1936, where she remained for about two years. Then Wason decided she would go to Europe and become a foreign correspondent.

This was becoming an increasingly popular idea. Young people, some of them with journalism backgrounds, felt that careers could be made by getting in on the action when war in Europe broke out. Some newspapers and wire services encouraged these hopes by agreeing to let the neophytes send stories back to them, paying on an "as used" basis. In Wason's case, she had a one-way ticket to Europe, $300, and a loose agreement with Transradio Press Service. Transradio was supplying wire copy, written in broadcast style, to radio networks and stations. If a correspondent was sending in useful material regularly, payment might reach $25 a week.

After some initial success stringing, Wason found that things quieted down following the Munich crisis in the fall of 1938, and she couldn't make enough to live on. Early the next year she returned to the United States and landed a position planning the food section of the new New York newspaper, *PM*, which was a creative, but not a commercial, success. Wason left before the first copy rolled off the presses, however, and went back to Europe for another try at foreign correspondence. Before she did, she stopped off at CBS and talked to Paul White, the network's news director. He had a policy of letting his European correspondents, Shirer and Murrow, do the hiring. But he also knew that war was coming, and the network needed to beef up its staff. So he suggested she stop off in Berlin and see Shirer on her way to Scandinavia, which she did in January 1940. This was the period of the war called the "Sitzkreig," when nothing much was happening, and Wason didn't have much luck getting work. Then the Nazis invaded Norway, and Wason had a perfect observation post in Stockholm.

> I was down to one Swedish krona, which was the equivalent of twenty-five cents, and I had a room in the Grand Hotel and I had tried everything and I thought "What am I going to do? There's a war on and I still can't get anything." I was literally weeping in my hotel room when a call came from Bill Shirer asking me to make a broadcast, and I hurriedly found a girl who could translate from the Swedish papers, and my first broadcast was a scoop.[18]

Wason had vowed to learn how to write for the ear instead of the eye after losing her last radio job, and her first report on CBS showed it.

> A Swede who had fled from the Swedish legation in Oslo, along with the rest, was standing by his car outside the house where the court and government were staying, when he saw a German plane coming. He gave the one and only air-raid alarm with his automobile horn. Down the road ran King Haakon, Crown Prince Olaf, the British and Polish Ministers, and all the other governments' officials. They had to stand waist-deep in snow beneath fir trees while bombs crashed.[19]

Wason continued to report for CBS as the fighting escalated. She managed to get into Norway and interviewed injured British soldiers who were being treated in a converted dance hall. CBS paid her $100 a week. However, in May 1940, news executives asked Wason to find a man to broadcast for her, saying her voice was too young and feminine for war news and that the public was objecting to it.

It is true that Wason did not have the strong delivery of a Breckinridge or a Rupli. She stumbled more often, for one thing, and her voice was higher in pitch. But she was perfectly understandable, and her writing was strong; and she was a better broadcaster than Schultz by far.

Wason felt that, had an American male in Stockholm been interested in working for CBS, she would not have had the opportunity to broadcast in the first place. Many men working for newspapers or wire services in Europe had not been in America to witness the increased importance of radio as a news source. They preferred the stability of a career in print journalism.

Wason did ask a man to voice her reports. Winston Burdette had taken over for Transradio in Stockholm when Wason decided to concentrate on CBS. She coached him on his first broadcast so successfully that she soon found she would have to move to another city to continue broadcasting herself. In contrast, Burdette was beginning a career with CBS that was to last four decades.

Wason went to the Balkans, which seemed promising for her until Burdette, also moving to where the action was, showed up. She moved on to Turkey, filing several stories for Transradio, and then on to Greece. With the Greeks defending themselves against the Axis troops, Wason once again was heard on CBS. She managed to get to the front, view the bombing, and file an eyewitness account on November 28, 1940. Before long, however, network officials again asked her to find a man to broadcast for her. Wason was outraged.

> I knew I was an excellent reporter, and yet they said my voice did not come across. Well, I have done so much broadcasting since then that I know my voice was good, and it was just the objection to a woman's voice giving news.

Wason located a man at the American Embassy in Athens to read her scripts. He used the radio name of Phil Brown, and would identify himself on the air as, "Phil Brown speaking for Betty Wason." She continued to file dispatches by wire when broadcasts could not be arranged. Wason stayed on in Athens when the Nazis occupied the city, not knowing they would put her under a kind of house arrest for two months before sending her and the few other remaining foreign correspondents on a long trip to Berlin, where they were released. Wason asked CBS about further work, but there was little interest in her services, and she returned to America.

Betty Wason on an Athens street, spring 1940. Since there were no correspondents' uniforms for women, Wason had this one custom-made. The Scottish band on her cap was just a remnant the tailor had on hand. Courtesy Betty Wason.

Wason kept her hand in broadcasting. She established a weekly round table program on WINX, Washington, D.C., late in 1945. The half-hour broadcasts sometimes originated from a place where news was happening, such as the Senate radio gallery. Its topics were chosen with the help of a nine-woman advisory committee. For several years in the late 1940s, Wason was the woman's editor for the Voice of America and moderated an interview program called "Woman's World." After that, she began to concentrate on print work, writing a number of cookbooks and a book about a difficult relationship with her daughter, who she raised while a single parent after a brief marriage. Wason continues to broadcast occasionally, moderating events such as National Press Club forums; she is writing a novel about female foreign correspondents in World War II.

## WOMEN'S VOICES: SHATTERING A MYTH

The notion women should not broadcast news because their voices did not carry enough authority surfaced long before Betty Wason started broadcasting. For while there were some women who gave news on the radio in its first two decades, the unwritten rule was that news was a man's game. Few stations were as innovative as KVOO, a Tulsa outlet that in 1938 began putting its woman news commentator, Dorothy McCune, "on broadcasts where it was believed heretofore that only men's voices were acceptable," such as news and special events programs. KVOO vice president and general manager W. B. Way found his listeners, especially women, liked McCune on the air, and that "her pleasing voice personality adds a long needed touch to some types of special events broadcasts, which have heretofore used only masculine, rapid-fire types of voices."[20] The majority of Americans, however, apparently did not agree with Way. A study in the mid-1930s found most people preferred hearing the news from a man; a woman's voice was more acceptable delivering a commercial or reading literature.

Most of the men who did the hiring agreed. Harry W. Flannery, CBS's Berlin correspondent in 1940, found that

> Columbia did not favor women on the air, especially from foreign points. That was probably because most of the listeners preferred male voices and had no confidence in women for such assignments, even though some of them . . . were as good reporters as any of us.[21]

One of the most prominent women behind the microphone in those early days also recalls the prejudice against the female voice. When Ruth Crane began her broadcasting career at WJR, Detroit, in 1929,

> each station usually had one woman personality on the air and at that time few of us had invaded the news or sports or other fields. You know, a man's voice was supposed to denote authority and knowledge and not very many of the women

did interviews even. This, too, was a man's field. . . . But early in the forties opportunities were expanded and women did take on the chores previously assumed to be a man's field.[22]

Those opportunities, created by the shortage of manpower as World War II claimed more and more American men to the draft, also brought on changes in attitudes about women on the air. But baritones continued to be the preferred tone for news for the next three decades. United Nations network correspondent Pauline Frederick gave a lecture to groups in the late forties titled, "A Woman in a Man's World," in which she concluded that technically, radio was geared to men. "Even the microphones are built to pick up men's voices more eloquently than women's." But beyond that, Frederick said women in the male domain of broadcasting were aware that the general opinion in radio was that women could not broadcast news. "This school of thought believes that a woman's voice doesn't carry authority, especially on international affairs; that a feminine voice immediately suggests a woman's program or strictly the sewing and cooking departments of life."[23]

### The Prejudice Continues

More than a decade and a half later in the mid-1960s, many broadcasting executives agreed with Elmer Lower, president in charge of news, special events, and public affairs at ABC, when he said,

> Many women may possess the knowledge and authority but they seldom can convey this through their voices. Even the best-trained actress can't compare with men in this respect. Her voice is naturally thinner, with less timbre and range. It's not as appropriate for reporting crucial events. For hard-core news, the depth and resonance of the male voice are indispensible.[24]

The voice problem, according to another network executive of the same era, stemmed from other feminine characteristics. Robert Wogan, vice president of the NBC Radio Network, said many women sounded fine in everyday conversation, but once they got in front of a microphone, "something happens to them. They become affected, overdramatic, high-pitched. . . . Not that they all put on an act. But with a man you seldom have this problem."[25]

### "She'd Rather Have Her Hair in Place"

Some men who did the hiring at that time did not want to put women on the air as newscasters for other reasons. "A woman's manner is not suited to news and serious discussion," stated Giraud Chester, NBC vice president in charge of television programming. He reflected a feeling in the industry that a woman was not effective in those roles because

she thinks it's unfeminine to be forceful. She is not in the habit of asking prob-
ing questions or getting tough with unruly guests. Not that she couldn't if she
tried. But she generally prefers to be the gracious, glamorous hostess. She'd
rather have her hair in place than her brains. The audience won't buy it so we
can't afford to do it.[26]

Those prejudices persisted even as more women began breaking into broadcast news in the late sixties. Jessica Savitch, who went on to become an NBC
correspondent and anchor, couldn't get a job at first because she was a
woman; besides, women didn't want to watch women on television.
"How," she questioned, "could it be determined that women did not want
to watch other women deliver news when they had yet to see any? And if in-
deed their voices were not perceived as authoritative, could it be because no
authority had ever been vested in women?"[27] Savitch's cry, echoing that of
the pioneers before her, was just beginning to be heard. But it did not yet re-
sound throughout the industry; long-held beliefs are slow to change, as evi-
denced by the attitude of NBC News president Reuven Frank in 1971: "I
have the strong feeling that audiences are less prepared to accept news from
a woman's voice than from a man's."[28] That theory has since been refuted
by several studies indicating Americans don't really care whether they get
their news from a man or a woman.[29]

## CONCLUSION

The women who broadcast in the early days of radio largely reflected the
roles of women in American society in general. Most of the women on the
air were involved in the less serious aspects of the new medium—entertainment rather than news and information. The few who did give information
were on programs aimed at those of their own sex, "homemaker" shows
that combined entertainment and household tips.

Timing was a major factor in the careers of women who succeeded on the
air; women such as Ruth Crane and Fran Harris were in the right places at
the right times and made transitions to new jobs.

World War II provided more opportunities for women in broadcasting.
Those who became radio foreign correspondents also had the breaks any
successful broadcaster needs. But most of them were well-educated, and
some spoke several languages or had travelled in other parts of the world.
Many of them, like their male counterparts, were trained in print. The majority got on the air because no man could be found to broadcast.

One reason those who did the hiring preferred men on the air was because
women's voices were not thought of as being authoritative. Another type of
discrimination in those early days was pay inequality. Historically, women
had been paid less than their male counterparts, and it was no different in the

broadcasting industry than in any other field. And, as we shall see, these prejudices remained a part of broadcasting even as more women broke into radio and television here at home.

**NOTES**

1. Morleen Getz Rouse, "Daytime Radio Programming for the Homemaker, 1926-1956," *Journal of Popular Culture* 12 (Fall 1978): 315.
2. Betty Parker, "Women's Place in Radio Advertising," *Broadcasting* 17, 1 (1 July 1939): 48 + .
3. Ruth Crane Schaefer oral history, interview by Pat Mower, 18 November 1975, tape recording and transcript, Broadcast Pioneers Library, Washington, D.C., p. 7.
4. Ibid., p. 12.
5. "Our Respects to Ruth Crane," *Broadcasting* 34, 4 (26 January 1948): 48.
6. Ibid., p. 50.
7. Rouse, "Daytime Radio Programming," p. 319.
8. These fictitious names were rather common in broadcasting, with many of the programs controlled by advertising companies. The air name meant the talent could be changed while the continuity of the character could be kept. At one point, the federal government had dozens of women at stations all over the country reading duplicate scripts which featured recipes for inexpensive meals created by government economists; the women all used the same name.
9. "Meet the Ladies: Kathryn Cravens," *Broadcasting* 23, 17 (26 October 1942): 38.
10. *Broadcasting* 28, 26 (18 June 1945): inside front cover.
11. William L. Shirer, *Berlin Diary* (New York: Knopf, 1941), p. 42.
12. Mrs. Jefferson Patterson (Mary Marvin Breckinridge), interview with David H. Hosley, Washington, D.C., 12 November 1981.
13. "CBS Appoints Taylor as Grandin Successor; Breckinridge also Quits," *Broadcasting* 18, 12 (15 June 1940): 33.
14. Margaret Rupli Woodward, personal papers, script, 9 May 1940.
15. Margaret Rupli Woodward, interview with David H. Hosley, Washington, D.C., 21 May 1981.
16. Carmen McCormack Simpson, "They're Roving Newscasters," *Independent Woman* 20, 5 (May 1941): 135-36.
17. Helen Hiett, "Helen Hiett Back from France." Library of Congress Sound Recording, Disc 20475A, Cut A2, Box 741-20, LWO 16798, R28, Washington, D.C., 31 March 1941.
18. Unless otherwise stated, quotations from Betty Wason are from an interview with her by David H. Hosley, Arlington, Virginia, 5 June 1981.
19. *Current Biography* (Detroit: Gale Research Company, 1943), p. 806.
20. "Women's Place in the Studio," *Broadcasting,* 16, 3 (1 February 1939): 55.
21. Harry W. Flannery, *Assignment to Berlin* (New York: Knopf, 1942), p. 108.
22. Schaefer oral history, pp. 7-8.
23. Nancy H. MacLennon, "Only One of Her Kind," *New York Times* (5 December 1948): II: 15, 4.

24. Lee Graham, "Women Don't Like to Look at Women," *New York Times* (24 May 1964): 1, 53.

25. Ibid.

26. Ibid., p. 50.

27. Jessica Savitch, *Anchorwoman* (New York: G. P. Putnam's Sons, 1982), p. 41.

28. "The New Breed," *Newsweek* (30 August 1971): 62-63.

29. See Vernon A. Stone, "Attitudes toward Television Newswomen," *Journal of Broadcasting* 18, 1 (Winter 1973-74): 49-62; Susan Whittaker and Ron Whittaker, "Relative Effectiveness of Male and Female Newscasters," *Journal of Broadcasting* 20, 2 (Spring 1976): 177-84; "The Press: Will the Morning Star Shine at Night?" *Time* (3 May 1976): 51-52 +; Kevin L. Hutchinson, "The Effects of Newscaster Gender and Vocal Quality on Perceptions of Homophily and Interpersonal Attraction," *Journal of Broadcasting* 26, 1 (Winter 1982): 457-66; K. Tim Wulfemeyer, "Interests and Preferences of Audience for Local Television News," *Journalism Quarterly* 60 (Summer 1983): 323-28.

# 2  The War Years at Home

The most famous woman heard on non-entertainment broadcasts in the late 1930s and early 1940s was Eleanor Roosevelt. The president's wife often had her own network program and was a frequent guest on others. News commentator Dorothy Thompson, however, was a close second. It wasn't until the United States entered World War II in late 1941 that women were heard in any numbers on domestic news broadcasts.

The opportunities for women in radio changed dramatically when America became involved in the war. The manpower shortage caused by the draft forced station owners in the United States to fill vacancies in almost all departments with women, including many in news.

Some women working in radio newsrooms were singled out in *Broadcasting*, a trade magazine. The only woman newswriter at WBBM, Chicago, Helen Oppegard, was noted for being named the 1941 outstanding woman graduate of the Medill School of Journalism at Northwestern University.[1] WGAR, Cleveland, reporter Kay Halle was known for her travels: "In eighteen months of broadcasting she has never missed a program. Her transcribed programs arrive by air express in time for her Saturday evening show, and chances are they'll arrive from any corner of the country. . . . Last fall she flew to South America, air-expressing her transcribed broadcasts from Mexico City, Buenos Aires, Lima and Santiago."[2] Wynn Hubler was singled out as one of the first female newscasters in her part of the country when, in 1942, she began a 10 A.M. daily newscast on WNAX, Yankton, South Dakota, where she was women's director.

It was not uncommon to hear of women taking over control room operations and announcing duties, and many stations recorded female firsts during the early years of the war: "Harriette Thompson becomes first full-time mike woman WROK, Rockford, Illinois"; "WING, Dayton, Ohio, assigns a woman, Jo Andrews, to a full-time announcer's schedule."[3] Many stations began preparing for the loss of male employees. Stations such as KGVO,

Missoula, Montana, trained a complete staff of female announcers, while others, such as WDAS, Philadelphia, reported many women were applying for jobs as announcers and production assistants. But 1942 still found WDAS experimenting with women as announcers for music programs, and WDAS president A. W. Dannenbaum said that "as a last resort women [would] be used to give news reports," claiming that female voices lack the authority required for newscasts.[4]

As the war progressed, women became even more common in radio newsrooms. The women tended to be the underlings, primarily because of lack of experience, while men held the management positions. This staff configuration would continue as the media developed, and it wouldn't be until the women's movement of the sixties and seventies that it would become an issue.

The news department at WHK-WCLE, Cleveland, was "all girl," with the exception of those in charge. At KVOO, Tulsa, the news staff headed by Ken Miller consisted of Polly Trindle, assistant news editor; rewrite women Marie Chauncey and Margaret Johnston; and teletype operators Maxine Henry and Emma Grace McHugh. Although their numbers were increasing, in 1942 newswomen were still enough of a novelty to call attention to them. CBS's news bureau in Hollywood, California, hired three young women and assigned them to handle the Associated Press teletype and other wire reports for network newscasts. Ruth Maxwell, Harriett Ginn, and Barbara McGee, wearing uniforms identifying them as part of the network's news bureau, worked where they could be seen by the public—in a specially installed newsroom in the window of a Los Angeles department store.

As the draft claimed American men, the fledgling television industry also began employing more women. Chicago station W9XBK, for example, announced its production and technical departments would be completely staffed by women for the duration of the war.

Many of these women new to the work force were getting good reviews from their bosses. At a San Antonio radio station, KABC, manager Charlie Balthrope said the efficiency record of women at the controls was higher than that of men for any corresponding period of time. CBS news director Paul White called several women in his newsroom from a journalism class he taught at Columbia University "capable," including writers Jane Dealy, Beth Zimmerschied, Margaret Miller, who went on to become a producer (and later married White), and Alice Weel, who became a writer for "Douglas Edwards and the News" and later a producer for "60 Minutes."

## WOMEN ON THE AIR

### Dorothy Thompson: News Commentator

The most well known female journalist on radio during World War II was Dorothy Thompson. She rivaled singer Kate Smith for popularity in the late thirties and early forties, and challenged any notion that a woman's voice did not carry authority.

Thompson gained her fame as a newspaper and magazine writer, however, and drew on that base of support to gain her place on the airwaves. She was born July 9, 1893, in Lancaster, New York. Both of her parents had been born in England, and she carried a trace of an English accent in her speech. Thompson's mother died when she was seven, and her father, a Methodist minister, remarried. Dorothy did not get along with her stern stepmother, so to keep peace in the family, her father packed the child off to live with an aunt in Chicago. A good athlete, Thompson played basketball in high school and at Syracuse University, from which she graduated cum laude in 1914.

Thompson was active in the suffrage movement in college, and her first job after school was in the Buffalo office of the New York State Suffrage Association. After holding jobs in public relations and advertising in New York and Cincinnati, she went to Europe in 1920 with a college chum. Thompson managed to sell several pieces to the International News Service. That led to other articles, for which she was paid per word or column inch. Thompson wrote for the Associated Press, *London Star*, *Westminster Gazette*, and *Manchester Guardian*. To earn a steady income, she took a job writing publicity in 1921 in Paris for the American Red Cross. The pay was a penny a line. Then she sold a story about refugees to Wythe Williams, the head of European service for the *Philadelphia Ledger*. One story led to another, and before long Thompson was costing the *Ledger* so much at space rates that they put her on salary.

*European Bureau Chief.*    Thompson soon became the *Ledger*'s bureau chief for Austria, Hungary, and Czechoslovakia, and was based in Vienna. There, in 1922, she met and married Josef Bard. She joined a group of writers who shared her interest in international politics and loved to talk about the world situation at dinner parties and other social gatherings. Bard didn't fit in well with that group and, within a few years, he and Thompson drifted apart. She went to Berlin in 1924 to become the central European bureau chief for the *Ledger* and its sister paper, the *New York Post*. There she met and became friends with Sigrid Schultz, who later broadcast for Mutual. While in Berlin, Thompson also wrote an interesting article for *The Nation*, which made her thoughts known about being a woman in what was basically a man's world.

> There seems to me to be nothing extraordinary or of significance in the fact that a woman should be a foreign newspaper correspondent. . . . It is high time women were taken for granted. The see-what-the-little-darling-has-done-now attitude ought to be outlawed.[5]

Thompson also felt that any difficulties she had encountered as a journalist were due to inexperience, not her gender.

On her thirty-third birthday, which was also the day she received her divorce papers, Thompson was given a birthday party. Novelist Sinclair Lewis attended and was captivated by Thompson. He proposed marriage almost immediately, but she refused. Determined in his pursuit, Lewis followed Thompson on her assignments, continuing to propose in a rather public courtship that took them all the way to the Soviet Union.[6] Thompson gave up her work in Berlin in March 1928 and went to live with Lewis in Naples. They were married in London that summer, moving to the United States in August. Lewis soon bought a farm near Bernard, Vermont, and they began an unusual sort of marriage that often found them happier apart than together. Thompson's best work was ahead, Lewis's behind. They had a son in 1930, the same year Lewis became the first American to win the Nobel Prize for literature. Thompson would later say that she enjoyed the birth of son Michael: "I felt it was something I could grit my teeth and go into battle about."[7] Thompson apparently had mixed feelings about motherhood. She seemed devoted to Michael, but often left for lengthy trips abroad. A good deal of his youth was spent in the care of nannies and at boarding schools.

Professionally, Thompson's career began to take off. She had written a controversial book about Adolf Hitler that resulted in her expulsion from Germany in 1934. She was in demand on the American lecture circuit, and in March 1936 she began a column for the *New York Herald Tribune*. The idea for the column came from the wife of the *Herald Tribune* publisher. After hearing Thompson speak at one of the newspaper's public forums, Helen Reid thought the writer could explain the world's events in a way women could understand so they wouldn't have to turn to their husbands for information. Called "On the Record," Thompson's column became a fixture of the *Herald Tribune* editorial page three days a week, alternating with Walter Lippman's column. Thompson also began writing a monthly column in the *Ladies Home Journal*, which she continued for a quarter century.[8]

*Starts with NBC.*    Later in 1936, Thompson began her career as a broadcaster, giving commentary on the Democratic convention in Cleveland and the Republican event in Philadelphia for NBC. A year later, she became a regular commentator on Sunday nights and then moved to Mondays at 9 P.M. Her audience for those broadcasts, which were sponsored by General Electric, was estimated at five million. Her income in 1938 was reported by *Time* magazine at more than $100,000, and Thompson was so popular that a collection of her columns and broadcasts, *Let the Record Speak*, was published. By 1939, she had added another broadcast on NBC, "Hour of Charm." In a *Radio Guide* poll of 729,000 listeners, Thompson was voted "most popular commentator" with 57.2 percent of the votes, compared to Kate Smith with 28.3 percent and Mary Margaret McBride with 9.4 percent.

Commentators were a peculiar kind of broadcaster. They ranged from those who stuck closely to the facts of the day's news, like Lowell Thomas, to ones who devoted almost their entire broadcast to venomous attacks on anything and everything, but mostly politicians. Thompson tended to broadcast her strong views. Program length ranged from five to fifteen minutes for most of the commentators, and some broadcast as frequently as six days a week. Others, like Thompson, were heard once a week. All the networks and some local stations had commentators, many of whom developed devoted followers who argued with friends and acquaintances about the merits of their favorite's stance on the issues of the day. The networks, of course, preferred that the commentators be sponsored so that the program time would generate revenue, but many of them were not.

*A Belligerent Tone.*    By the eve of World War II, Thompson was devoting the majority of her columns and broadcasts to the coming war, in particular to Adolf Hitler. Every broadcast seemed to bring a new attack against somebody, and General Electric officials got nervous about what they felt was an unnecessarily belligerent tone in her commentaries. First they put a disclaimer at the beginning of her broadcasts. Then they tried to soften them with music immediately before and after Thompson spoke. None of this seemed to change things. One important affiliate, KWK, St. Louis, once cut her off in mid-commentary. When her contract with General Electric came up for renewal in late 1939, neither side was eager to continue the relationship, and Thompson took a rest from radio.

Thompson had cut back on her lucrative lecturing while working on a play that winter. She also made a curious political switch. Initially, Thompson supported Wendell Wilkie for president in 1940, but suddenly flip-flopped to supporting Franklin Delano Roosevelt for a third term, a maneuver that undermined some of her credibility, especially with the Reids; her association with the *Herald Tribune* ended the next year. Thompson's column then was picked up by the Bell Syndicate and put in the *New York Post*, but that was not the prestigious paper that the *Herald Tribune* was.

*Broadcasts from Britain.*    In the summer of 1941, Thompson returned to Europe to see firsthand how the British were holding up. Thompson had a wide following in Britain, where her column was published, and she had done some shortwave broadcasts that attracted notice. One of the broadcasts was a speech she gave in Montreal urging Winston Churchill to stand tough. The British prime minister did not hear it, but friends brought a recording to his country estate; when Churchill heard it, it brought tears to his eyes. In the address, Thompson placed Churchill in impressive company.

Around you, Winston, is a gallant company of ghosts. Elizabeth is there, and Raleigh, and Wellington. Burke is there, and Walpole and Pitt. Byron is there, and Wordsworth and Shelley. Yes, and I think Washington is there, and Hamilton, two men of English blood whom gallant Englishmen defended in your Parliament. And Jefferson is there, who died again the other day in France. All the makers of world freedom and of law are there.[9]

In going to England, Thompson was repeating a pattern she had followed throughout her career as a journalist: going to see things for herself. She was always a whirlwind of activity, keeping a staff of three secretaries busy in the United States. Things weren't much different during her four weeks in England. In addition to preparing her newspaper column and her magazine column, Thompson was back on NBC. She did several London broadcasts for the network, at the early hour of 2:30 A.M. Actually, this fit right into Thompson's schedule, for she tended to get up late and stay up half the night. On a typical day in England she would rise by 10 A.M., digest the newspapers and work for a few hours, lunch with an old friend or a news source, tour some military facility or hospital, write some more, and then dine with more friends before heading out to see an air raid shelter or defense position. At any social occasion she might abruptly excuse herself to jot down a column or commentary, emerging a half hour or so later to pick up where she'd left off, usually dominating the conversation, which was almost always about world events.

Thompson also did some broadcasts for the BBC. Her words were very much wanted by the British officials, who promoted her broadcasts quite heavily. The BBC magazine, *The Listener*, described Thompson as having "an unusually attractive voice, low in register, beautifully clear, and wide in its range of tones."[10] Though an experienced broadcaster, Thompson seemed surprisingly nervous before her first British broadcast in which she explained why she had gone to Britain. She always suffered from a dryness in her throat before going on the air, but more so this time because she felt it was especially important for her to boost British morale.

James Drawbell, who was editor-in-chief of the *Sunday Chronicle*, the British paper that carried her column, ended up accompanying Thompson most of her time in England. He was somewhat of a social secretary for that month, and was amazed at the hundreds of people who wanted Thompson's ear. Some were old friends from earlier days in Europe; others were representatives of nations overtaken by the Nazis and now in exile in London. While traveling, Drawbell received bits and pieces of Thompson's views, including a rather revealing conversation about careers for women. He quotes Thompson as saying:

> If I'd a daughter, I'd tell her: Think twice before you prefer a career to a marriage. Society at this moment has a bigger need of good mothers than it has of more secretaries and movie stars. It's a better thing to produce a fine man than a second rate novel, and fine men begin by being fine children. . . . If I'd a daughter, I'd warn her not to bite off more than she could chew. A lot of women of my generation did that. In the joy of the new chances open to them, thousands of them have tried the impossible. They've thought they could "lead their own lives," enter occupations, competing with men, enjoy social and even sexual freedom and, at the same time, have happy and productive

marriages. Well, they just can't! One woman in a thousand can do it, even though they may be gifted; and most of those who try what is, by nature, too much, just break their hearts.[11]

Thompson's marriage to Lewis had soured by this time, and perhaps she felt the price of her professional success had been failure in her personal life; after all, few women of her time had the career she did, and Thompson seemed to have accomplished what she would advise a daughter not to attempt. Eventually, though, she would be happy in matrimony. In 1943, she married Maxim Kopf, an artist with whom she was very contented until his death fifteen years later.

*"Listen, Hans."*   A few months before she went to Britain, Thompson had begun broadcasting to Germany over CBS's shortwave facilities. These broadcasts were part of an American propaganda effort and were addressed to a friend from her newspaper days in Europe, whom she called "Hans." He was actually Count Helmuth von Moltke, who was executed by the Nazis in 1945. These weekly broadcasts were the idea of a writer friend of Thompson's. Thompson spoke rather good German and, in the form of letters or conversations directed at Hans, described Nazi atrocities or gave lectures about the inevitability of Allied victory.[12]

*On the Decline.*   Thompson's popularity was waning by the war's end. At the beginning of 1945, she broadcast on NBC's Blue Channel and then stayed through its transition to ABC. By summer, she was with Mutual, still broadcasting in a "crisp, metallic voice rich with scorn and irony."[13] She and her husband went to Europe to witness the last days of the war. Thompson began to write extensively about Palestine, taking a position that was perceived by some to be anti-Jewish. Her views became such a problem for the *Post* that it dropped her column in 1947. She became active in the American Christian Palestine Committee, further raising questions about her objectivity on the issue.

Thompson was no longer on the radio, and her column was carried in a declining number of papers. She continued it, however, until shortly after the death of her husband in 1958. Thompson died January 30, 1961, in Lisbon, while visiting her former daughter-in-law and grandchildren.

### Lisa Sergio: Trilingual Broadcaster

Not all the female news broadcasters during World War II reported from overseas. Lisa Sergio had special expertise that allowed her to broadcast from both sides of the Atlantic. Sergio had been an insider during Italian leader Benito Mussolini's early years, broadcasting for him in Europe. But she became disillusioned with his politics and fled to the United States where she interpreted news of the war to the American people.

Lisa Sergio, being introduced on WOV by commentator Quincy Howe. She did newscasts and commentary in Italian on the station in the late 1940s. Courtesy Lisa Sergio.

Sergio was born in Florence, Italy, in 1905, the only child of a well-to-do baron and his American wife. Fluent in Italian, French, and English, Sergio studied for a career in archaeology. But she turned to literature at the age of seventeen, editing *The Italian Mail,* an English literary weekly. For the next seven years she also translated several plays, saw them produced, and wrote short stories. In 1930 Sergio moved to Rome, where she combined writing and archaeology, becoming the bibliographer for the magazine of the Association of Mediterranean Studies and working for archaeology professors.

Broadcasting became Sergio's profession in March 1932 when Mussolini decided to initiate English radio broadcasts to tell the story of fascism. He asked Guglielmo Marconi, inventor of the wireless, whether it was feasible. When the reply was affirmative, Mussolini asked Marconi whether he knew anyone who spoke English well. Marconi, an old friend of Baron Sergio, thought of Lisa. Believing it was an afternoon job, she agreed to it.

> I remember so well that first night. I had never seen a microphone. I had never been on the air before. And the engineer said to me, "Now you see this box on this table. If you punch that button, it's red, and it means you're on the air. And if you punch *that* button, it's green, and it means you can cough.[14]

Sergio never returned to archaeology. Mussolini's idea was a success, and soon fascist messages were being broadcast in twenty languages.

Sergio turned from fascism after Italy attacked Ethiopia in 1936. The following year she was forced to flee her homeland and with Marconi's help escaped to the United States in July 1937. Her old family friend gave her a letter of introduction to David Sarnoff, head of NBC. Ironically, the first broadcast Sergio did for the network in the United States was a tribute to Marconi, who died July 20 of that year.[15]

Sergio continued to broadcast for NBC in a variety of capacities. She was the voice of Elizabeth Arden on "The Elizabeth Arden Show," the announcer on "Radio Guild," the narrator of "Tales of Great Rivers," and the first woman to do commentaries from the Metropolitan Opera House. Sergio also conducted interviews with people in cultural affairs for "Let's Talk It Over." But she never did any women's programs. "I've never believed in the division between men and women; we don't in Italy. . . . I just didn't think that there was any purpose in doing programs for women, because programs for women in those days meant kitchen pointers or . . . ridiculous things."

When war broke out in Europe, Sergio went to work for WQXR, New York, as a news commentator. She thought it was inevitable that the United States would become involved and believed many Americans agreed with her and wanted to know what was going on. Sergio felt she could tell the American people what the events overseas meant for them because "the people who were playing leading roles were mostly known to me. I knew

Mussolini well. I had come to know Hitler. I knew what they were thinking. I knew DeGaulle. I knew some of the English people.''

Sergio's broadcast was heard Monday through Friday, at first at 10 A.M. and a couple of years later, in 1942, at 7 P.M. It opened with music, followed by a male announcer welcoming the audience. Then Sergio would come on, and in a clear, low voice, analyze the latest events in the war. Her delivery was deliberate and calm, and though she had no trace of an Italian accent, her pronunciation was European, and her voice sounded cultured. A contemporary of Sergio's at CBS, Helen Sioussat, remembers it as "the most beautiful voice, and she was a very brilliant woman."[16] Sergio's knowledge, authoritative style, and contralto voice led to her acceptance on the air. Though one of only a few women news commentators heard across the nation, her gender didn't seem to make much difference; *Variety* magazine called her "the only woman among thirty male commentators in the U.S.A. qualified to interpret the news." Her career as a news commentator had come naturally for her. She was raised believing men and women were equal, and "if you had brains, that was what counted."

After the war, in 1947, and by now an American citizen, Sergio returned to Europe to gather information for a series of lectures. She took up writing, lecturing, and consulting as her primary occupations and never again broadcast full time. But Sergio did not give up her place on the radio entirely. She broadcast news in Italian and English on New York radio station WOV and in the 1950s broadcast for NBC on "Frontiers of Faith," a religious program, and for ABC's "New Nations of Africa." Since 1960, she has volunteered her time and thoughts on "Prayer through the Ages," a fifteen-minute program heard on WMAL, Washington, D.C., at 6:45 Sunday mornings.

Sergio was a unique broadcaster. Her heritage gave her entrees in both Italy and the United States, allowing her to broadcast equally well in Italian and English. That attribute was responsible for her brief time in radio's limelight, but like most of the women who broadcast during the war, her career as a radio journalist faded after the fighting stopped.

### Esther Van Wagoner Tufty: The "Duchess"

Like many of the other broadcast newswomen of her time, Esther Van Wagoner Tufty had a hand in print as well as radio and television. Although she made a contribution to news on the air, she was primarily a newspaperwoman during most of her career.

Tufty began in the news business just after graduating high school in 1914, getting a job as assistant society editor on her hometown newspaper, the *Pontiac* (Michigan) *Press*, for $7.50 a week. After a year there she decided to go to Michigan State University but completed her degree at the University of Wisconsin because she liked its journalism school. While there, she worked on the *Madison Democrat* and *Capital Times*.

In 1921, Esther Van Wagoner married Harold Tufty, an engineer, and they moved to Chicago. She became managing editor of the *Evanston News-Index*, and then they moved to Washington in 1935 when Harold took a job with the Federal Radio Commission. Her brother Murray, who later became governor of Michigan, suggested she open her own news bureau and serve Michigan newspapers. She took his advice, and the Tufty News Bureau had twenty-six dailies for clients. Eventually she served more than 300 papers, including some in New Jersey and New York.

During the war, Tufty got into radio. She broadcast "Headlines from Washington" over the Atlantic Coast Network from WWDC, Washington. The fifteen-minute program aired at 12:45 P.M. Monday through Saturday, and she described it as not a "woman's program, but the news as reported by a woman."[17] From there she went to NBC and, when the network split, stayed with the Blue Network, which became ABC. Her program then was called "Tufty's Topics."

In 1952 Tufty also took on television broadcasting, working for NBC at the 1952 Chicago conventions. She went on to become Washington news editor for Arlene Francis's "Home" program, and also did a daily spot for a program hosted by Mike Wallace.

Tufty was known around Washington as "The Duchess" and looked the part; she wore her hair in a braided crown. But she actually got her nickname when an innkeeper in Europe mistook her for a real duchess who was arriving later in the day.

In a career that spanned more than seventy years, Tufty covered everything from President Franklin Roosevelt's news conferences—she was one of the few women to do so—to the Vietnam War. She also gave dozens of lectures every year, and she was the only woman to be president of the top three Washington press clubs for women, the Women's National Press Club, the American Newspaper Women's Club, and American Women in Radio and Television.

Tufty also was known for her physical endurance. She walked with a cane after a broken leg didn't heal properly, survived breast cancer, lost an eye, and had nine pacemakers. She suffered a stroke in February 1984 at the age of eighty-seven and died in the spring of 1986.

### Elizabeth Bemis: CBS's First Female Newscaster

The scarcity of men at home during World War II launched many women's broadcast news careers at local stations, but it was not as easy for women to break into the network ranks on the air. Network executives generally did not

Elizabeth Bemis, before a mike at KLZ, Denver. Her proud father, Edwin A. Bemis, looks on. Courtesy Bemi DeBus.

want women's voices delivering the news and made little effort to recruit women for on-air work. But Elizabeth Bemis changed those notions at CBS, and her career flourished during the war years. She was hired as CBS's first West Coast woman news analyst in 1942 after she had been reporting and reading the news on several local stations.

Elizabeth Louise Bemis was raised in a home where literature and the arts were important. She was born August 5, 1916, to the owner and publisher of the weekly *Littleton Independent* in Colorado and a concert singer who "was an artist to her fingertips."[18]

Bemis was an inquisitive child, interested in everything going on around her—"they said I couldn't let anything go by without knowing about it." Although she wrote her first newspaper article at the age of eleven and worked summers at her father's newspaper and did a bit of acting and poetry on two Denver area radio stations, Bemis decided her curiosity suited her to the medical profession. She graduated from the University of Colorado in 1937 with a double degree in zoology and psychology, then won an exchange scholarship to the University of Paris to study medicine.

While overseas, Bemis traveled quite a bit. Her adventures included a trip to Africa, where she was arrested as a suspected spy after a stamp in her passport mysteriously was erased. She was on her way to Eastern Europe when the Munich crisis occurred, and she returned to Paris. Later that year her mother visited, and deciding it was too dangerous for them to remain in Europe, Mrs. Bemis took Elizabeth home.

*Newscaster at KLZ.*    It didn't take the twenty-two-year-old long to find a news job in Colorado. Bemis heard that one of the radio stations was planning to put a woman on the air doing news, so she headed for the CBS affiliate, KLZ, where she had done some entertainment broadcasting before and convinced the head of the news department to hire her. "I had just returned from Europe and I knew something about the situation over there, and I had sent home articles from Europe." If that wasn't enough to get her the job, she also told him to "give me a test and you'll find my voice drops two octaves"—an argument she was to use more than once in the future. Several weeks later Bemis discovered it was not KLZ but another station that had wanted to have a woman newscaster. But at that point it didn't make a difference—she had a job.

Unlike most women of the time, Bemis did not broadcast "women's news." It was quite rare in 1939 for a woman to do hard news as she did, but from the outset she refused to do anything else; "there were plenty of cooks and household hints. I was a news gal." For several months, she was paid $27 a week to be heard over the airwaves as "Betty Lou Bemis."

In 1940 a news editor at KLZ got a job in Cincinnati at WLW and, without Bemis knowing it, gave his boss a tape of her reading the news. Soon she got a telegram asking how soon she could get there and what she wanted to be paid. For $50 a week, the union minimum in Cincinnati, "Betty Lou" became "Elizabeth Bemis," giving the news for fifteen minutes every afternoon at three.

Cincinnati brought another change in Bemis's life. She met Louis DeBus, the brother of a friend. It was love at first sight, and a week later he proposed. She refused at first, but the next night she said yes; they were married in September 1941.

After two years at WLW, Bemis moved to Southern California with her husband, who was in the military and had been transferred. She tried to get a job as a newscaster at several of the bigger stations, but they all turned her away. Finally she got an interview with Ira Copley, who owned radio stations in Southern California.

> The first thing he asked me was what I read. So I called off a list of magazines that I read. He said, "No, I mean *Ladies Home Journal, Colliers, Women's Home Companion*"—stuff like that. And I said, "I don't read them." He said, "You don't? Well, why not?" And I said, "Because that's narrow stuff. That's not the way I go. That's not what I've been doing." And he said, "Well, I really would want you to do 'From the Woman's Point of View.'" And I said, "Mr. Copley, we have nothing to say to each other." And I walked out. I was so furious.

But it fired up Bemis to convince KNX, the CBS-owned station, to hire her. Again, the argument that her voice was deeper on the air helped her get the job.

*Joins CBS.*    Bemis started out doing a fifteen-minute commentary that was heard in the early evenings over CBS's West Coast stations. A few months later, CBS network head William Paley heard her and, impressed, asked her to work for CBS in New York. Bemis had no reason to stay in Los Angeles since her husband was stationed in the Pacific during the war, so in May 1943 she packed her bags and moved East to become the first woman news anchor on CBS. Her fifteen-minute program aired every afternoon at three, and she also did some reporting. Although she had a CBS press card, it was not always honored because some authorities did not believe a woman was gathering the news. She recalls one assignment, covering war maneuvers in Louisiana, when she was forbidden to ride in a tank because no woman had ever been in one there. In spite of what other people thought, however, Bemis did not consider herself an anomaly.

*A Feeling of Equality.*    Although the public might have seen Bemis as unusual in her profession, she never felt singled out by her male colleagues. She says they always treated her as an equal perhaps because, she says, she didn't play on her femininity and so was accepted for what she was.

In the afternoons, after I got off the air, very often we sat down with [William L.] Shirer or Doug Edwards, even occasionally Bob Trout would poke his head in. We would sit down and talk about the news and quite often I would bring up an idea of some sort and they would say, "Gee, that's great. Can I use it?"

Edwards recalls the same feeling of equality and respect among the men and women who worked in that newsroom. Shirley Wershba, who was just starting out then as a desk assistant, recalls how helpful Bemis was the first time Wershba was given a chance to write a 4:25 P.M. newscast.

She looked at me and she said, "Shirley, just pretend that you've gone home after a whole day of reading the wires here and one of your friends says to you, 'You're up on the news. What happened today?' " And I sat down at the typewriter—and she did that for me—and I sat down and just [snapping fingers] went.[19]

*CBS Lets Her Go.*    Wershba did not have Bemis's counsel for long. In July 1944, Bemis was let go "because they had not sold me. This was sort of a mutual thing [leaving CBS] because they said they'd tried and I said that I had my spies around and knew that they hadn't." Bemis wasn't really told she was out of a job. One of her supervisors said, " 'There's an extra check for you down in accounting.' And I said, 'Gee, does that mean they finally have sold me?' He said, 'I don't know. They just called to tell me there's an extra check.' So I went down into accounting and the extra check was a termination check." Bemis was paid two weeks severance, $300.

Bemis believes her gender was ultimately responsible for her being fired, because the network would have sold a newscast by a man. She got a lot of supportive fan mail, however, from both men and women. Not all the reactions to a woman delivering the news were positive, though. "Occasionally people would call in and ask what the hell I thought I was doing. But you get that kind of thing all the time, even today, I'm sure."

After Bemis left CBS she took a job with the Office of War Information in New York, broadcasting news to American troops in Europe. She worked there until Christmas of 1944, when her husband returned to the States. She accompanied him when he was sent to Malden, Missouri, where she did weekly radio news updates and wrote a column called "Pertinent, Impertinent" in the Army newspaper. When her husband was transferred to Texas, Bemis left her career in broadcast news for good. After the war they moved back to Southern California and raised a family. Bemis has turned her energies to community activities and a volunteer society aimed at educating the public about whales, dolphins, and porpoises.

Though Elizabeth Bemis was not with CBS long, she paved the way for other women on the network's airwaves. CBS's Los Angeles station, KNX, promoted a two-year veteran of its news bureau, Katherine Carr, to become its first woman news reporter in 1943, and Carr went on to have her own daily news program, fifteen minutes in the early morning. Still, Bemis's departure from the network left a lot of questions about whether a woman could be accepted as a newscaster.

## BEHIND THE SCENES

### Helen Sioussat: The First Female Network News Executive

While the war provided a catalyst for many women to broadcast news and commentaries, those years also saw America's first female network news executive earning her reputation. Again, CBS led the way. Helen Sioussat took over as director of talks for the network when Edward R. Murrow went to London in 1937, a position she held for more than two decades.

The Talks Department was under the direction of Paul White, part of a division that included news, sports, and special events. Under Murrow it handled educational and religious programs as well as public affairs broadcasts. By the time Sioussat took over, CBS had decided to split the department, so she was responsible only for talks—all non-commercial public affairs broadcasts such as debates, roundtable discussions, and cultural programs. The only commercial time the Talks Department controlled was political programs during election periods. Since it was a relatively new department, Sioussat also had a hand in formulating policy, and as the popularity of radio grew, she helped set the standards of fairness in granting air time.

Helen Johnson Doyle Sioussat grew up in Baltimore, where she was born February 11, 1902. Her mother, for whom she was named, died when Helen was seven, and the child was raised by her aunt. After her debut to society, Sioussat attended secretarial school. She then held a series of office jobs—assistant to the dean of Goucher College, a dentist's assistant in Philadelphia, the business manager of two Kansas City, Missouri, firms, the Buschman Company and the National Professional Bureau, and assistant to the treasurer of the Petroleum Industry's Planning and Coordinating Committee in Washington, D.C. Sioussat also had danced professionally for a year as half of the Spanish Adagio Team. By the time she returned to the Washington area in 1934, she had been married and divorced twice.

After a year with the Petroleum Industry, Sioussat began looking for another job. She heard of an opening as an assistant to radio producer Phillips H. Lord and, along with about 200 other women, applied for the job. When he interviewed her, she was honest, telling him she knew nothing about radio, didn't like radio, and didn't even own one. In spite of that, Lord decided to hire her at $50 a week.

> And I said, "Well, I won't do it for $50. I want more." And he said, "Well, you haven't got any experience." I said, "That's why I want more, because it's

going to be much harder for me to do it than one of these other people." And he said, "That is the damndest thing I ever heard. How can you possibly?" I said, "Well, that's it. I'm sorry, but this is the first time in all the jobs I've had that I ever told my employer that I didn't know anything about the job. Heretofore I wouldn't say anything and I'd struggle through it and they would say that I was doing a perfect job. But I almost died trying to get it done!"[20]

Sioussat went on to tell Lord he would be happy with her work or he could fire her, but he decided he couldn't afford her and she drove on back to her father's house in Baltimore. Just as she pulled up, she got a telephone call. Her spunk had paid off; it was Lord, convinced he had to find out whether she could do the job, and offering to pay her $65 a week.

Sioussat began as the Washington manager for Lord in 1935. Her office was in the FBI building, right next to that of J. Edgar Hoover; the director had given it to her so she could easily get official information from the FBI files for the radio series, "G-Men," which was heard every week over NBC. While "G-Men" was on the air, Sioussat commuted between Washington and New York, where the series was broadcast. After it ended, she moved to New York and was promoted to manager of all Lord's productions, which included "Gang Busters," "Seth Parker," and "Mr. District Attorney." Her duties had expanded to include researching shows, writing and rewriting scripts, casting, and directing rehearsals.

*Hired By Murrow.*    Working with Lord was exciting, but it also was taxing. The veteran idea man was "tireless," and Sioussat didn't want to work twenty-four hours a day. So in the spring of 1936, she headed for NBC to see if there were any jobs there. Since CBS was across the street, she stopped in. Sioussat interviewed with Ed Murrow, then director of talks, and he hired her as his assistant—a move he later called "my greatest contribution to CBS," in an inscription to her of a collection of his London broadcasts. Within a month or two she became the associate director of the department.

Although there weren't many women at CBS, Sioussat didn't have any trouble getting hired. She says CBS founder and then president, William Paley, had no problem with her gender, and Murrow treated women as equals. "I didn't find that he felt that men were superior, and he was always very encouraging. And if you didn't do exactly the right thing, he would be very patient about it, explain it and be patient about it . . . and he was a good teacher."

Murrow played an important role in the careers of several early women in broadcast news, for he seemed to be open to the contributions of women at CBS. He came from a family with a strong mother. Before joining the network he had worked in student organizations where women had played important roles. Throughout his career, Murrow encouraged women in broadcasting. However, it should be remembered that his colleagues covering World War II overseas were known as "Murrow's Boys"—no women.

Helen Sioussat, Director of Talks, CBS, chats with her boss, William S. Paley, in New York. During the war, Paley served in the military while maintaining control over the network he founded. Courtesy Helen J. D. Sioussat.

*The Struggle for Acceptance.*   A year after Sioussat first began working for CBS, Murrow was promoted to European director for the network. At Murrow's suggestion, Sioussat was chosen to take over the department—"he didn't insist upon it, but he suggested it. He said I was a natural for it." She also began editing the CBS quarterly digest, *Talks.* It was not an easy transition for her; other male managers at CBS were not as supportive as Murrow. Vice president Douglas Coulter "did not like women in any kind of an executive position, and he fought it. And while he was fighting it, he finally admitted that I was the head of the department, I was the director of the department. But he didn't want me to have it on my letterhead. He didn't want me to have it on my cards." With no business cards and no official stationery—essentially, with no official recognition of her position—Sioussat found it awkward dealing with politicians and business people. Finally she got support from CBS's legal department, and Coulter was overruled.

Executive vice president Edward Klauber also "was very much opposed to women in offices," and Sioussat believes he was insulted by having a female executive on the network staff. It was eight years before Klauber accepted her.

> Up until the night that [President Franklin] Roosevelt died, he had been really very rude to me and showed his displeasure at my being there. I stayed because everybody else wanted me but he did not want a woman. It wasn't particularly me because he didn't even really know me, but he just didn't like the idea of a woman executive. So the night that Roosevelt died . . . he came down and walked around the floor seeing what was being done. And ordinarily I would have been a little self-conscious because of him. He was a little man, but he was very, very pompous. But this was so important that I just said, "I'm sorry, but I haven't time to talk with you. I'm doing thus and so and thus and so, and so if you don't mind I'll come get you when I can talk." And I went ahead with what I was doing, which was extremely urgent. And he said, "May I stand in the door and watch?" And I said, "Yes." And the next day he called and he said, "I remove all of my complaints against having a woman. I thought you did a wonderful job." And we became awfully good friends then.

In her early days as director of talks, Sioussat experienced another kind of discrimination, one that many other women pioneers in broadcasting felt: unequal financial compensation. She was paid $50 a week, the same wage, she says, that Murrow got when he was first hired by CBS. She didn't get a raise when she was promoted, and then the network brought in a man to be her assistant. "And I found out they were paying him more than me [$75 a week]. And he was my assistant! And that's the only time that I did really get very angry and demand that this be changed."

Still, Sioussat's fight for pay parity continued.

> I was a woman. Every time I would ask for a raise, they'd say, "Well now, you know you're a woman and you're head of a department, and it's an honor."

And I said, "To heck, I can't eat the honor!" I got raises later, but I didn't get raises then. This was supposed to be the reward that I got for working like a dog. But I loved every minute of it.

By the time Sioussat retired from CBS in 1962, she was earning about $260 a week. She didn't really care whether she ever reached pay parity with men because it wasn't that important to her. What counted the most was that "it was the first job and only job I really loved. And when I retired it was worse than any divorce you could possibly have. I was heartbroken. I think it was because I was given complete responsibility and they backed me up on everything."

Sioussat found that for the most part, the people she put on the air treated her the same as they would have treated a man in her position, "provided I went to the head. I mean, I used to refuse to go to an assistant. I would go to the head because the assistant would be very patronizing, but not the head." Only twice does she recall people treating her condescendingly, and one of those times was by a woman. She did, however, get special treatment when she traveled on the French Steamship Line. She was always put at the captain's table, "and they made a tremendous lot to do over the fact that I was the head of a department in a radio network and I was a woman. And they just couldn't believe it! In those days, I mean, you were almost famous because you were a woman."

Interestingly, though Sioussat treated male and female newsmakers in the same manner, she drew a difference between the sexes on her own staff. "I refused to have a man assistant. That's the one place I insisted upon a woman. I thought—this is going to upset you, I'm afraid—but I thought it sort of demeaned a man to work under a woman." Sioussat felt she was reflecting the social conventions of the times and that working for a woman might hinder a man's chances for career advancement; and so her one assistant and three secretaries were women.

*"Table Talk" on TV.*    As radio was enjoying its golden days, television was just beginning. Sioussat experimented with it by starting up the first question-and-answer discussion program on CBS, "Table Talk with Helen Sioussat." The program was on the air for a year, from 1941 to 1942, and was broadcast from the CBS television studio at Grand Central Terminal.

When Sioussat began as director of talks, women's groups were "delighted that a woman was there because they thought they could get more time." But she told them they would only get time if they had something to say and could present it well. However, she found most of their programs "very, very dreary," and didn't put many on.

*Honored for Her Accomplishments.*    Sioussat's achievements were recognized within the industry when she received a Peabody Award in 1954 for the best educational program, a series, "Man's Right to Knowledge." Her accomplishments already had won her a place as *Good Housekeeping* magazine's "Girl of the Month" in March 1938. Throughout her career, she devoted herself to her work and was so concerned about being perceived as politically impartial that "I didn't even vote the whole time I was at CBS. They don't know that, but I didn't because I was so afraid that I'd get all interested in this side or that side."

After twenty-one years as director of talks, Sioussat was transferred to the network's Washington offices. She was reluctant to leave New York, a city she loved, but agreed to go at the request of CBS president Frank Stanton. From 1958 to 1962, Sioussat was the network's liaison with Congress and federal agencies, retiring in April when the aunt who raised her became ill. After her aunt died, Sioussat was a self-employed consultant on integrated public and government relations. She retired in 1983.

*Words of Advice.* One of the founders of American Women in Radio and Television, Sioussat often got calls from young women asking for advice and assistance. Some she would help with recommendations, but if she didn't think they could do the job, she would tell them so and steer them in another direction. Had she recommended someone who she didn't think would work out, "I would have been doing a disservice to the rest of the women who had come along. . . . You can hurt people by not using judgment in recommending them."

Sioussat had more advice in her book, *Mikes Don't Bite*, published in 1943.

> You've got to "show 'em," girls. Not by affecting low-heeled shoes and masculine garb, by acting self-important or bossy. If you have the stuff of which executives are made, don't be tactless or step on other toes or over the boys ahead. Swaggering females are even more intolerable than swaggering males. Be modest and natural; never fluttery, hysterical nor late. Win respect for your abilities rather than demand it. Men can be your most valuable guides, as well as your most powerful foes. In most cases it's up to you to decide.[21]

A book and several pamphlets and articles on broadcasting weren't Sioussat's only endeavors in writing. She also composed the music and wrote the lyrics to four copyrighted songs—"Unathletic Me," "My Beloved," "Meet Me at the Waldorf," and "Beautiful Cat Cay."

Sioussat got offers to leave CBS during her twenty-six years with the network; NBC's David Sarnoff told her he'd double her salary if she'd work for him, and President Dwight Eisenhower offered her a position on the Federal Communications Commission or an ambassadorship to Brazil. "But I had at last found what I wanted to do, and I said in my book, and I still mean it and think of it, that success is getting what you want. Happiness is wanting what you get."

### Marian Glick: The Fourth TV Network's News Director

Had the DuMont Network prospered in the 1950s, perhaps Marian Glick would be recognized today as the first woman to head a network news organization. While that is literally true, it's an accomplishment for the DuPont Network was never more than a handful of stations and went out of business in 1955 after selling its Pittsburgh station, which became KDKA.

Marian Glick graduated from Indiana University and moved to Portland, Oregon, to work for the United Press. After four years with the UP she quit, went to New York and worked in a Greenwich Village restaurant, and then joined the syndicated Women's National News Service. While there, a friend who worked at experimental TV station W2XJT on Long Island asked her to become news director of the fledgling DuMont Network, and she started with the weekly salary of $45 and only herself to direct. "Nobody said a word about my being a woman. They just said, she knows news."[22] The network's news commitment was modest: initially a Sunday report read by an announcer and then a daily fifteen-minute broadcast that she wrote, edited, and directed. DuMont was so strapped for equipment that Glick shared a typewriter with the casting director for the network's entertainment programming.

Glick lasted through four management turnovers in four years, but the fifth general manager fired her, and she went to work for the Associated Press as a writer and editor in 1954. Two years later, she became a writer at CBS. Glick says she was treated as an equal to the men there, adding that her greatest compliment was "when the fellows said I was a good newsman." After thirty years with CBS, she retired in early 1986.

### Alice Weel Bigart: Network Nightly News Writer

CBS was also the home of the first woman to become a full-time writer for a network evening news program. Alice Weel, later Alice Weel Bigart, joined "Douglas Edwards and the News" in 1948 after working on some of the network's top radio programs.

A native of New York, Alice Jane Weel graduated from Bryn Mawr in 1943. During her senior year, she taught a course in map making and worked briefly during the war as a map maker for the government. She went on to graduate school, receiving her M.S. in journalism from Columbia University in 1944. She worked briefly as New York correspondent for the *London Daily News* before joining CBS later that year.

While at CBS Radio, Weel wrote for several major news programs. Shortly after CBS established a television network, she moved into that news department as a writer and associate producer for "Douglas Edwards and the News," a fifteen-minute program broadcast in the early evenings. Edwards remembers her as a quick study and a talented writer who often won praise from some of the top correspondents, including Edward R. Murrow. She occasionally substituted as editor of the evening news.

Weel worked with Edwards, producer-director Don Hewitt, editor William Porter, and writer Sanford Sokolow on "Douglas Edwards and the News," and though she was one of the only women in TV news then, she found few handicaps because of her gender.

> If there are any, it's my own fault. . . . I think that being a woman, you have to be a little more careful. Once in a great while, you come up against a man who resents women in this business. But it's unusual. You may decide yourself that there are certain restrictions that apply to you. But if you do, it's your own fault.[23]

Weel went on to work on several documentaries for CBS, including "The Face of Red China," a critically acclaimed program that she wrote in a weekend. She was co-producer of the CBS Special Events Unit, handling such assignments as national political conventions, space shots, and the Army-McCarthy hearings of 1954. She also produced CBS's year-end round-up of 1963, the network's first two-hour news program. That same year she married Homer Bigart of the *New York Times*.

Alice Weel Bigart wound up her career at CBS as a producer for "60 Minutes." She died of cancer in 1969.

### Shirley Wershba: Starting Out as a Desk Assistant

One of the few women to work her way up from an entry-level position at a network during the war was Shirley Lubowitz Wershba. Wershba began as a desk assistant at CBS, juggled a marriage and a career, became a full-time mother, then, after her children were in school, returned to the work force.

A native New Yorker who had graduated from Brooklyn College in 1943 with a degree in English, Wershba got her first job at the *Daily News* as a copy girl. Soon she was hired by a neighborhood publishing company, where she worked up to an editor's position. But Wershba wasn't happy, and after a few months she quit to go into radio. She applied to be a page at CBS, but there were no openings, so she took a job in the mail room. Six weeks on the job she discovered the newsroom and fell in love with it. When a desk assistant's job opened up, she got it, earning $19 a week. Eagerly she took on the duties of ripping wires, keeping the newsroom supplied, and getting coffee.

But Wershba had higher aspirations: She wanted to be a writer. She found the atmosphere at CBS News encouraging; if she practiced, she could get her copy critiqued. After about a month as a desk assistant she began writing a 4:25 P.M. newscast on the regular writer's day off. Ten months later, at the end of 1944, she was promoted to junior writer on the overnight shift, and her wages were hiked to $35 a week. She worked from midnight to 8 A.M.; hours were not assigned according to gender. Wershba wrote at least five two-minute newscasts a night for the next nineteen months, deciding which stories to include in the summaries. Eventually she was moved to a day shift. Wershba remembers a fairly egalitarian attitude in the newsroom; the work of the few women on the news staff was respected—"highly regarded," as CBS anchor Douglas Edwards recalls. But though there were women writing, and one had even been on the air at CBS News, it was still a man's field.

> A man could aspire to be on the air and it was unusual for a woman to be on the air, even though there had been precedent for it. And women were not promoted to editor. I mean, you were a writer and that was it. I can remember executive Ted Church saying to me, "If we ever get around to making a woman an editor, you're the first one I'm going to make an editor." And you accepted that.[24]

By the time Wershba left CBS News in 1949, there still were no women on the desk. But the opportunities would come. "More women did come in after the war, and I guess maybe we had paved the way. We proved we could do anything."

*Raising a Family.*    Wershba resigned to join her husband, Joseph, in Washington, D.C. They had known each other in college and met up again when he joined CBS News as a senior writer a few months after she did. Romance blossomed, and in April 1948 they married. They kept it a secret to avoid a CBS policy forbidding married couples from working for the network. Soon Joe was transferred to Washington as a correspondent, and for several months they had a commuter marriage. During a round of budget cuts, manager Ted Church asked Shirley to resign, saying she would eventually want to join her husband, and her departure at that point would save someone else's job. She agreed, expecting to find work in Washington. "My experience in New York had been so favorable given that I had set my own limitations because that was the realistic approach. But Washington I found not only a Jim Crow town, but a very male chauvinist town, and I didn't like that." Unable to find a job in broadcasting, she did freelance magazine work.

In 1951, Wershba became a full-time mother when she and Joe had a daughter. Two years later they returned to New York, and the following year had a son.

*Back in the Work Force.*    When the Wershba children were in school, in 1962, Shirley went back to broadcasting. She had tried returning to work a couple of years earlier, writing and producing for an NBC documentary series, "Assignment America," but discovered that though "it was very exhilarating

... the night that I came home and found my son and the housekeeper kicking each other, I knew where my priorities were and I quit." When Wershba returned this second time, she wrote for a new CBS program, "Dimension of a Woman's World." Within the year, a sort of informal networking got Wershba back in news. Alice Weel, a writer and friend from Shirley's early days at CBS, asked her to help produce "The Midday News with a Woman's Page" for the network if a newspaper strike materialized. She agreed, it did, and when the strike was over, Wershba stayed in news, moving to CBS's local television station in New York as entertainment news editor.

Dissatisfied with local news, Wershba moved to ABC in 1965 as a writer. She worked on "Feature Story," a five-minute broadcast at the end of a soap opera, then wrote and produced for Marlene Sanders's "News with a Woman's Touch." At one point, during a strike of on-air personnel, Wershba was asked to substitute for Sanders, but refused and wouldn't even cross the picket lines because Sanders was her "team mate."

Tiring of spot news, Wershba left ABC in 1971. She freelanced a bit for CBS—the no-marriage rule had been abolished—and soon was hired as an associate producer for the morning news program. The business had changed for women since Wershba had first stepped into a newsroom more than a quarter of a century earlier.

> Originally there was no education on the part of women to get into the business, to get ahead as fast as men. There was no sense of, "Hey, what about me?" And when I came back twenty-five years later, there were women saying, "We're just as good and we want equal opportunities." And they were fighting for it. They had women's groups; they hadn't had that earlier.

*A Difference in Pay.*    Although there were more opportunities for women, discrimination still existed. Wershba was shocked when she discovered big salary differences in public television. She had gone to WNET as a producer when her contract at CBS expired in 1974. One year, when most people got a 7 percent salary increase, she got 8 percent. She was told it would bring her closer to parity. "That's when I discovered that I was making less than somebody they had hired after me with far less experience, and they had paid him more money. So I really raised holy hell at that point."

The pay differences in public TV, Wershba believes, were based on society's values. "The policy is get people as cheap as you can. Somehow, they seem to feel that they can't get men as cheap as they can get women."

*Back to CBS.*    Wershba returned to CBS News in 1981, working first for "Up to the Minute," a program that folded after thirteen weeks, then for special events, and finally for the morning news program. She was laid off in the summer of 1986, again the victim of staff cuts. After thirty-two years in the industry, she sees the biggest change for women is opportunity.

At first they went out of their way to put women in positions of power whether they should be there or not. I think now the time is coming it seems to me in the women's movement in general not just to sit back on your laurels but to stop making a point of it's a *woman* in that job. We should accept it. We're there, we belong there, we'll work our way up or out depending on our abilities.

## GETTING IN THE BACK DOOR

### Anne Denton Blair: From Volunteer to Bureau Chief

Not all the women who broke into broadcasting during the war did so intentionally. When Anne Denton Blair had her first brush with broadcasting, she never thought it eventually would lead to covering the nation's capital and becoming the first woman bureau chief for two different broadcast organizations. She got there in a circuitous way, and her path would only have been taken by a woman.

Blair was born February 4, 1914, in Oakmont, Pennsylvania, the only child of the editor of the *Pittsburgh Post* and his wife. The family moved to Cleveland before Anne was two, where her father did publicity throughout the Midwest for war bonds and later started up the *Summit County Democrat*.

The Cleveland area was hit hard by the Depression, but Blair's family made sacrifices so she could attend Bryn Mawr. After her freshman year, however, she persuaded her family not to send her back. The next January— 1933—her father died of a heart attack, and Anne and her mother moved to Connecticut where a grandmother lived. Blair got a job in New York, selling junior sportswear at Macy's for $15 a week. She went on to a couple of other sales and modeling jobs, then worked as an assistant registrar at Brearly School. In 1939 she married Robert Farnham Blair, a Washington patent lawyer. They had a son in 1943, and were divorced in 1949.

The Red Cross gave Blair her entree on the air during World War II. Fighting had broken out in Europe, and it looked as though the United States would soon get involved. Her contribution, as a member of the Red Cross's public relations committee, was to clip newspaper and magazine articles about what the chapter was accomplishing. That didn't seem to be helping the war effort much, so she decided to try to recruit new volunteers. The volunteer chairman suggested she check out a new radio interview program, "The Magic Carpet," moderated by Arthur Godfrey. Her efforts were successful; the Red Cross got more volunteers and Blair briefly became Godfrey's assistant. Soon NBC's affiliate in Washington asked Blair to produce "Red Cross Cavalcade," which was a success. But Blair did not pursue broadcasting again for several years.

Blair's next broadcasting experience came after the war. She met a woman at a cocktail party who had a program on a new radio station in Washington,

WQQW. Called "Capital Shopping," the daily fifteen-minute show featured the two women hosts telling people where to find different products. That night, after Blair got home, she got a call from the woman, who was at the airport on her way to Boston where her son had appendicitis. The woman asked Blair to fill in for her the next morning. Blair did that for several weeks, then the woman moved to New York and Blair continued the show.

Blair eventually became woman's program director of the station, which changed its call letters to WGMS. The station was part of the "Good Music Network," with four other stations, in New York, Philadelphia, Boston, and Richmond, Virginia. Blair did all sorts of shows in her decade there, from interviews to music programs to religious ones. She also provided live coverage of special events, such as the Eisenhower inaugural parade—"hanging out a second story window on lower Pennsylvania Avenue, I described the scene steadily, except for station breaks," for more than seven hours.[25]

*Washington Bureau Chief.*  The Red Cross had continued to get Anne's attention over the years, and after WGMS changed hands, she went to work for the association full time, becoming its director of radio and television. In 1962, a friend urged her to get back on the air and introduced her to the manager of Triangle Stations. That led to Blair becoming "the first Washington bureau chief ever for a 'group' of stations. Networks had had them—always men, of course—but the Triangle Stations, eighteen radio/TV outlets in seven states—the Annenberg group—was the first group not only to have a bureau chief, but a *woman* bureau chief!"[26] The bureau consisted of Blair and her assistant, and they had access to a camera crew. Her beat took her all over Washington, from the White House to the Pentagon to Capitol Hill. She covered events of national interest as well as those requested by individual stations. Though one of a handful of female bureau chiefs in Washington, Blair felt very little discrimination in those early days. "There were so few women, really, that the men felt quite courtly. . . . The senators and congressmen couldn't have been nicer. They loved having women reporters."[27]

Blair's behind-the-scenes view of the nation's capital turned into a regular syndicated program, "Windows on Washington." It was based on the premise that Washington is the hometown of all Americans. "I tried to appeal to everybody, and the idea that Washington belongs to them." She enjoyed the combination of hard news reporting and a public affairs program; "you have to do the news bang-bang kind of stuff if you're going to do the other, otherwise you won't know what's going on."

Television was making big technological gains then, and Blair was in the forefront with videotape. Triangle had taken its new mobile videotape truck to the 1968 Republican convention in Miami Beach, and Blair found anyone she wanted to interview willingly came to her camera. "Alas, it was not my charm or skill; it was the sheer fact that we were using videotape, and for the first time, they could see themselves played right back—no waiting!''[28]

After a decade with Triangle, Blair was out of a job when Capital Cities Communications bought the stations. She wasn't unemployed long; Blair soon got a call asking her to become Washington bureau chief for Tele-Prompter, at that time, 1972, the largest cable company in the country. Again, she was the first woman in her position there. Blair continued her ''Windows on Washington'' program, which aired on about a hundred stations throughout the United States and Canada. Two years later, though, TelePrompTer was spun off and, once again, Blair was out of a job.

Blair left politics and hard news when she left TelePrompTer, but she didn't leave broadcasting. After working as the radio/TV director for the Environmental Protection Agency and then as press secretary to the chairman of the telecommunications committee on Capitol Hill, she returned to the station at which she had begun, WGMS. She introduced ''At the Corcoran,'' a weekly rundown of what's happening at the art gallery. Blair also has written several children's books, including one about the adventures of a White House mouse.

### Fay Gillis Wells: World Traveler

Like Anne Denton Blair, Fay Gillis Wells first broadcast long before she became a regular on the radio. Her off-and-on romance with the airwaves began in the 1930s, but it wasn't until 1964 that she became the first woman broadcaster to cover the White House exclusively, a beat she picked up at the age of fifty-five.

Wells was in the air long before she was on it. Born October 15, 1908, in Minneapolis, she learned to fly as a young woman. Her first days as a pilot were quite exciting; the day after she first soloed, she and her instructor were forced to bail out of their plane over New York City after the tail, wings, and engine broke away. She was not hurt, and her performance in the emergency landed her a job as a demonstrator and saleswoman for Curtis Flying Service. That was the first of her many colorful careers. The following year, 1930, she went to Moscow with her father, where he taught mining technology. For the next four years she freelanced from Russia for the Associated Press and several aviation magazines and newspapers, including the *New York Herald Tribune.*

*A Honeymoon Covering a War.*   While in Moscow, Wells met the International News Service's correspondent there, Linton Wells, and three years later in 1935, when they were back in the States, they eloped. They spent their honeymoon covering the Italian-Ethiopian war for the *Herald Tribune,* she in the south and he in the north. They even had front-page byline stories on the same day—from different cities. The Wellses headed back to the United

Fay Gillis Wells began her broadcasting career in the 1930s, and ended it four decades later as a Washington correspondent for Storer Broadcasting. Reporting from the White House in winter called for gloves and fur-lined coat. Courtesy Fay Gillis Wells and Storer Communications, Inc.

States after the war, Fay detouring to Damascus to cover Syrian riots. Then while Lint wrote his autobiography, she covered Hollywood for the *Herald Tribune.*

The year 1938 saw the Wellses on the road again, this time because Lint was the roving reporter for the program, "Magic Key of RCA." It was Fay's indoctrination into radio, for that year RCA chief David Sarnoff sent the couple to Latin America to prove the feasibility of shortwave radio. They would stay in a country for a week, broadcast Sunday afternoon, then fly to the next country. Fay was the engineer, Lint the talent. But when they couldn't find a guest who could speak English well enough to be understood, "we used to chat back and forth on the culture of the country and the politics."[29] Lint was under contract at this point, and Fay worked for free, as she often was to do. But "we always worked together, no matter what the job was. He wouldn't go anyplace without me."

After helping found the Overseas Press Club in 1939 and going on two safaris, the Wellses went to Angola during World War II, buying strategic war materials such as copper and industrial diamonds for the U.S. government. When they came home in 1946, Fay became a full-time mother to their son, Linton II, who had been born in Africa earlier that year. They lived on a farm in Mount Kisco, New York, then in 1958 moved onto a houseboat. Fay designed yacht interiors, then wrote a syndicated boating column, "Nautical Notebook," for the *Herald Tribune.*

On a trip to south Florida in 1962, the Wellses met broadcast executive George Storer, who asked Lint to open his company's Washington bureau. Fay stayed in New York with their son, but after he went to the Naval Academy the next August, she moved to Washington, D.C. There the Storer company got the same kind of deal that RCA had; Fay "sort of helped out in the office, learned how to splice tape and help with the morning news and do little interviews with senators' wives."

One day in 1964 George Storer visited. "He looked around and he said, 'We don't have anybody at the White House. Why don't we send Fay over?' And so I said, 'Well, if he wants me to cover the White House, I'll cover the White House.' " So Fay was put on Storer's payroll at $500 a month.

Fay was given complete freedom during those early days with Storer and that was one of the things she enjoyed most about her job. "They never told me what to do. They just said, 'You're the correspondent. You're there. You decide what you think the news is.' " So she covered briefings and state dinners, and when there was time, the First Lady as well. Wells broadcast primarily on the radio in what she calls an "informal" style, tailoring her reports for each of Storer's seven stations. Later, around 1969, she did a little television, too, but radio was her first love because it was less complicated—when "something came up, you just went in and broadcast."

Though Fay had broadcast before, covering a beat like this was new to her. Much of her training was on the job. Her colleagues—nearly all of them were male then—treated her well, perhaps because she was older than most of them, perhaps because "I wasn't vying with anybody for time on the air." She never expected special treatment because she was a woman. "Everybody carried his own bags. . . . The boys would say, 'Could I help?' and I'd say, 'No, I can do it.' Because you're out there doing a job, and so you do the job. . . . I mean, if I can't do it, well then get somebody who can." Wells remembers the same treatment from newsmakers—courteous, but not preferential.

The most exciting presidential trip Wells took was to China with Richard Nixon. Two thousand newspeople applied, so the White House kept narrowing the criteria by which it chose who would go. Thirty-seven correspondents finally were selected, and while some news organizations sent their big guns instead of their White House regulars, "Storer said, 'Fay's the White House correspondent. She has done all these things. She's been with the president. She knows him better than we know him. She's to go.' " Wells was one of three women journalists to make the trip, Barbara Walters of NBC and Helen Thomas of the UPI the other two.

After more than thirteen years with Storer, Fay Gillis Wells retired. The company had sold its radio stations, and she wasn't interested in pursuing television. So on June 30, 1977, she left her "job in heaven" for another career, this one involving solar energy. Linton had died in 1976, and Fay has spent much time since then traveling and working with aviation. She is very involved with the Ninety-Nines, an organization of women pilots, and helped establish the International Forest of Friendship in Atchison, Kansas, where Amelia Earhart was born. Most of the numerous awards she has received recognize her contributions to aviation.

Though broadcasting, like flying, has been a part of Wells's life for five decades, unlike her adventures in the air she has no desire to go back on the air. "It was just an exciting episode in my life that was fascinating and the best time that ever was."

## CONCLUSION

The years leading up to World War II marked the beginning of the first of the two most progressive periods for women in broadcast news (the other being the age of affirmative action in the 1970s). The tensions of the times created special opportunities for women. A few women were knowledgeable about international affairs and put the events in Europe in perspective for the American public. CBS became the first network to hire a woman as a news executive. The war years also saw a woman break the network news barrier on the air.

Times of national stress often bring about major societal changes, and this certainly was true for American women during World War II. Some patterns also began to emerge for women in broadcast news. An increasing number of women made inroads into radio news, though it was often because men were not available. But most still followed traditional family patterns; many abandoned professional opportunities to accommodate their husbands' careers, while others were able to take advantage of opportunities presented for the same reason. Others felt their professional success had come at the cost of personal happiness.

The successful broadcast newswomen of this period, like their colleagues before and after them, had time and place on their sides. But because these women were trailblazers, they didn't expect anything; no precedent had been set, so they were free to establish their own standards. It was a difficult charge, however, for like females in most non-traditional jobs in general, women in broadcast news had a hard time finding acceptance and equality in a male-dominated profession.

## NOTES

1. "Behind the Mike," *Broadcasting* 20, 22 (9 June 1941): 26.

2. "Meet the Ladies: Kay Halle," *Broadcasting* 20, 19 (26 May 1941): 28.

3. *Broadcasting* 22, 13 (30 March 1942): 55; and "Announcerette," *Broadcasting* 22, 13 (30 March 1942): 38.

4. "Women Installed in Station Jobs," *Broadcasting* 22, 15 (2 February 1942): 14.

5. Dorothy Thompson, "On Women Correspondents and Other New Ideas," *The Nation* (6 January 1926): 11.

6. The articles Thompson wrote about the Soviet Union became *The New Russia* (New York: H. Holt, 1928).

7. Margaret Case Harriman, "The 'It' Girl, Part 1," *New Yorker* (20 April 1940): 30.

8. A selection of Thompson's *Ladies Home Journal* columns became *The Courage to Be Happy* (Boston: Houghton, Mifflin, 1957).

9. Marion K. Sanders, *Dorothy Thompson: A Legend in Her Time* (Boston: Houghton, Mifflin, 1973), p. 261.

10. James Wedgwood Drawbell, *Dorothy Thompson's English Journey* (London: Collins, 1942), p. 37.

11. Ibid., pp. 104-6.

12. A collection of Thompson's broadcasts to Germany was published as *Listen, Hans* (Boston: Houghton, Mifflin, 1942).

13. Dixon Wechter, "Hearing Is Believing," *Atlantic Monthly* (July 1945): 41.

14. Unless otherwise stated, all quotations from Lisa Sergio are from an interview with her by Gayle K. Yamada, Washington, D.C., 17 August 1986.

15. Sergio first broadcast for NBC from Rome on April 19, 1935. The broadcast, on Easter Sunday, told the story of the Colosseum and the role it played in Christian history. The commentary was interspersed with recorded music. Sergio did several other broadcasts from Italy for NBC and CBS. Lisa Sergio, letter to Gayle K. Yamada, 17 September 1986.

16. Helen J. Sioussat, interview with Gayle K. Yamada, Washington, D.C., 18 August 1986.

17. "Meet the Ladies: Esther Van Wagoner Tufty," *Broadcasting* 24, 9 (1 March 1943): 42.

18. Unless otherwise stated, quotations from Elizabeth Bemis are from a telephone interview with Gayle K. Yamada, 18 September 1986.

19. Shirley Wershba, interview with Gayle K. Yamada, Manhasset Hills, New York, 25 August 1986.

20. Unless otherwise stated, quotations from Helen Sioussat are from an interview with Gayle K. Yamada, Washington, D.C., 18 August 1986.

21. Helen Sioussat, *Mikes Don't Bite* (New York: L. B. Fischer, 1943), p. 249.

22. All quotations from Marian Glick are from an interview with her by Gayle K. Yamada, New York City, 23 August 1986.

23. "Woman in a TV World of Crises," *New York Times* (16 October 1960), p. 16.

24. All quotations from Shirley Wershba are from the interview with her.

25. Anne Denton Blair, speech at a fund raiser for the Hancock Point Library, Bangor, Maine, 3 July 1985.

26. Ibid.

27. Unless otherwise stated, quotations from Anne Denton Blair are from an interview with Gayle K. Yamada, Washington, D.C., 16 August 1986.

28. Blair speech.

29. Unless otherwise stated, quotations from Fay Gillis Wells are from an interview with Gayle K. Yamada, Alexandria, Virginia, 18 August 1986.

# 3  After the War

World War II did more to change the role of American women in the work force than any other event in the first half of this century. The shortage of manpower created opportunities for thousands of women, but for many it was temporary. When the men came home they took back their jobs, and many women returned to being wives and mothers full time. But women had gained a foothold in the workplace in general, and in broadcast news in particular, and a lot of them wanted to stay on. Their biggest struggle right after the war, then, was to be accepted as serious newswomen and to have their work respected. No longer would only the exceptions be noticed; the numbers of women in the field also began to attract more attention.

Women in radio benefited greatly from World War II. A 1944 survey found one female announcer for every twelve men, a ratio which station managers directly attributed to the war. Most of those managers believed that "the female announcer has proved her worth and will continue to find her place in radio announcing and increasingly so as commentators." It was not unusual to see in *Broadcasting* magazine notices such as "Marie Wathen, formerly with AP and UP, is in charge of the now fulltime newsroom of WMPS, Memphis"; "Margaret Sharpe, former feature writer for *Boston Tribune*, is new reporter with news bureau of KPRO, Riverside, California"; or "Mrs. Frankie Walker, assistant manager and news director of WFOY, St. Augustine was praised for her success in building local news shows, with three quarter-hour and one ten-minute local newscasts sponsored six days a week."[1]

Not all the women were singled out for professional accomplishments. *Broadcasting* also recognized "beautiful and bright . . . 'Miss Radio News of 1946,' Ina Shippey, KPO-NBC San Francisco news writer. She was voted 'most beautiful news-writing girl from coast-to-coast' by *Newscaster*, INS magazine."[2]

At the same time, *Broadcasting* also records instances of women who left news jobs to follow their husbands: "Mary Waller, news reporter at WMAZ

Macon, Georgia, resigned her position to marry Captain Bruce Ross on October 19''; and "Ina Stephenson, member of news and public service section of KPO San Francisco, has resigned and also has announced her engagement to Burt Leiper, member of NBC New York news staff."[3]

While *Broadcasting* chronicled the rise of women in broadcast news for members of the industry, the public followed a glamorized version of a woman reporter's life in an unusual CBS radio soap opera, "Wendy Warren and the News." Debuting in June 1947, the broadcast told the story of a big city "girl reporter" and her adventures. The soap opera was preceded by a two- or three-minute real newscast, anchored for many years by Douglas Edwards. When he was done, he would ask Wendy, who was played by New Jersey radio actress Florence Freeman, to give the ladies' news. As "Wendy Warren" she read a minute of women's news followed by a commercial, and then she launched into the day's drama.

## ON THE AIR

### Pauline Frederick: United Nations Correspondent

The difficulties Pauline Frederick experienced making her mark in broadcasting so much resembled a soap opera that her story could be called "The Perils of Pauline." Frederick persistently fought sex discrimination and rejection in the largely male world of broadcast news and carved a niche for herself covering the United Nations at a time when it was making headlines nearly every day. Her career spanned more than forty years, and she served as a role model for countless numbers of others.

Frederick was born February 13, 1908, in Gallitzin, Pennsylvania, the second of three children. Though neither of her parents was formally educated beyond the eighth grade, Frederick's father, a postmaster in Gallitzin and later a state labor mediator, was an avid reader who encouraged his daughter's interest in international affairs. A strong Methodist upbringing instilled a sense of integrity and honesty that characterized her professional ethics.

Frederick was a shy, sensitive child. Though she matured into a tall, handsome woman, as a girl she was taller than the boys and skinny, with buck teeth and allergies. She saw herself as an "ugly duckling."[4]

Pauline's interest in covering news blossomed early. As a teenager she reported society news for the *Harrisburg Telegraph*. At the age of seventeen, Frederick was offered the position of social editor at the paper but turned it down to study political science at American University in Washington, D.C.

The nation's capital was the perfect place for a serious young woman captivated by politics. Frederick soon mastered the town, learning about the buildings and their histories as well as memorizing the names of the legislators. She considered going into journalism, but political reporting was a field closed to women then, so she decided to pursue law. As she was completing her master's degree in international law, a history professor encouraged a return to journalism, suggesting she combine her interests by reporting on diplomats' wives. After receiving her degree in 1931, she took his advice and called it the best decision she ever made.

*NBC Network Debut.* Frederick sold her first interview to the *Washington Star.* Soon she was writing weekly features on diplomats' wives that were syndicated through the North American Newspaper Alliance (NANA). Her stories caught the attention of NBC's director of women's programs, Margaret Cuthbert, who had the network's Washington bureau audition Frederick in 1939. The following week, Frederick made her debut on the airwaves, interviewing the wife of the Czechoslovakian minister just after Hitler invaded that country. Frederick was so nervous she didn't sleep the night before; neither did her guest. After sharing a glass of sherry, the two went on the air. Although Frederick remembers it as "frightening since I had never been on the air before," she was asked to do more and continued them until they were dropped after the war began.[5]

With that entree, Frederick became an assistant to NBC commentator H. R. Baukhauge. She did research for him and wrote scripts. In April 1945, she had a chance to go on a journalists' tour to North Africa and Asia. Baukhauge did not believe a woman should go on the trip, but Frederick ignored his protests and went anyway. While overseas she broadcast from Chungking, China. Two months and eighteen countries later she decided to quit her job with Baukhauge and cover the Nuremberg trials in Germany, freelancing for NANA, the Western Newspaper Alliance, and ABC radio. But she only got on the air once, when Hermann Goering took the stand, and then only because the first-string male reporter wasn't there.

*Rejected by Murrow.* Though she had managed a few scoops—such as the Goering testimony—Frederick's tenacity and reporting skills still didn't get her regular news assignments. In fact, she couldn't even get a regular job with a network. Frederick still has a copy of the staff memo, dated August 27, 1946, that Edward R. Murrow wrote after she applied to CBS News.

> I have listened to the records submitted by Pauline Frederick. She reads well and her voice is pleasing but I would not call her material or manner particularly distinguished. We have a long list of women applicants and, as you know, little opportunity to use them. I am afraid that Miss Frederick's name cannot be put very near the top of the list. E.R.M.[6]

While looking for a network staff job, Frederick was stringing for ABC, where she was relegated to women's stories. Her first assignment: a forum on "How to Get a Husband." Next: a market rush on nylon hosiery. "They just couldn't understand why I wasn't content to do women's news—fashion shows and that type of thing. I don't think they were trying to keep me down;

they just felt the public wouldn't accept it at the time, and I'm not sure they weren't right." Still, Frederick believed women cared about more than "women's interest" stories, and she wanted to cover a news beat like a man. "I tried every way to convince the powers that be that I could broadcast news. . . . This was very difficult because it was unheard of for a woman to want to enter this man's world." She recalls trying to compete with her male colleagues, but was not allowed on the air unless she had exclusive stories. The reason, she was told, was that "a woman's voice doesn't carry authority."[7]

Frederick soon had her opportunity to disprove that premise. One night, ABC found itself with two big stories to cover in New York—a truckers' strike and a foreign ministers' conference—and only one male reporter. Because of the possibility of strike violence, local news manager Paul Scheffel sent Frederick to the conference. It was her big break. After that, she was allowed to cover the United Nations, but again she went on the air only if she had exclusive reports. Finally her hard work paid off; after several months she was given the United Nations as a regular beat, and was signed to an ABC staff contract in 1948.

Frederick's determination to win a hard-news beat drove her to work long hours boning up on the issues and cultivating sources. Ironically, her single-minded approach to her career was due, in part, to her feeling of feminine inadequacy. She did not think anyone would marry her because she was unable to have children. At the age of seventeen, Frederick underwent exploratory surgery after suffering severe stomach cramps. After discovering two grapefruit-sized cysts on her ovaries, doctors performed a hysterectomy. But they didn't tell her about it. A few weeks later, she realized what had happened when she felt the physical changes. "For a long time I felt like a freak. It wasn't until ten years later that I realized I was just like any other woman, except I couldn't have children."[8]

*TV: Make-up, Too.*    Actually, most other women were not like Pauline Frederick. Her training, talent, tenacity, and timing won her a place in broadcasting history as the dean of women electronic journalists. Among the many precedents she set was that of women broadcasting at political conventions.

In 1948 a notice was posted at ABC asking employees to sign up for TV assignments. Since she'd just started getting better radio assignments, Frederick ignored the invitation. Most male reporters wanted no part of the new medium either. Frederick's news director called her in and told her she'd be covering the first televised Democratic convention.

> I nearly fell off my chair! I didn't know what to do. I went to Elizabeth Arden and asked how I should make myself up for TV. Nobody knew. Eventually I wound up doing the makeup for all of the women—Margaret Truman, Helen Gahagan—I'm sure we all looked terrible, but we got through it.[9]

Frederick continued with both radio and television at ABC, her reports airing on both morning and evening newscasts. In 1948 she was on six regular ABC radio broadcasts each day, and three television programs every week, including a non-news television show on Saturdays, "Pauline Frederick's Guest Books." She preferred radio, however, because she found less prejudice against women there. "When a man speaks on television, people listen. But when a woman speaks, people look, and if they like her looks, *then* they listen."[10] Beyond the cosmetics, Frederick found radio permitted more time for background and analysis.

Frederick's international political expertise and reportorial skills attracted the attention of NBC, which hired her away from ABC in 1953. In addition to her U.N. beat, Frederick covered the 1956 political conventions. Though most of the network's executives apparently were satisfied with her performance at the conventions, a few were not, reportedly because she did not ad-lib well, and they prevented her from covering future conventions.

Frederick was well compensated for her work. During the mid-sixties, she was one of the most highly paid broadcast newswomen in the United States, earning an estimated $60,000 a year from NBC and various speaking engagements.

*United Nations Beat.*   Frederick was inextricably linked to the United Nations. From her U.N. post she covered international crises, including the Korean War, conflicts in the Middle East, the Cuban missile crisis, the Cold War, and the Vietnam conflict. The American public associated her so closely with the international organization that when Secretary-General Dag Hammarskjold was killed in an airplane crash, many people sent her sympathy notes. She continued on the U.N. beat for NBC until her compulsory retirement in 1974 at the age of sixty-five. But her broadcasting career was not over. Within the year she returned to the airwaves, this time on National Public Radio, and for the next five years, her clear and confident contralto voice could be heard commenting on international affairs. Frederick was still making "firsts"; on October 6, 1976, she became the first woman to moderate a debate between presidential candidates when Jimmy Carter and Gerald Ford squared off in San Francisco.

Frederick's long list of accolades includes twenty-three honorary doctorate degrees in the humanities, law, and journalism. She was the first woman to receive the Paul White Award from the Radio-Television News Directors Association, the first woman to receive the Alfred I. duPont Awards' Commentator Award, the first woman named to the journalists' Hall of Fame by the New York chapter of Sigma Delta Chi, and the first woman elected president of the United Nations Correspondents Association. Frederick also has been named to the Gallup Poll's "Ten Most Admired Women" in the world and has received the George Foster Peabody Award for her coverage of the

United Nations, McCall's Golden Mike award for outstanding women in broadcasting, and a special commendation from Theta Sigma Phi, a national professional fraternity for women in journalism, for her coverage and interpretation of significant national and international events.

Frederick might not have achieved such distinction in broadcast journalism had she married at a young age. Her romantic relationships with men had not brought her happiness. A foreign service officer she dated after college broke off their relationship after he learned she could not have children. Another died in a plane crash, and a third died of a heart attack. Frederick remained single until the age of sixty-one.

> My situation is quite different from other women who have had children or who have come into their career in an earlier stage in their marriage. I think with the kind of career I've had, something would have had to be sacrificed. Because when I have been busy at the United Nations during crises, it has meant working day and night. You can't very well take care of a home when you do something like that, or children.[11]

On March 31, 1969, Frederick married Charles Robbins, former president of the Atomic Industrial Forum and former managing editor of the *Wall Street Journal*. Matrimony has changed her life, she says, because now she is "sharing my experiences with an understanding mate who had been a newsperson."[12]

### Dorothy Fuldheim: Just "Dorothy" in Cleveland

If Pauline Frederick is the dean of national newswomen, Dorothy Fuldheim is her counterpart at the local level. Fuldheim was the first woman in the United States to anchor a television news program and she remained on the air until she was ninety-one.

Fuldheim began her television career relatively late in life, at the age of fifty-four. She was born Dorothy Violet Schnell on June 26, 1893, in Passaic, New Jersey. Her father was a German immigrant. Their family was so poor that when her sister died at the age of one, they couldn't even afford a coffin, and the child was buried in an orange crate. When she was twelve, Dorothy went to work as a cashier at a local department store on Saturdays. She attended Milwaukee Normal College, graduating with a teaching degree in 1912. After teaching for four years, Fuldheim's interests turned to the stage. She went into acting, first gaining recognition as Juliet in "Romeo and Juliet," and later taking on leading roles in several other plays, including "Man and Superman" and "Hedda Gabbler." From drama she turned to public speaking at the insistence of social reformer Jane Addams, who saw Fuldheim perform one day in 1918 and was convinced Fuldheim was needed to deliver a lecture on peace. Soon, others, drawn to Dorothy's dramatic delivery, also asked her to give public talks.

Dorothy Fuldheim interviewing Helen Keller on WEWS, Cleveland. The woman on the right is Keller's assistant, Polly Thomson. Courtesy Donald Perris/Scripps Howard Broadcasting.

*Joins WJW and ABC.*    Also in 1918, Fuldheim married an attorney from Cleveland, Milton H. Fuldheim. They had one daughter, Dorothy Louise. For nearly three decades, Mrs. Fuldheim continued on the lecture circuit in the United States and Europe. She became a commentator on WJW in Cleveland in 1944, and in 1947 began commentaries heard over the ABC Radio Network on Saturdays, following the Metropolitan Opera. "I charged $5,000 for the year and they questioned me as though I were out of my mind. 'Is that your fee?' I thought it was too much, but they had expected me to ask for $25,000. I was so simple them."[13]

About the same time, the Scripps Howard station, WEWS-TV, was getting ready to go on the air in Cleveland. Fuldheim was asked to anchor its evening newscast. When the station signed on December 17, 1947, she reported for work. Her duties included doing news commentaries and interviews which were part of the fifteen-minute news program. It was an unusual move— asking a woman to anchor the news—but the station, headed by general manager James C. Hanrahan, was "very progressive and was considerably ahead of its time in the employment of women."[14] The commercial sponsor was not as open in its attitude toward women.

> The sponsors, Duquesne Beer, wanted a man. But the head of the station told them, "If you want the time, you'll have to take her." When they handed me the script and asked if it was satisfactory I said, "I guess so, but it's not what I do." They said they never had anybody work without a written script, and I said, "Then you've probably never had anybody competent."[15]

Duquesne gave in and it turned into "one of the great client-performer romances of all time."[16] Fuldheim anchored the evening news for a decade, and after she stepped down from the anchor chair in 1957, she continued to contribute to the program with her interviews and commentaries and later did specials, primarily issue-oriented programs.

*"You Think Like a Man."*    Objections to her gender were not new to Fuldheim. She had encountered them as a lecturer. "A woman orator is a rarity, and one of the reasons is that the female voice is often a liability. . . . A director once taught me how to deepen the tones of my voice. . . . I used to drill and practice every day; the difference is discernible if I neglect to do so." But in spite of the prejudices against women, she was proud to be one. "If there is one thing that really irks me, it is to be told, 'You think like a man.' I doubt if one's brain were removed from the body whether it could be identified as male or female. My emotions are female, not my brain."[17]

As a woman in a man's world, Fuldheim was occasionally the victim of unwanted sexual attention. But she was not about to be embarrassed by such behavior. One of her colleagues discovered that on a trip to Taiwan in 1955, when Fuldheim was the only female correspondent along. He gallantly gave up his room for her, but later that night stopped by for a visit. Fuld-heim loudly rebuked him and, as all the rooms were along one corridor, the other correspondents heard the exchange. The would-be tryster found he was the victim of teasing throughout the trip.

While she was building her reputation as a newswoman, Fuldheim suf-fered some personal losses. Her first husband died in 1952; she married Wil-liam Ulmer the following year, and they remained together until his death in 1969. Many years later, in 1980, Fuldheim's only daughter died of a heart attack.

*A Lonely Time.*    Fuldheim's early days in male-dominated television news were sometimes difficult for her. She was "very lonely. I always felt like an outsider."[18] But Fuldheim persevered, gaining a reputation for being "a complete person who read everything and was interested in everything and had a complete background in the arts, in history, in literature, and in sci-ence. . . . She knew more than was in that day's paper or on the wire that day."[19] Fuldheim also gained fame and some degree of notoriety for her out-spokenness and her peppery interviews. She talked with all sorts of news-makers, from President Franklin D. Roosevelt to Albert Einstein to Zsa Zsa Gabor to Barbara Walters. One of her most memorable moments came when she interviewed radical activist Jerry Rubin in 1971. Fuldheim listened as he told her why people should smoke marijuana, but then

> he wanted to show me a picture of a nude with all the pubic hairs showing, right on the show, and I said no. I was sick of the subculture that was living off those who took care of the lighting and sewage. I said, "Get off my show, just get out."[20]

If Fuldheim could be tough with an interview subject, she could also be sensitive. She recalls one of the interviews that touched her the most deeply, when she talked with Helen Keller. "She never saw any sunshine, never saw a smile, never heard the ripple of water, the sound of music, and yet this woman understood everything. . . . It was a moment of emancipation from the senses that left me awed; I've never gotten over it."[21]

*A Sense of Loyalty.*    Fuldheim remained with WEWS despite other offers, some for considerably more money. She felt "a curious sense of loyalty. . . . They took a gamble with me."[22] That gamble paid off for decades; Fuld-heim kept an active schedule until 1984, reporting for work at 9:30 every morning and leaving at 6:30 in the evening. In addition to the interviews she had done for the noon news since 1958, Fuldheim delivered two commen-taries, one live on the six o'clock news, and one taped for the eleven; those she had been providing since 1957.

At times, Fuldheim hosted other programs. In 1949 it was "Shopper's Guide," and from 1957 to 1964 she co-hosted a live variety show, "The One

O'clock Club.'' In her spare time she gave lectures and appeared at fund raisers.

While network newsmen were getting headlines when they retired, Fuldheim attracted newspaper attention when she signed a new contract with WEWS that ran until she was eighty-nine years old. ''But I will never retire. Life will have to retire me.''[23] Fuldheim last broadcast on July 27, 1984. Late in the afternoon, after interviewing President Ronald Reagan by satellite, ''she started having what she thought was a severe headache. But she did the 6 anyway.''[24] After the broadcast she was taken to the hospital. Fuldheim had suffered a stroke. She has not returned to work.

Donald Perris, now president of Scripps Howard Broadcasting Company, worked with Fuldheim for all but a few months of her television career. He was a news writer and reporter at WEWS in 1948 and he says, over the years,

> she was exactly the same. Very warm, very friendly. Very temperamental and full of storminess if she thought her turf was being invaded, but most of all if she thought something was not first class. She just hated anything that was mediocre.[25]

Fuldheim's vitality, says Perris, drew people with whom she worked as well as viewers.

> Everybody used to go in there to philosophize, to talk shop, to get help with personal situations. She definitely was the ''glue'' person in the building all the time she was here. . . . The women found her very friendly and supportive, but so did we.[26]

Perhaps the greatest compliment to Fuldheim and her unique style is that after nearly four decades on Cleveland television, ''she was just known to everybody as 'Dorothy.' ''[27]

### Zona B. Davis: Effingham's Beacon

Zona B. Davis was to Effingham, Illinois, what Dorothy Fuldheim was to Cleveland. Davis never intended to be a newscaster for more than a few weeks, but ended up as news director of WCRA-AM for twenty-nine years. She was so well known that everybody in town just called her ''Zona B.'' Only the station announcer was left with the formality of introducing her as ''Zona B. Davis.''

The B. stands for Buchholz, her maiden name. Zona Buchholz was born in rural Effingham County in 1911. She wanted to be a writer and had sold stories to the local paper when she was still in high school. Her father, a farmer, thought writers starved to death and would not allow his daughter to attend college if she was going to be a writer. So she went to work at a newspaper, not as a journalist, but a linotype operator on the *Effingham*

Marian Glick began her journalism career with United Press, and went on to become news director of the DuMont Network before joining CBS for three decades. Courtesy Marian Glick.

Zona B. Davis during her first weeks as a newscaster on WCRA, Effingham, Illinois, in April 1949. One of the first women news directors in the country, Davis had the unique right to vote for her son, Paul, for president of the Radio-Television News Directors Association. Courtesy Zona B. Davis.

*Daily Record.* For Zona, that was her journalism school, because she was able to see dozens of stories every day and decide for herself what made news.

After five years on the *Record*, she quit, but almost immediately got a reporting job on the *St. Elmo Banner* a couple of towns away. That lasted a year, and then Davis became assistant editor of the *Effingham County Review.* The title did not indicate that she was also the only journalist on the weekly's staff, which included a linotype operator, press man, and the often absent publisher. Her duties included selling advertising.

In 1937, Zona married Plaford Davis, a car salesman she had dated for seven years. She decided to get out of the newspaper business, perhaps hoping to write books, and the Davises bought a historic old house and started a tourist hotel. Soon, their only child was born. Cars and tourists were their businesses for the next decade.

*Beginning with a Blaze.*    In 1949, a huge fire swept through the local hospital. In a matter of minutes, seventy-six people lost their lives. Nearly every family in the town of 8,000 was affected in some way by the fire. Davis saw firemen whose boot soles had burned through while fighting the fire and learned of other acts of heroism by nurses, administrators, and patients. She called up the local radio station, WCRA, then just two years old, to tip it off about these stories. Davis reached owner F. F. McNaughton, who had rushed down from Pekin, from where he managed his chain of papers and radio stations. This was the same man who many years earlier had encouraged Helen Hiett's interest in journalism. McNaughton asked Davis to tell what she knew on the radio and help in the effort to identify the dead and let relatives and friends know where survivors were. In some cases, patients had been taken to private homes; others had been moved to out-of-town hospitals.

WCRA could be heard in about a hundred-mile radius in Illinois, which meant that the emergency broadcasts went just about border to border, east to west. The fire coverage, with the station serving as a community billboard, nearly made Zona B. a household name in her first days as a radio reporter. A business card was made up identifying her as news director, but Davis told McNaughton she would only stay on until someone permanent could be found. She was concerned about Paul, her ten-year-old son at home. McNaughton said she could bring the boy along if necessary. Often working from her home, Davis balanced motherhood, innkeeping, and broadcasting. She remembers Paul taking old wire copy out of the station's wastebaskets and practicing reading for hours. He memorized the music library, and at the age of fifteen made his debut on the station as an announcer.

*"If You Want a Miracle. . . ."*    Zona B., as she was soon known to her listeners, became a community beacon for three decades. She became so well known for initiating good deeds that it was said, "If you want a miracle, call Zona B."[28] She initially delivered the news on a fifteen-minute program at 10:15 weekday mornings. It was so popular with advertisers and listeners alike that it was expanded to forty-five minutes and included guest interviews, contests, and commentary. To accommodate more sponsors, a second broadcast from 11:20 to 11:30 was added. Zona B. also was responsible for the morning drive newscasts. She usually would prepare scripts at home the night before and have them picked up for reading by the morning announcer. She'd go into the station from 10 A.M. or so until early afternoon, writing the afternoon newscasts before she left.

One of Zona B.'s first "miracles" was a surprise for a local man who returned home after being a POW in Korea. She got the idea after another veteran who had been a POW during World War II told Davis how disappointed he had been upon returning from war to no fanfare. He suggested that a new car for the Korean veteran might be a proper honor, and Zona B. discussed the idea on her broadcast. The community rallied behind her effort, and when the veteran arrived at the train station, he found a shiny automobile waiting for him.

Another fund raiser involved listeners sending in dollar bills for patients at a nearby veterans' hospital. There were 1,700 men there, and they had little cash to pay for incidentals like candy bars. At Thanksgiving one year, Zona B. urged her listeners to write a note thanking the men for serving their country and enclosing a single dollar. More than $1,700 was raised.

*Vietnam Letters.* Davis's biggest project again involved servicemen, this time during the Vietnam War. It started with a conversation with a friend about a letter a local woman had received from her son in the service. Davis was dismayed to hear that the young man questioned the value of what he and his fighting comrades were doing and whether anyone back home supported their efforts. Zona B. urged her listeners to write any servicemen they knew overseas, and to send her addresses of local fellows in the military so she could write them, too. The next day, she recalls receiving a peck of letters, which she dumped on the station manager's desk. He remarked that Zona B. always seemed to start with a molehill and end up with a mountain, but also agreed to duplicate a letter to be sent to the servicemen if she could come up with the stamps and address them. Before long, assisted by a group of volunteers, Zona B. was sending out 3,000 letters full of hometown news every other week. Servicemen who had never been to Illinois were asking to be put on her mailing list. For her efforts, Davis received a Golden Mike Award from the American Legion Auxiliary.

Davis carried her activism to state broadcasting associations. She was the first female officer in several of them and president of the Illinois UPI Broadcasters in 1967.

Zona B. retired in 1978, knowing that broadcast news has stayed in the family. The little boy who used to empty the wastebaskets at WCRA went on to become news director of WGN-TV in Chicago. Paul Davis is also a past president of the International Radio-Television News Directors Association and was responsible for the nomination of Pauline Frederick as the first women recipient of the RTNDA's highest honor, the Paul White Award. Davis died June 3, 1987, of congestive heart failure.

### Lucy Jarvis: Pioneer Producer

While Pauline Frederick, Dorothy Fuldheim, and Zona B. Davis made inroads for newswomen on the air, Lucy Jarvis pioneered the ranks of network news producers for women. Jarvis developed an interest in the world around her at a young age, and as an adult combined her knowledge of other peoples' cultures and histories with broadcasting to bring the world to the American public.

She was born Lucile Kirsch Howard in New York City, the daughter of a mechanical engineer and "an extraordinary woman [who] had the philosophy that if you want to do something badly enough . . . you can find a way to do it."[29] It is her mother Jarvis credits with giving her

> a great sense of myself. . . . She said, "The best thing you can do for a child is give her all the tools that she will need in later life. I want you to be the kind of person that can walk into a room anywhere in the world and not feel inadequate." Now when I was growing up, that was a very unusual thing to say.

Jarvis became interested in broadcasting as an undergraduate at Cornell University. Though her major was biochemistry of foods, she was active in the drama club, which led to a founding role in the campus radio station.

*Speaks for* McCall's.  When Jarvis graduated in 1938, she got a job as a food and nutrition expert at Cornell Medical School. She soon left for *McCall's* magazine, where she became associate food editor for $35 a week. While at *McCall's* Jarvis was invited to speak or be interviewed all over the country; some of the talks were on radio and television stations.

> When I was . . . being interviewed on a national broadcast, instead of half a million or a million at most—a million readers, that was the entire subscription of *McCall's*—I could reach eight, nine, ten million people! And I thought to myself, "I'm in the wrong business."

Jarvis eventually became an editor at *McCall's*, at a salary of $75 a week. The magazine, impressed with its young nutrition expert, sent her to Columbia Teacher's College, from which she received an M.S. in food and nutrition. In 1944, she married an attorney, Serge Jarvis, and they soon had two children. The couple decided Lucy would stay at home with their children, and they built a house in Stamford, Connecticut. In 1958, after the children were in school, Lucy decided to return to work. Rather than going back to print, though, Jarvis chose radio. She got her start with one of her husband's clients, Martha Roundtree, who had created "Meet the Press."

The two women brainstormed and worked out two or three programs. One of them, "Capitol Close-Up," they successfully pitched to WOR/Mutual Broadcasting Company. Their first guests exemplified the kind of newsmakers they wanted for their daily broadcast: President Dwight Eisenhower, Vice President Richard Nixon, and FBI Director J. Edgar Hoover.

*Washington Shuttle.*  "Capitol Close-Up" was broadcast from Washington, D.C. The two women bought a house on R Street; Roundtree lived on the bottom two floors, and the top floor became a studio with direct lines to New York. For the next two years, Jarvis maintained a grueling schedule. Mondays she would spend at the network in New York. Tuesdays she'd take a helicopter from her Connecticut home to La Guardia Airport, then catch a shuttle to Washington. On Thursdays she would return to Connecticut and on Fridays would be back at the network.

About this time, a friend, David Susskind, began urging Jarvis toward network television. He suggested she watch a new program on CBS called "The Woman." Jarvis thought it was "abysmal," and wrote a five-page critique blasting it. Susskind showed the critique to the producer, Irving Gitlin, who not only agreed, but wanted to hire its author. Gitlin was on his way to NBC at this point. He was taking his team from CBS and wanted Jarvis in the line up. But with the political conventions coming up that summer, she didn't feel she could leave Roundtree. Finally though, convinced that Gitlin would have a much harder time hiring her after he went to NBC, Jarvis agreed to work for him one day a week, which she did until Roundtree found someone to replace her and bought Jarvis out.

Jarvis spent the next two-and-a-half years producing "The Nation's Future," an hour-long debate program that aired from 9 to 10 on Saturday nights. During that time she began to develop ideas for documentary films. One day she went to Gitlin and suggested a broadcast on the Kremlin. With her mother's philosophy imprinted on her personality, Jarvis was confident that she could pull it off through contacts she had made on a trip to Europe with President and Mrs. John F. Kennedy. Gitlin was excited, but to protect her in case she failed, he officially sent her to Moscow to get Soviet leader Nikita Khrushchev for "The Nation's Future." The result was the American public's first look inside the Soviet seat of power, "The Kremlin," for which she was associate producer. Her coup won an Emmy and *McCall's* Golden Mike Award.

"The Kremlin" was the first of many award-winning documentaries Jarvis worked on; dozens of programs, including "The Louvre," "Who Shall Live," "Dr. [Christiaan] Barnard's Heart Transplant Operations," and "The Forbidden City" would follow.

*"He Hit Me."*    Drama seemed to follow Jarvis as she pursued her documentary subjects. In 1964 she convinced the British to let NBC do a film on Buckingham Palace, promising to do it "in a most dignified way. . . . But my instinct told me I should not tell this to the [senior correspondent] in the bureau in London, that that was not going to sit well with him." He learned of the Palace plans anyway and called Jarvis in to talk with him about it.

> I'll never forget it. He said, "Do you know that I have been working for twelve years to do that project?" And I said, "No, I didn't know that." I really did not know that. And I said, "I don't understand. I mean, the first thing I would do as I did in Russia and in Paris, the NBC correspondent in each of those cities became a part of the project. So if I accomplish this, of course you will be the NBC host in the film." He said, "That's not good enough." And he struck me! He hit me. Wham! Everybody ran into the room. Of course he was nonplussed; he was devastated. . . . I said to him then, "Would you have done

this if I were a male producer?'' And he said, ''I probably wouldn't have gotten away with it.'' I said, ''You're not going to get away with it with me.'' He said, ''Well, I'm sorry. I am terribly sorry. I lost my temper. I apologize. Please let us put this behind us.'' And I said, ''It's behind us, but as far as I'm concerned, you're not part of this project any longer.''

That was the only time Jarvis was harmed physically because she was a woman, but she recalls other, more subtle, slights. Sometimes when she was waiting to see NBC's president or chairman, she says a male colleague would breeze past her to see him. It angered her, particularly since the men did not see it as an insult.

In spite of any obstacles her gender might have presented, Jarvis succeeded at NBC. Encouraged by Gitlin, she became executive producer of documentaries. Gitlin died of cancer in late 1967, but he had given her the freedom to grow, and set a tone for her work at NBC. She continued to work on projects she thought were different from what everyone else was doing. She ''always chose something that was a challenge and that made newspaper stories. And for the network that was very important.'' Once she was told that it didn't matter how good a show was as long as it made headlines the next day. But she disagreed, saying both were necessary. ''And he said, 'Well, that's because you're a woman.' And I said, 'That's right, if those are the standards of a woman' ''—awards, headlines, and good programs.

*A Head Count.*    When Jarvis started producing documentaries in the early 1960s and began hiring women, she did not find resistance up front.

> The way they handled it was not to say they don't want me to hire women. The way they handled it was to say, ''Well, you know there's a head count and we can't hire other people until there's a space.'' And the head count didn't matter whether it was producers, writers, directors, street-sweepers, secretaries. . . . When I started to revamp my whole team because ''The Nation's Future'' was finished . . . I said . . . ''We're starting from scratch. So if I'm allowed six people I have to be allowed to hire whom I want.'' So there was a lot of *Sturm und Drang*, especially if I would give them titles, like associate producer or line producer.

Jarvis liked to hire women because she believed they brought two important qualities to broadcast news, qualities she believes contributed to her success: innovation and perseverance. She also found they tended to pay attention to detail in their work, making sure their facts were solid. When large numbers of women broke into broadcast news in the late sixties and early seventies, many of them went to Jarvis, by that time an award-winning producer for NBC, for advice.

> I was the one thing that the network could have said, ''Well, what are you talking about? We allow women to make it.'' I gave them all the reasons why [the women] should not accept that. They didn't *allow* me to make it. I committed them to a situation and they had to go along with it.

*Financial Parity.* One situation Jarvis had to force was pay, for she didn't make as much money as her male counterparts. In addition to their salaries, producers received a fee for programs that were sponsored. When Jarvis got a $20,000 fee, she remembers a man would get $35,000. After the internationally acclaimed program, "The Louvre" in 1964, Jarvis got a lawyer, a contract, and finally, financial parity with male producers.

After sixteen years with NBC, Jarvis left in 1976. Her contract at the time allowed her a great deal of freedom, and she could do dramatic work, theatrical productions, and movies outside NBC—just about anything but documentaries. At that time, Barbara Walters was leaving NBC for an anchor seat at ABC and wanted Jarvis to produce four interview specials Walters also would do. Though it appeared Jarvis could do them under her NBC contract, her lawyer advised her to tell the network about them anyway. Management vetoed the idea: Jarvis would have to choose between NBC and Walters. Believing that she and Walters would own the rights to the programs and be able to syndicate them, Jarvis decided to leave NBC. Then they discovered ABC owned the shows. Jarvis produced the first special anyway, then started up her own production company, Creative Projects, Inc. Today, her New York-based agency handles a wide variety of projects from television movies to international video conferencing to industrial films.

A stylish, self-assured woman with a flair for the dramatic, Jarvis is proud of the distinction she has achieved in what was a man's world when she began. Displayed in her company's reception area are some of the many awards she and her staffs have won for their programs, honors that include Emmys, Peabodys, the American Film Festival Award, the Ohio State Journalism Award, the National Headliners Club Award, and the Christopher Award.

## CONCLUSION

The broadcast newswomen who gained prominence in the years right after World War II set high standards. Through a combination of skill, determination, and luck, they added more proof that women could succeed in this male-dominated field. And, importantly, they had staying power.

The most successful of these pioneers had broad backgrounds, came from different disciplines, and often got into broadcast news later in life. But they continued to face discrimination in employment. However, in spite of the odds against them, they stuck with broadcasting, which is one of the keys to having a major impact on the media and the communities being served.

While the war's shortage of men no longer provided an entree for women into broadcast news, society was getting used to large numbers of women in the work place and on the air. Though relatively few in number, their impact was being felt. They would become the role models for the women of the breakthrough generation of the 1970s.

## NOTES

1. "1200 Years of Broadcasting Announcing," *Broadcasting* 27, 11 (11 September 1944): 13; "News," *Broadcasting* 29, 4 (23 July 1945): 52; "News: American Shifts Men," *Broadcasting* 29, 15 (8 October 1945): 58; and "Improved Handling of Local Newscasts Urged at Meeting of Florida Stations," *Broadcasting* 30, 22 (21 January 1946): 34.

2. *Broadcasting* 30, 22 (3 June 1946): 89.

3. "News," *Broadcasting* 33, 17 (27 October 1947): 64 and "News," *Broadcasting* 33, 7 (18 August 1947): 54.

4. Gay Talese, "Perils of Pauline," *Saturday Evening Post* (26 January 1963): 3 and Gioia E. Diliberto, "Profiles of Three Newswomen," Master's thesis, University of Maryland, 1975, p. 5.

5. Pauline Frederick, letter to Gayle K. Yamada, 13 November 1986.

6. CBS memorandum from Edward R. Murrow to Mr. Kennett, 27 August 1946, National Press Club, Washington, D.C.

7. Diliberto thesis, p. 10 and Judith S. Gelfman, *Women in Television News* (New York: Columbia University Press, 1976), pp. 31-32.

8. Diliberto thesis, p. 14.

9. James Brown, "Pauline Frederick Back on the Beat," *Los Angeles Times* (8 April 1979): Calendar 92, 1.

10. Philip Nobile, "TV News and the Older Woman," *New York* (10 August 1981): 15.

11. Gelfman, *Women in Television News,* pp. 135-36.

12. Frederick letter.

13. Nancy K. Gray, "Before Barbara Walters There Was Dorothy Fuldheim," *Ms.* (December 1976): 40.

14. Donald Perris, telephone interview with Gayle K. Yamada, 9 September 1986.

15. Gray, "Before Barbara Walters," pp. 40 + .

16. Perris interview.

17. Dorothy Fuldheim, *I Laughed, I Cried, I Loved* (Cleveland: World, 1966), p. 152.

18. Harry F. Waters with Jon Lowell, "The First Lady of TV News," *Newsweek* (11 June 1979): 91.

19. Perris interview.

20. Gray, "Before Barbara Walters," p. 45.

21. "The Non-retiring Ways of a Nonagenarian Newswoman," *Broadcasting* 105, 1 (4 July 1983): 103.

22. Ibid.

23. Waters and Lowell, "The First Lady of TV News," p. 91.

24. Perris interview.

25. Ibid.

26. Ibid.

27. Ibid.

28. Unless otherwise stated, quotations from Zona B. Davis are from a telephone interview with David H. Hosley, 12 September 1986.

29. Unless otherwise stated, quotations from Lucy Jarvis are from an interview with Gayle K. Yamada, New York City, 25 August 1986.

# 4 Taking Off with TV

The newswomen watched by America's first television generation can be counted on one hand. Despite presenting some opportunities for women because it was unproven, television was a man's world. The women in it, with few exceptions, were expected to cover women's news. Those who insisted on covering hard news, like Pauline Frederick, stand out. Although they were small in number, their impact was great, for the broadcast newswomen of the 1950s became the role models for the wave of women on the air two decades later.

## THE FIRST TELEVISION NETWORK NEWSWOMEN

### Nancy Dickerson: "Hello, Nancy"

Nancy Hanschman Dickerson became CBS's first female television correspondent by knowing the right people and creating her own opportunities. As network news was expanding on American television in the early sixties, she was the most visible woman on the air. She was described in a *Saturday Evening Post* article as "Slim (five feet seven and 120 pounds) and social (she is a member of Washington's exclusive F Street Club), chic and charming, she looks and dresses like a fashion model, speaks like a professional actress, and goes about her job like a veteran newsman."[1]

Nancy Hanschman was born in Milwaukee and grew up in nearby Wauwatosa. She studied music for two years at Clarke College, a Catholic school for women in Dubuque, Iowa, and then transferred to the University of Wisconsin, graduating in 1948 with a concentration in Spanish and Portuguese. She spent that summer in Europe through a U.N. program for students. Toward the end of the summer, she took part-time jobs as a model and secretary in Paris and was hoping to stay on until her parents reminded her that she'd agreed to teach in the Milwaukee school system that fall. During the summers of the two years she was a teacher, Dickerson took courses at Harvard.

*From Foreign Relations to Public Affairs.*   Dickerson wanted to do something more exciting than teaching and felt Washington might be the place to find a position in foreign relations work. Her first job, however, was as a registrar at Georgetown University. Three months later she became a secretary to the Senate Foreign Relations Committee, even though her secretarial skills were limited. Her ability to make political contacts was sound, however, and soon she was a popular date for some of the most powerful men on Capitol Hill. After three years with the committee, Dickerson started looking for a new challenge.

> I had been going out with the UPI reporter covering Congress, and he told me that CBS was looking for a man who knew Capitol Hill. My only reporting had been as editor of the Hawthorne Junior High School *Echo*, I wasn't a man, but I got the job. In April 1954, I was put in charge of two CBS radio network programs, "The Leading Question" and "Capitol Cloakroom," both of which were radio versions of "Meet the Press." My title was "Producer, Public Affairs," and we had a corny laugh at the committee about my leaving foreign relations for public affairs.[2]

Later that year, Dickerson became assistant producer of "Face the Nation," a new program that competed with NBC's "Meet the Press." Willing to work long hours, Dickerson volunteered for assignments others at CBS didn't want. She worked every Thanksgiving and Christmas during her first six years at the network. Her diligence paid off when Dickerson was assigned to both political conventions in 1956 and worked election night as well.

*Producer for Murrow.*   In 1957, Dickerson became a producer for Edward R. Murrow. He was at the peak of his power as America's leading broadcast journalist. It is ironic that while working with a man who had strong feelings about ethics, Dickerson got so involved with politician Kenneth Keating that she called herself a "secret, unofficial campaign manager."[3] Keating and Dickerson had dated for several years, but her involvement in his 1958 Senate campaign intensified their relationship. When he won, Keating gave her his official certificate of election. The victory, says Dickerson, ended that phase of their friendship, and she says they never went out again. But her close friendships with politicians, particularly Lyndon Johnson, would bring her ethical values into question as her broadcast career developed.

Like the female foreign correspondents of twenty years before, Dickerson's big break came overseas. She convinced network officials to let her report on women in the army in Europe during the summer of 1959. Her first piece, from West Berlin, was followed by one on East Berlin preparing for a visit from Soviet leader Nikita Khrushchev. A third report was done in Vienna. When she arranged for a papal audience and His Holiness commented on Khrushchev, Dickerson had her fourth report. She believed she had greater opportunity to broadcast by going abroad. But some people at the network didn't appreciate the effort. "It was pointed out to me that since I was a woman and unmarried and didn't have a family to support, I should stop trying to broadcast."[4]

Dickerson was determined to succeed on the air. She arranged for an exclusive interview with House Speaker Sam Rayburn in January 1960, and her work so impressed Don Hewitt, then the producer of CBS's nightly newscast, that he pushed for her to become the network's first female correspondent. Hewitt, who would later be blasted by Sally Quinn for his treatment of her while covering a royal wedding, also made it clear that he didn't want Dickerson covering "women's news" because that would typecast her.

Murrow also gave some advice to Dickerson. He advised her to dress conservatively, suggesting that it was a shock to have a woman giving the news on television, and that "frilly clothes might suggest frivolity."[5] He also said that the substance of what she would say in a report was only 51 percent of a broadcast, while how she said it was 49 percent.

*First on the Floor.*    Politics continued to be Dickerson's beat, and at the Los Angeles Democratic convention in 1960 she became the first woman reporter to work a convention floor. She had a powerful ally in Senator Lyndon B. Johnson, who would favor her with interviews, often to the exclusion of others. It became a standard scene for Johnson to step off a plane, walk directly to the only female reporter in a crowd of newsmen, and drawl into her live mike, "Hello, Nancy."

Dickerson reported exclusively that Johnson would accept the vice presidential nomination after he had publicly maintained he would not become Kennedy's running mate. While covering the inauguration, she was favored with brief interviews with Kennedy immediately before he was sworn in as president, and right afterward. Dickerson accompanied Vice President Johnson on his around-the-world tour in 1961, again using her strong relationship with him to beat her competition.

In 1962, Nancy Hanschman married C. Wyatt Dickerson, a businessman who was a widower with three children. Her engagement was announced at a dinner co-hosted by Johnson, Supreme Court Justice Arthur Goldberg, and Senator Abraham Ribicoff. The new family life required a good deal of coordination but also provided satisfactions that her career did not.

At this point, Dickerson was becoming concerned about where her work was appearing; it somehow always seemed to be sidetracked to radio and the morning television shows.

> I realized that being a woman was sometimes helpful, but more often a hindrance. There were no effective anti-discrimination laws then, no groups to fight women's battles; television was having growing pains, and sexism was not of paramount concern in broadcasting. There were literally dozens of problems

arising from being female in that world, and from the stereotype expected of women. To take a trivial example, if a male correspondent complained, he was merely analyzing his situation; if I were to do so, I was automatically "a bitch."[6]

*The Switch to NBC.*    That frustration led Dickerson to consider switching networks. Vice President Johnson, who wanted her to stay with CBS, even got involved in the negotiations with NBC. Dickerson joined the older network in May 1963. Part of her concern about the transition was that she was pregnant. But NBC officials assured her that was not a problem and, after the birth of a son, she added a weekday afternoon newscast to her political duties. She also had a daily three-minute radio network broadcast. Dickerson earned around $40,000 a year, making her the most highly paid woman in the broadcast news industry.

Dickerson covered most of the big political stories of the next few years, including the civil rights march on Washington, D.C., President John F. Kennedy's funeral, and Johnson's presidency. She and her husband were invited by Congressman Wilbur Mills to visit Fanne Fox where she worked as a stripper, and the Dickersons witnessed several of Mills's escapades, that developed into the Tidal Basin scandal.

Dickerson believes the women's movement hurt her professionally; that men felt threatened by the movement and started to treat her differently than they had in the years when she was the "Princess of the Press." In 1970, her afternoon newscast was canceled, and Dickerson decided to leave NBC. She felt that her own syndicated political reporting and analysis would open new opportunities for her, and she wanted to write a book. She also became a regular on the lecture circuit.

But the syndication effort was less successful than Dickerson had hoped, and her days as a fixture on American television were over. Her decade of prominence did lead, however, to participation in January 1971, on behalf of PBS, in a nationally broadcast interview with President Richard M. Nixon. She shared the spotlight with correspondents from the three commercial networks. Dickerson established her own production company and received several awards, including a Peabody, for a 1982 broadcast on Watergate. She and her husband were divorced in 1983.

Dickerson's close social ties to her sources might be objectionable in today's atmosphere of adversarial Washington coverage. But in the turbulent decade of the sixties, her personal approach to news gathering was an effective way to make a mark in broadcast journalism as one of the medium's first news personalities.

### Lisa Howard: "A Confessed Egghead"

ABC's answer to Nancy Hanschman Dickerson was Lisa Howard. For four years in the early 1960s, she scored a series of impressive exclusives and grabbed headlines for the way she got her stories. But Howard also had problems with ethics and politicians and died in her late thirties of an overdose of sleeping pills shortly after a miscarriage.

Born Dorothy Jean Guggenheim in Cambridge, Ohio, she attended a year of college at Miami of Ohio before beginning a career as an actress. She studied at the Pasadena Playhouse, adopting Lisa Howard as a stage name that she kept when she turned to broadcasting a decade later. By then Howard had been married twice and had two daughters. She had appeared in a number of summer stock productions, including "Private Lives," an off-Broadway staging of " 'Tis a Pity She's a Whore," and had acted in television soap operas such as "The Edge of Night" and "As the World Turns." There was another side to Howard; she also had been writing magazine articles for progressive journals since college, including *Progressive World,* and wrote a novel about life in the theatre, *On Stage Miss Douglas.*

*Khrushchev and Castro.*    Howard decided she was more interested in current events than history and wrangled a job covering the Los Angeles Democratic convention in 1960 for the Mutual Broadcasting System. She got her break later that year when Khrushchev visited America. Howard sneaked into the Soviet embassy in New York and surprised the Soviet premier with a request for an interview.

The exclusive made news but it also got her suspended, for many inside and outside broadcast journalism thought her naive questions allowed Khrushchev to propagandize. But after a day she was reinstated.

James C. Hagerty, ABC's vice president for news, signed the husky-voiced Howard to a one-year contract in May 1961, saying, "She works like a beaver. She'll be tops."[7] Howard got a second exclusive interview with Khrushchev, this time in Vienna, and one with President Kennedy. She quickly became a frequent contributor to ABC's evening news, which was a distant third to NBC and CBS. Her biggest scoop came early in April 1963, when she managed to get into Cuba and then land an interview with Fidel Castro. Howard had been aided by a friend, Ghana's ambassador to Cuba and the United Nations, in getting a visa. Then she had contacts bombard Cuba's leader with requests for an interview. Three weeks after she arrived, Howard had an all-night conversation with Castro in a restaurant. They discussed everything from literature to political philosophy, and she obtained a commitment for a formal interview. Howard got forty-five minutes on film with Castro, the longest interview with him in more than two years. She interviewed Castro several other times, and a documentary aired April 19, 1964, was singled out for praise.

> The real news lay in the making of the documentary itself and its presentation on ABC. For in simply showing what she had seen and heard during her tour of Cuba and talks with its leaders, Miss Howard offered evidence to challenge

some of our most treasured notions about the island. By her own statement, she—and producer Harry Rasky and the crew—were allowed to go anywhere they wanted (except military installations); to interview anyone, including an outspoken critic of the regime as well as a political prisoner; and to take their film home intact. True, Premier Castro was cagey in discussing one or two political matters, and Miss Howard occasionally found it necessary to couch her questions in State Department cliches. But the total effect was one of freshness, and our only real protest is that such objectivity should be rare enough for commendation.[8]

Howard had her own television newscast, five minutes at 2:55 each weekday afternoon, "Lisa Howard and News with the Woman's Touch." She was receiving about $25,000 a year. But she also had a number of detractors. One profile found that

Lisa operates with all the canvas-backed insensitivity of the trained newshound, but personally she is as sensitive as a gouty toe. She suspects darkly that newsmen want to write her off as a pushy Clairol blonde who forges ahead by making more sex than sense, and because she was once an actress in TV's daytime serial, "The Edge of Night."[9]

Another carped: "Though lacking polish and a real reporter's knack for the trenchant question, she packs plenty of punch: a mixture of sass, brass and self-confidence wrapped in a package guaranteed to lure males." Howard felt that her good looks were a handicap as a newswoman: "I have to fight certain things because I look the way I do."[10] She resisted the stereotype: "I stand before you as a confessed egghead, not as ABC's jazzy bombshell."[11]

*Off the Air.* Howard's career nose-dived after she became so involved in a New York political campaign that ABC suspended and then fired her. Howard had supported Kenneth Keating against Robert Kennedy in the Senate race. She had helped form a committee that publicly endorsed Keating despite warnings from ABC. The network suspended her in September and, after several disputes over assignments, she was terminated. She sued the network for reinstatement, asking $2 million in damages, and lost.

Devastated by the loss of her job, Howard and her husband, film producer Walter Lowendahl, were buoyed when she became pregnant. She had lined up a job as publicity director of the New York State anti-poverty program. But a miscarriage put Howard in the hospital in early June, and she became very depressed. She was released in time to spend the Fourth of July at the family's vacation home in East Hampton, Long Island. While under medication for depression, Howard also had gotten a prescription for sleeping pills. The number of pills had been altered from 10 to 100 before being filled. The morning of the Fourth, friends found Howard in a parking lot next to a pharmacy, glassy-eyed and nearly incoherent. She was rushed under police escort to a nearby clinic, where she lost consciousness and died. The death was ruled a suicide.

Lisa Howard wanted desperately to be considered a broadcast journalist and not the actress she had been before beginning her brief career in television news. She benefited at times from being an attractive woman, for it certainly played a part in her exclusives with Castro. But Howard did not understand the ethics of network news reporting. And the men who ran ABC News may not have understood Howard and what made her want to succeed despite her good looks.

## Marlene Sanders: First Network Vice President

When Howard was suspended by ABC she was replaced by Marlene Sanders, who had just been hired by ABC News vice president Jesse Zousmer. Sanders was thirty-three years old and had a wealth of experience in broadcasting, going back to 1955. It had been a solitary ten years in one respect; as a writer, producer, reporter, and news administrator, she had no female peers where she worked. "Being the only woman on the premises is a distinction of a sort, but a lonely one."[12] Within months of her hiring at ABC, she became the first woman to anchor a network nightly newscast and her more than three decades in the business have made her a role model for many.

Sanders was born in Cleveland, Ohio, January 10, 1931. She attended Ohio State, and then Cleveland College, where she majored in speech. She says she was "stagestruck" growing up and tried a career in acting. While doing summer stock in New England in 1955, Sanders met Mike Wallace, then a newsman on WABD, New York, soon to become WNEW-TV. He introduced her to the newscast's producer, and Sanders landed a job politely described as a production assistant. She has described it as a "go-fer" and "flunkey-type job," but adds it gave her a chance to learn quickly about television. Wallace soon moved on to a nightly interview show, called "Nightbeat," and Sanders and several others who had worked on the news went to the new show. By 1957, she was "Nightbeat's" associate producer. When Wallace left the program later that year, he was replaced by John Wingate, who failed to excite the audience in the same way the tough-questioning Wallace had. "Nightbeat" was canceled in 1958, and Sanders became the producer of "Probe," which looked at a particular subject in depth. She also married Jerome Toobin, and they had two sons. The next year she worked on several programs, including one interview show that was hosted by Monty Hall, the man who would become famous for "Let's Make a Deal."

Sanders moved on to a new program for the Westinghouse stations in 1960. Called "P.M.," it featured segments for the East and West coasts;

again, Wallace was the talent. Sanders produced the East Coast portions. She felt that her later success would be due in large part to a solid foundation as a producer.

> In the early years, I worked for very good people, men who really didn't care that I was female. . . . There was opportunity to be upwardly mobile, which a lot of people don't have. So I was lucky in the first people I worked for and I got through the first five years making great career advances. And that was partly because I was doing a great job. I worked very hard, very long hours. I liked what I was doing. I was enthusiastic and I hope intelligent about it. But I also had people around who were not a hindrance, because you do run into them at certain points in your career, and sometimes that's a very difficult problem.[13]

*The Only Woman Again.*    With those underpinnings, Sanders moved into hard news at WNEW-AM in 1962, serving as assistant news and public affairs director. She was the only woman broadcaster on the station. Her duties included street reporting, anchoring, and producing a weekly half-hour program called "News Closeup." Her documentary, "The Battle of the Warsaw Ghetto," won a Writers Guild of America Award, one of more than two dozen awards she's won in her career. Sanders's coverage of the funeral of President Kennedy attracted the attention of ABC News executives, and in the fall of 1964, she joined the network as its second female correspondent. The man who hired her, Jesse Zousmer, had been a crack writer for CBS. He took interest in Sanders's work, providing helpful critiques of her early anchoring.

On December 2, 1964, just three months after joining ABC, Sanders became the first woman to anchor a network nightly newscast. Anchorman Ron Cochran became ill, and started to lose his voice. Sanders pinch hit, and the event was duly noted in the *New York Times*: "People who should know report that never before has a distaff reporter conducted on her very own a news broadcast in prime time. For the record, then, the courageous young woman with a Vassar smile was crisp and businesslike and obviously the sort who wouldn't put up with any nonsense from anyone."[14] Sanders says the precedent-setting event had no impact.

> It was as if it had never happened. So I continued as an afternoon anchor; no other woman got anything there or on the other networks. People didn't begin to say, "Gee, what a great idea. Why don't we get a woman to anchor the evening news?" Of course, 1964 was the Dark Ages as far as women's progress was concerned. Not only were women not an issue; no one was even thinking about them at all.[15]

Sanders also was perturbed about how much attention was being paid to the way she looked rather than her reporting. She had to look no further than her family for a critique. "Even my own mother writes me long letters about how I look rather than what I talk about."[16]

Sanders co-anchored ABC's coverage of the inauguration of President Johnson in 1965, and was sent to Vietnam in 1966 for three weeks. Her reports were broadcast on the ABC evening news as well as during her afternoon "News with a Woman's Touch." That broadcast was canceled in 1968, perhaps a sign of the times, and Sanders was free to travel more as a correspondent. She covered Senator Eugene McCarthy's campaign for the presidential nomination, the assassination of Robert F. Kennedy, and that summer's political conventions. And she began to do more documentaries, which provided a satisfaction the shorter news pieces did not. One 1970 documentary was titled "Women's Liberation," a subject of special interest to Sanders as a charter member of the National Organization for Women. Another of her reports that year, "We Have Met the Enemy and He Is Us," explored the population explosion, taking its title from the comic strip, *Pogo*.

Sanders chalked up another milestone in 1971 when she was chosen as the substitute for Sam Donaldson, who had been anchoring ABC's late newscast on Saturdays. Donaldson was assigned temporarily to Vietnam, and Sanders filled in for three months. Again, there was no lasting change because of the assignment.

Sanders moved to the network's documentary unit on a full-time basis later in 1971. She continued to focus on social problems, turning out award-winning documentaries on child abuse, women in politics, birth control, breast cancer, the evolving role of women in America, and the impact of television. Many of the broadcasts were done as part of ABC's "Closeup" series, overseen by Av Westin. When he resigned in early 1976, Sanders was named to replace him. As head of the documentary unit, she became the first female vice president in any of the network news divisions.

Sanders continued to make her interest in social issues felt on the air. ABC examined the Equal Rights Amendment, the fairness of the American legal system, and the battle over the development of nuclear power. When Roone Arledge took over the network's news division, Sanders felt that she wasn't getting the kind of cooperation she desired from the top and resigned two years after becoming a vice president.

Sanders soon joined CBS, where she did a number of "CBS Reports" and segments on "60 Minutes" and "Sunday Morning." More recently, Sanders anchored TV updates in prime time and hourly broadcasts on the CBS Radio Network. She often substituted for Douglas Edwards on the radio network's roundup, "The World Tonight," before leaving CBS during a round of cuts in early 1987. She has been named the Woman of the Year by the American Women in Radio and Television, and is a former president of Women in Communications, Inc.

Sanders feels there may be some disadvantages to being a trailblazer for women in broadcast news. She thinks that others may have benefited more from her breakthroughs as an anchor and news executive than she did.

### Local Anchors

Local stations had been faster to add women to their staffs in the 1950s and early 1960s. Some of them were already in place when the big push of the women's movement teamed with civil rights advances to open the floodgates in the late sixties and early seventies. For others, it was too late.

At KPIX in San Francisco, Wanda Ramey was twenty-nine years old when she was teamed with anchorman John Weston in 1957 and became known as Channel 5's "Girl on the Go." She left to have a baby a decade later and after returning to work decided to devote herself instead to raising her family. A brief comeback in 1969 at KGO-TV was unsatisfactory because Ramey, then forty-one, felt she was not getting the kind of stories she deserved and wasn't being treated equally.

Marie Torre, who had gone to jail for ten days in 1959 rather than disclose a source for a *New York Herald Tribune* story, joined the news staff of KDKA-TV, Pittsburgh, in the summer of 1962. She hosted a morning news and talk program and did reports for the station's other news broadcasts. Torre had started her journalism career in 1942 on the *New York World Telegram and Sun*, and had been a syndicated radio-TV columnist for the *Herald Tribune* before joining KDKA. She was in her mid-fifties when she left the station after fourteen years to return to New York.

Ruth Ashton Taylor was the first woman to report live on television in Los Angeles. Taylor stayed with KNXT more than three decades after her start in 1951. After undergraduate work at Scripps College in southern California, she went to Columbia Graduate School of Journalism, where a professor convinced her to try television.

## EQUAL EMPLOYMENT OPPORTUNITIES

In the mid-1960s, new impetus for hiring women was provided by Congress, with a healthy push from President Johnson. The Civil Rights Act of 1964, originally drafted to forbid racial discrimination, was changed at the last minute so it would outlaw sex discrimination as well. Southern members of Congress thought they could defeat the bill if it included women, so it was quite a surprise when the amended bill became law. When the Equal Employment Opportunity Commission, the federal agency charged with aiding enforcement of the law, began functioning in 1966, a third of the complaints filed involved sex discrimination, most of them revolving around compensation and terms of employment. Coupled with the rise of the women's movement in the mid-sixties, the creation of a ready forum for such complaints provided momentum for women, especially black women, to move into broadcast newsrooms in increasing numbers.

Lady Bird Johnson, the president's wife and chair of the board of LBJ, Co., owned 57 percent of the stock in the company that had interests in stations in Austin and Waco, Texas. She was active in its operation and so when she spoke to the 1963 annual convention of American Women in Radio and Television about women in broadcasting it made news. "Today, doors are opening wider for the woman performer in entertainment and in news and it's long overdue. If the industry is to do its best it must have fuller use of their brains and ability."[17] A survey of news directors in 1964 found that most of the women in broadcast news were presenting news for women and that one radio station in three, and half of the TV stations had women on their news staffs.

The women hired in local and network broadcasting in the mid-sixties came from a variety of backgrounds. Some, particularly blacks, had been working in other media while waiting for the doors to open. The advantages of hiring black women were obvious to station managers, who could count them in two EEO categories.

### Trudy Haynes: Weather First

A few, like Trudy Haynes, had a good deal of experience. Haynes had been broadcasting since 1956, when she became an announcer at Detroit radio station WCHB. Born in New York and a graduate of Howard University, Haynes had been an investigator for the New York City Department of Welfare and for the U.S. Special Services in Germany before starting her broadcasting career. In 1963, she became a weather girl at WXYZ, Detroit and in 1964 a reporter. In 1966 she moved to KYW-TV, also as a reporter and remains there now as entertainment reporter. The ranks of the weather girls, a popular concept in the late fifties and early sixties, produced several other reporters, including Jeanne Parr at WCBS-TV, New York.

### Joan Murray: Striking Opportunity

Joan Murray came up through the secretarial ranks. Born November 6, 1941, Murray had grown up in Ithaca, New York, in a well-to-do black family. Her father had gotten through college in two-and-a-half years. Murray was an identical twin and also had a younger sister. She learned shorthand at age fourteen, was working part time for a Cornell professor at fifteen, but only dabbled in college before joining her twin in New York, where they lived at a YMCA-sponsored complex for young women. Murray's first job was at a company that made cosmetic carrying cases. Then she worked as a secretary at a theatrical agency before joining CBS as a secretary in the publicity office. Her boss handled public relations for CBS News and Public Affairs.

Murray transferred to corporate headquarters when her boss got promoted, but soon moved on to become secretary to Allen Funt of "Candid Camera" fame. She appeared in some industrial films and had a bit part in a movie. She worked both in front of the camera and behind the scenes on "Women on the Move" on WNBC-TV, a broadcast co-hosted by Kitty Carlisle and Murray, which lasted only four months. After a long vacation in Europe, Murray returned to New York and got part-time work on WCBS-TV's local news. Six months after she became a reporter, in September 1965, a newspaper strike in New York prompted local stations to increase their newscasts. A new show on WCBS went on at 1 P.M., and Murray co-anchored it with a rotating group of men. After the strike was settled, the newscast stayed on as "Two at One," and Murray continued to be the co-anchor.

A bright woman who went back to college while working in television, Murray also became a private pilot as part of a feature story. Her participation in the 1967 Powder Puff Derby cross country became a feature. By then, the novelty of a woman reporting the news had worn off.

> When I initially began reporting, there were a few women in the field, but not enough to shake a man's confidence and job security. All of the men were extremely polite, would help out with a story, and sometimes make sure that you, as a girl, had a good microphone vantage point, or let you have first crack at the questions. Now, however, with more and more females competing with the men, it's everyone for himself.[18]

Murray added a syndicated radio show to her duties, won dozens of awards, and served on the New York Governor's Commission on Employment of Minority Groups and Women in News Media. In the early seventies she formed her own advertising agency and has devoted the bulk of her energies to her business since then.

### "Twofer" Hiring Goes On

The pattern of hiring women who were also racial minorities would continue in broadcast news. A study of news staffs in 1977 found that a quarter of the women in television news was also minorities; 16 percent of the women in radio news were minorities as well.

Still, it was a singular experience for most of these women entering broadcast news. White, black, Asian, or Hispanic, they still were breaking into a field dominated by men. Their assignments continued to be lighter stories, perhaps not just women's news but nothing too serious. They had to learn the techniques of reporting, then make their opportunity to move into hard news.

### Marya McLaughlin: Solo at CBS

Marya McLaughlin became the only female reporter at CBS when she was hired in May 1965. She wasn't joined by another woman on the air for six years. Born in Baltimore, she attended Catholic University, then transferred to Marymount College in New York where she received her degree in political science and economics. McLaughlin had been an associate producer on a CBS documentary, "1945," and had worked on several other documentaries, including a BBC series on World War I. She worked as an assistant on CBS's 1964 election coverage and for six years was an assistant to David Brinkley. After a few weeks break-in time working days, McLaughlin pulled a midnight to 8 A.M. shift in the network newsroom, handling the desk duties. She had three women companions in the newsroom, perhaps more a factor that the rookies worked crummy shifts then trying to hide the women in the journalistic Siberia of the overnight shifts. Later, McLaughlin began street reporting, and on what seemed like the routine "woman's story" of interviewing a new cabinet member's wife, Martha Mitchell suggested that America's anti-war protestors should be sent to Russia, an exclusive that made headlines around the world. McLaughlin was made a correspondent in 1971. She has been with CBS for more than twenty years now and has been a general assignment reporter in the Washington bureau for most of the last decade.

### Liz Trotta: Newspapers to TV

A number of the new broadcasters came from print backgrounds. Liz Trotta was hired in 1965 by WNBC-TV, New York, becoming the station's first female reporter. She was hired as the station expanded to an hour of news from 6 to 7 P.M. Trotta, who was twenty-eight years old, came from *Newsday* and had been a reporter for the Associated Press and *Chicago Tribune.* To make her debut on camera, WNBC had consultants change her hairstyle; she emerged from the session with bangs, which she'd never worn before. Her first on-camera appearance was a disaster, as she was brushed off on live TV by Congressman John Lindsay, who was not talking to reporters. The next day he announced that he was a candidate for mayor of New York City. A few days later she had another embarrassing incident. Shooting a feature story, she had to go back a second day for more interviews. Trotta forgot about wardrobe continuity for the story and wore a different outfit. She had to be driven home to change.

The presence of women in visible positions on newscasts provided role models. In Trotta's case, she was the inspiration for Phyllis Haynes, who became a reporter in New York City. When Haynes was a seventeen-year-old scholarship winner, Trotta covered the story. Haynes recalls that "meeting a woman who was telling her crew what to do and shaping a story really might have been my initial motivation to go into broadcasting."[19]

Trotta continued her career in broadcasting for two decades, covering the Vietnam War, among other assignments, before being laid off by CBS in 1985. She sued on grounds of age discrimination and received a settlement.

### Edith Huggins: "Eddie" Won't Do

Other women were plucked from obscurity. Edith Huggins, a black woman whose real first name was Eddie, was spotted by WCAU-TV General Manager Bruce Bryant in New York and invited to audition for a news job, which she got. A striking black woman, Huggins was a nurse and part-time actress, who had been born in St. Joseph, Missouri, and had been a disc jockey as a teenager. She also had done some educational TV while majoring in music at the University of Nebraska. Huggins switched to nursing at the State University of New York and graduated cum laude. While nursing in New York City, Huggins had gotten acting work portraying a nurse on NBC's soap opera, "The Doctors." She was also a technical advisor for the program.

When Huggins joined WCAU-TV in 1966, station executives made her change her first name because they thought "Eddie" was a boy's name and would confuse viewers if she used it. While working at WCAU, she continued her acting, appearing in "Edge of Night" and "Love of Life" as well as additional episodes of "The Doctors."

### Belva Davis: From Black Media to Mainstream

The breakthroughs in broadcast news for women continued into the late sixties. The timing varied from market to market. In some communities, the amount of pressure applied by organizations such as the NAACP affected hiring of minorities and women. Belva Davis, who had been working in the black media in San Francisco since 1961, knew very well that local black leaders had been pressuring stations to hire more blacks. While the NAACP's efforts were directed mainly at KGO, she got her break at KPIX-TV.

Davis was born in October 1933 in Monroe, Louisiana, and was raised in the San Francisco Bay area, graduating from high school in Berkeley. She was working as a supply clerk with the navy when she began writing a social column for a small community newspaper, *Bay Area Independent*. Except for two radio stations that served the black community, most of the information was communicated in these weeklies. Davis reported on community events on radio station KSAN, San Francisco, and became a stringer for the Johnson Publications' *Jet* and *Ebony*. In 1963, Davis gave up the security of a full-time government position for the more than full-time commitment of her media jobs: stringing for Johnson Publications, writing a column in the *Sun Reporter*, and working as a clerk at KJAZ, Alameda. Davis switched to KDIA, Oakland, where she was traffic manager and on the air from 10 to

11 A.M. weekdays and two hours on Saturdays as a disc jockey and public affairs hostess.

KDIA had special significance for Davis, for listening to that station while growing up, she had heard a black woman giving news for the first time. The voice was that of Tarea Hall Pittman, the wife of a prominent dentist who broadcast a fifteen-minute program on Sundays for a half century, starting in the 1930s. "Negroes in the News" was known far and wide, yet Pittman was not paid for the broadcast. She felt the 9:45 A.M. program was a public service. Its popularity continued long after "blacks" had succeeded "Negroes" in American speech, for Pittman stepped down only when she reached her eighties and the station was sold.

KDIA's news director, Lewis Freeman, had helped Davis with her newscasting skills, and she looked for a television job for several years before landing the one at KPIX in 1967. Finding out that one of the station's two newswomen, Nancy Reynolds, was leaving to work for Ronald Reagan, Davis called the news director, told him she knew there was going to be an opening, and asked for the job. Sixty-seven people applied for the position, but after auditions, Davis got it. The NAACP and other community organizations made their support known by publicly congratulating the management of the station, and Davis got her introduction to TV news on her first story. It was a "hot chase" in which the station's mobile unit got between the police and a suspect who was firing a weapon at the cops. Fortunately, the only harm done was to her nerves. Even today, Davis remembers it as the most harrowing story she's ever covered.

Within a year, Davis began anchoring and before long was handling all the newscasts. In fact, it was not rare for her, in a pinch, to anchor the noon, 6, and 11 P.M. shows. Long hours were common at the station, and after she worked every day in the month of February one year, the union used her time card to successfully argue for a forty-hour work week for the news staff. Davis also established a public affairs broadcast at 7:30 P.M. on Saturdays. The time slot, away from the public service ghetto of Sunday morning, gave the broadcast a lot of visibility, and "All Together Now" became a model program for stations trying to cope with the emerging power of minorities in America.

After a decade at KPIX, Davis moved to KQED-TV, a PBS affiliate, to anchor an in-depth nightly news broadcast, "A Closer Look." She returned to commercial television after funding for KQED's news department was lost in 1980. Davis has been "Urban Affairs Specialist" at KRON-TV since 1981. It is a position created especially for her and includes "Weekend Extra," KRON's Sunday morning public affairs program, which Davis would like to see moved to a better time slot. And she would like more than one minute and fifteen seconds to explain her stories about the changes in the San Francisco and Oakland communities.

Belva Davis and Sylvia Chase are two veteran broadcasters among dozens who are breaking the traditional age barriers in television. Davis was the first black woman anchor on San Francisco television and is now an urban affairs specialist for KRON-TV. Chase returned to local news in 1986 after fourteen years with CBS and ABC. Courtesy KRON-TV and Chronicle Broadcasting Company.

The mother of two grown children, Davis is married to KTVU-TV, Oakland, cameraman William Moore. In her mid-fifties, she reflects on her battle for equality as a woman, a minority, and now as someone confronting the age issue: "I just wonder where the period was when I was free of all the shackles. I don't know if it ever happened."[20]

### Ponchitta Pierce: Mixed Media

Ponchitta Pierce attributes many of her career opportunities to the civil rights movement and the women's movement. Like Belva Davis, Pierce made her broadcast news debut in 1967. She had been spotted on a television talk show by a CBS executive. New York bureau chief of Johnson Publications, Pierce spoke about racism in American society on the program. The executive wondered whether she'd consider broadcasting, and soon Pierce was doing special pieces for CBS, mostly interviews for the "CBS Morning News," but also some for the evening newscast.

Born in August 1942 in Chicago, Pierce moved to New Orleans as a baby. Her parents, a contractor and a teacher, were appalled that she wanted to major in journalism. They didn't feel there were enough opportunities for a black person to make a living in the field. In fact, they were so upset about it that she switched to foreign languages as a freshman at the University of Southern California. But the idea stayed with her, and she ended up graduating cum laude in journalism, studying at Cambridge one summer. Pierce was yearbook editor. By the time she graduated she had been recruited by Johnson Publications and had a job waiting in New York.

By 1967, Pierce had become *Ebony*'s New York editor and bureau chief for the parent company. When she started working for CBS, Pierce was twenty-six. "What made the final decision for me was that I really thought I was young enough that I could fail . . . and go on with my life."[21]

Though Pierce remembers the people at CBS as supportive, her actual training to be on the air was minimal. One reviewer found that "Ponchitta is obviously learning by doing and has awkward moments, as if suddenly numbed by awareness that the staring camera eye is on her."[22] Network executives also wanted her to change her name; Ponchitta was thought to be too ethnic. She felt, "If that was good enough for my parents and me, it was going to be good enough for everybody else."

When the network had staff cutbacks in 1971, Pierce was laid off. She had continued print work while with CBS, however, and became a contributing editor to *McCall's* for several years. Then she worked for *Reader's Digest* until 1981. Pierce also continued to broadcast part time, doing a program called "Sunday" on WNBC-TV with Dick Reeves from 1973 to 1977 and then hosting, with Joe Michaels, a public service broadcast for seniors, "The Prime of Your Life," from 1977 to 1980. In 1982, she began to host "Today

Ponchitta Pierce while special correspondent for CBS News in the late 1960s. She primarily did interviews for "CBS Morning News with Joseph Benti." Courtesy Ponchitta Pierce.

in New York,'' a daily early morning interview program on WNBC-TV. She also co-produced it until March 1987, when it went into reruns.

### Melba Tolliver: Black First, Woman Second

Another television news career began amid controversy in 1967. Melba Tolliver made her anchoring debut as a strike breaker at ABC. Born in Rome, Georgia, Tolliver grew up in Akron, Ohio, and graduated with honors from Bellevue School of Nursing in New York. Looking for something new, she had gotten a job with ABC as a secretary in 1966, hoping to become a researcher. When an AFTRA strike loomed early in 1967, Tolliver's boss was one of those making contingency plans. But when the news people walked out, the planners still didn't have a woman to broadcast "News with a Woman's Touch," which Marlene Sanders normally anchored. A man had been lined up to do the newscast, but the sponsors wanted a woman. Tolliver was asked to fill in for just one day. She had a little experience modeling and doing television commercials and did well enough to be asked to continue until the week-long strike ended. Sanders was not happy about Tolliver's initial strike breaking; when there was a technicians' strike in the fall and AFTRA members honored their picket lines, Tolliver again filled in for Sanders, who never forgave her.

By the end of the year, the Kerner Report on the causes for racial unrest in America had been issued. It provided more impetus for advancing minorities, and Tolliver was to benefit. She had expressed interest in learning to become a newsperson, and now entered a minority training program at ABC. In the summer of 1968, Tolliver became a vacation relief reporter at WABC-TV and within a few months was on the permanent staff. Tolliver feels that being black was more important than being a woman in her case. While she takes exception to the term "twofer" to describe minority women who were hired to fill two voids in news staffs, she does acknowledge that's what happened.

> I'm black and I'm a woman. And if you're a news organization and people are accusing you of not having any blacks or not having any women, if you can get the two together [in one woman], you'd be a fool not to hire them. I'd do it. And if they could speak French or something else on top of it, great. The more talented, the more slots they fill, terrific.[23]

Tolliver thinks she benefited because the WABC-TV news staff was smaller than those of the other two network-owned New York City stations. She believes she was given assignments commensurate with her abilities and, as she got better, so did the assignments.

Tolliver got in trouble with station management when she wore a "natural" to work in the early seventies. She was taken off the air, but eventually management backed down in the face of growing community criticism.[24] Tolliver remained with WNBC-TV for a dozen years. She is now a freelance writer.

### Gloria Rojas: Hispanic Pioneer

Another response to the demand for increased opportunities for minorities in general and broadcasting in particular was the establishment of a training program in the summer of 1968 at Columbia University. Sponsored by a grant from the Ford Foundation and directed by former CBS News president Fred Friendly, the program lasted eight weeks, with twenty minority group members participating. A few had media backgrounds, but most did not. The intensive program trained them in broadcasting techniques in the hope they would be able to go out and get jobs when the summer was over. Two of the students were women; one of them was Gloria Rojas, who was hired by WCBS-TV, and thus became the first Puerto Rican reporter in New York City.[25]

### Progress

By 1970, 45 percent of TV newsrooms in America had women reporters, and 94 percent of the news directors who participated in a national survey said they would hire a woman reporter. Some of the ones in smaller markets said they would not because women couldn't carry camera equipment and most of their reporters also shot their own stories. And the bigger the city and the larger the staff, the more likely women were to be on the station's staff.

When the "Today" show marked the fiftieth anniversary of the passage of the Nineteenth Amendment that year, NBC devoted the entire two hours to women. The broadcast was presented on the air by Barbara Walters, Aline Saarinen, Pauline Frederick, Liz Trotta, and Nancy Dickerson. Neither ABC nor CBS could match that kind of strength in numbers, but the ranks of women at all three networks and at local stations across the country would swell dramatically in the next two years.

## CONCLUSION

Women in broadcast news often got assignments men didn't want. But even though television was not the preferred source for news in the late 1950s and early 1960s, it still was rare to see newswomen on the air. Professional positions still belonged largely to men, and broadcast journalism in the relatively new medium was no exception.

Nancy Dickerson, Lisa Howard, and Marlene Sanders were among the first television women to gain national recognition in hard news. Like many of their predecessors in radio, they started with "women's" assignments but were determined to cover hard news. They had to prove themselves by scoring exclusives and doing exceptional work. These early television newswomen showed they were like many of their female contemporaries in other fields who felt they had to be better than their male counterparts to be considered equals. Their work did get them noticed, and they began to accustom the American public to women in TV news.

The push to hire women on the air might not have happened in the mid-1960s had it not been for the civil rights movement. As employment doors opened for minorities, they opened for women. Black women in particular benefited, for many employers hired people who counted in two equal employment categories.

The influx of women in broadcast newsrooms in the mid-sixties foreshadowed the boom that should come in the next decade; the civil rights movement was the beginning of the women's movement, and the number of women in broadcast news would skyrocket in the 1970s.

## NOTES

1. B. Gottehrer, "Television's Princess of the Press Corps: Nancy Dickerson, Correspondent in NBC's Washington Bureau," *Saturday Evening Post* (31 October 1964): 36.

2. Nancy Dickerson, *Among Those Present* (New York: Random House, 1976), p. 20.

3. Ibid., p. 26.

4. Ibid., pp. 32-33.

5. Ibid., p. 135.

6. Ibid., pp. 86-87.

7. "The Beaver," *Time* (28 July 1961): 56.

8. "Viewing the Unseeable," *Nation* (27 April 1964): 407.

9. "No One Dodges Lisa," *Time* (25 October 1963): 68.

10. "The Beaver," p. 55.

11. "Fidel and Lisa," *Newsweek* (13 May 1963): 69.

12. Marlene Sanders, "Women in TV News—Where We've Been and Where We're Going," *Television Quarterly* (Spring 1981): 49.

13. Judith S. Gelfman, *Women in Television News* (New York: Columbia University Press, 1976), p. 74.

14. Jean Gaddy Wilson, "What It Takes to Be a Pro," *Working Woman* (October 1985): 130.

15. Ibid., pp. 130-31.

16. Angela Taylor, "Demands of the Camera Limit Choice of Clothes," *New York Times* (24 May 1965): 35.

17. "Doors Are Finally Opening for Women," *Broadcasting* 64, 18 (6 May 1963): 88.

18. Joan Murray, *The News* (New York: McGraw Hill, 1968), p. 80.

19. Gelfman, *Women in Television News*, p. 106.

20. Belva Davis, telephone interview with David H. Hosley, 14 September 1986.

21. Unless otherwise stated, quotations from Ponchitta Pierce are from an interview with Gayle K. Yamada, New York City, 22 August 1986.

22. "Newscasting: Duel at Daybreak," *Time* (25 April 1969): 89.

23. Melba Tolliver, telephone interview with Gayle K. Yamada, 25 August 1986.

24. A decade later, a similar beef involved Dorothy Reed at KGO-TV in San Francisco. Reed wore her hair in cornrows to cover a story. The result was the same; after being taken off the air with pay, Reed reestablished the right to wear it in "rows," compromising in that she agreed to take the beads off the ends of the braids.

25. Maureen Bunyan, Washington, D.C., anchor, and Isabel Duran, Chicago TV newswoman, were later graduates of the program.

# 5 The Explosion

While the Civil Rights Act of 1964 and the EEOC had prodded broadcasters to hire more women, the breakthrough came in the early seventies when the Federal Communications Commission decided to include women in minority staff counts. The new rule made it possible to challenge licenses if women were not given equal opportunity for employment or training for advancement.

An indication of the battle ahead came in the summer of 1970, when the American Civil Liberties Union sued ABC News on behalf of Sharon Neiderman, a secretary in the news department. Twenty-two years old, Neiderman was a 1969 graduate of George Washington University who had attended Harvard graduate school. She claimed she had applied to ABC for a position writing and producing news broadcasts but was assigned as the secretary to the director of public relations for the news division and that her attempts to advance into news positions were met with laughter or ignored. Neiderman said her case was symbolic of the plight of the American working woman. The ACLU sent a four-page letter to the chair of the New York Commission on Human Rights, asking for an investigation. The complaint maintained that of 250 employees in the news division, only 50 were women, and 33 of those were at the bottom of the hierarchy as secretaries or researchers.

But the major salvo was fired on December 4, 1970. The National Organization for Women filed a petition with the FCC asking that station operators be required to file plans to assure equal employment opportunities for women and that women be included in the count of minorities each station had to file with the commission when applying for license renewal, sale of a station, or a frequency allocation to build a new station. Almost all of the two dozen groups and individuals sending in comments on the proposed rule favored it. Those opposed were the National Association of Broadcasters and Mrs. Virginia Pate, president and general manager of the Chesapeake Broadcasting Corporation.

Among those favoring the rule change was Bella Abzug, soon to take her seat in the U.S. House of Representatives, who charged that women had been deliberately excluded from the section of the rule designed to provide equal opportunity and that few women were in positions of responsibility at the networks. She further predicted that if women did become employed in sizeable numbers, programming would improve.

Others filing in support of the petition included the Office of Communication of the United Church of Christ, which would continue to be very active in pushing for improvements in broadcasting; the American Newspaper Guild; and John W. Gardner, chairman of Common Cause. An individual filing in support of the change was Audrey Hansen, a university administrator and president of the Winnebago, Wisconsin, chapter of NOW. She told the commissioners she had left broadcasting because it became clear her income would be limited after a station manager told her, "No woman, no matter what she does, will ever be worth more than $500 a month at this station."[1]

### NOW vs. WRC

While the rule change was being debated at the commission, three women's groups, including NOW, filed charges in March 1971 with the FCC and the federal EEOC, contending that NBC's Washington, D.C., stations, WRC-AM-FM-TV, discriminated against women. The charges claimed that of the twenty-four major job categories at the stations, only one had a woman in it. That these stations served the nation's capital only underlined the significance of the November 10, 1971, response by the Washington district office of the EEOC. The eighteen-point ruling found that managerial jobs at WRC were virtually reserved for men, that word of management job opportunities was withheld from female employees, that most women in supervisory categories presided over all-women staffs, that the one female manager earned less than twenty-three of the twenty-four male managers, that several job categories at the stations—including that of announcer—had never been filled by a woman, and 43 percent of the men earned more than $15,000 a year, while only 5 percent of the women did. It was also reported that at the time the complaint was filed, women were not allowed to use accumulated sick leave for maternity, but that men had unlimited use of accrued sick leave; that policy had been changed by the time the ruling was made. NBC officials claimed there had been a steady advancement of women at the stations, and they intended to continue a policy of advancement for women. While the EEOC upheld the class-action charges brought on behalf of twenty-seven women at the stations, including TV reporter Catherine Mackin, it ruled against the women in their individual claims.

## TESTING THE NEW RULE

On December 21, 1971, the FCC adopted the proposed rule change. The commissioners found that "the history of employment discrimination is amply demonstrated by the comments in this proceeding."[2] The only stations excepted from compliance were those with fewer than five employees.

Three license challenges in the spring of 1972 tested the strength of the new rule. In Syracuse, New York, a group of thirteen community organizations challenged the transfer of ownership of WNYS-TV and the license renewal of WSYR-TV. In June, the transfer opposition was removed after the prospective new owner, the Outlet Company, agreed to a broad range of concessions about how they would treat women, both on the air and in employment. The company's executives agreed to actively recruit minorities and women, to set up scholarships at Syracuse University for minorities and women, to expand public service programming, and to include minorities and women in those programs whenever possible. They also promised to limit racial or ethnic identification in news stories unless it was essential to the understanding of the story and promised to limit disparaging references to sex roles, including banning the phrase "women's libbers."

## NOW vs. WABC

A challenge that gained a good deal more attention about the same time was the 239-page petition by NOW to deny the license renewal of WABC-TV, ABC's flagship station in New York. It was a broad challenge that included charges of sex bias in employment and distortion of women's news coverage and alleged that daytime programming was condescending to women. Anchor Roger Grimsby was singled out for making snide comments about women, and the style of the news broadcast, called "happy talk" in the industry, was called a "locker room format."

### WRC Is Hit Again

In August 1972, ten Washington area women's groups asked the FCC to deny the license renewal application of WRC-TV. Along with the usual allegations, the petition included statistics about the number of news items reported by women and the lack of hard news assignments to women. NBC officials defended the network's record, claiming its programming complied with the Fairness Doctrine, and that its record of employing women was among the best in the broadcasting industry. The FCC rejected the petitions to deny, and the women's groups appealed to the U.S. Court of Appeals. Friend of the court briefs were filed by the EEOC, contending the FCC had erred in granting the renewal. But the FCC decision was upheld.

## THE IMPACT OF THE CHALLENGES

While most of the license challenges did not result in loss of license to station owners, the challenges, or even the threat of challenges, had an immediate impact on hiring and programming in broadcast news. In September 1972, KDKA-TV in Pittsburgh became the first station to agree to a code of conduct without a license challenge. The local NOW chapter had been ready to challenge the station's license renewal, but after presenting station management with the findings of its monitoring effort, an agreement had been reached. The station's officials signed a promise that they would increase coverage of the women's rights movement, improve coverage of women's sports, and, wherever possible, have those stories reported by women. A similar agreement was made between Scripps Howard, owner of WMC-AM-FM-TV, and the Women's Media Project in Memphis, Tennessee in 1973. Women there also were able to get the local cable company to allocate a channel to women. The following year, KPRC-TV in Houston worked out a similar agreement with the local NOW chapter.

## CBS: ONE PLUS FOUR

CBS executives had been watching the legal action against the other networks, perhaps wondering if they were next. They were moving to hire more women reporters and had been been keeping tabs on several prospects. In the summer of 1971, about the time of the first WRC action, CBS started hiring more women. First, in August, was Sylvia Chase, who had been at all-news KNX in Los Angeles. Within a matter of weeks, Michele Clark and Connie Chung joined the staff, and early in 1972, Lesley Stahl. In six months, CBS went from a network with one female reporter, Marya McLaughlin, to five newswomen on the air, including a black, Clark, and an Asian, Chung.

### Sylvia Chase: A Step Ahead

A graduate of UCLA in English who had been raised, in part, by a suffragette grandmother in Northfield, Minnesota, Sylvia Chase was first on radio when she was eleven. Her older sister and she had given school news on a Saturday morning radio show sponsored by a local drug store. In high school, Chase was a debater, editor of the school paper, and co-editor of the yearbook. In college, she took a few journalism classes but after graduating went into political work for the Democratic party in California. She also was married briefly. Chase was already in her thirties when she started as a writer and producer at KNX radio. The only woman on the air at the station then was Barbara Reigle.

Chase knew CBS was interested in hiring newswomen and, on a vacation to New York, she was invited to audition. Shortly after submitting it, she was offered a job. It was so easy that she decided to check around and see what else was available, and quickly had offers in television from both KNXT and KNBC in Los Angeles. But the network seemed to offer the best opportunity. Her ascent was rapid. Chase became a correspondent in 1974 and stayed with CBS until 1977, participating in many of the efforts to increase the presence of women and women's programming on the network. At ABC from 1977 until 1985, she anchored the "ABC Weekend News Report," and was a general assignment reporter before joining "20/20." In January 1986, Chase returned to local news as lead anchor at KRON-TV, San Francisco.

### Michele Clark: Unfulfilled Promise

Michele Clark was twenty-eight when she joined CBS in September 1971. A native of Chicago, Clark had been an airlines reservations clerk before going into journalism. After completing Columbia University's summer journalism program for minorities in 1970, she was hired as a writer and general assignment reporter at WBBM-TV, CBS's Chicago station. She immediately impressed the news people at CBS, and while based in Chicago was assigned to cover the 1972 presidential primaries in New Hampshire, Wisconsin, and California. Clark also covered the party conventions that summer and, at the Democratic convention in Miami Beach, Clark was promoted to correspondent. Continuing her fast track, she began anchoring the morning news from Washington that fall, commuting home to Chicago where her family lived. With a seemingly unlimited career ahead of her, Clark was killed December 8, 1972, in a commercial plane crash near O'Hare Field in Chicago. Michele Clark's story is that of promise unfulfilled.

### Connie Chung: First Asian-American

Constance Yu-Hwa Chung was born in the United States while her father, a diplomat representing Chiang Kai-shek's Chinese government, was stationed in Washington, D.C. When the Chinese communists gained power after World War II, William Chung decided to keep his family in America, and he got a job with the U.S. Department of Commerce. Her four older sisters set high academic standards, and Chung followed the family pattern of straight A's. She studied biology at the University of Maryland but after working as an intern for a congressman decided to switch her major to journalism. She wrote for the campus paper and was on its radio station. While still in college, Chung got a part-time job as a copy clerk at Metromedia's WTTG-TV, Washington. When she graduated in 1969, she took the only full-time job available, as newsroom secretary. Soon she became a writer and, in 1970, a reporter.

In October 1971, Bill Small hired Chung for the CBS Washington bureau. She became, at age twenty-five, the first Asian-American network reporter.

Also the youngest reporter at CBS, Chung joined a Washington staff that featured Dan Rather, Daniel Schorr, Marvin Kalb, and Roger Mudd. Although Chung managed to make the Cronkite broadcast her first week on the job, she was more often the reporter who picked up the scraps after one of the senior correspondents did the evening news piece; she would be left to do radio and the morning news television package. But she impressed colleagues like Dan Rather with her desire and hard work.

> She really wanted to be good. In those days, you couldn't be around her five seconds and not know that she was willing to do anything. No assignment was too gritty or grimy, no weather too inclement to send her out. I mean she was literally the first person off the bench to tug at Bill Small's sleeve and say "Send me in, coach." That was very impressive.[3]

On the network staff a few months, Chung received a break for which some reporters wait years: she was assigned to cover a presidential candidate. For six months she followed Senator George McGovern around the country as his effort gained momentum. Later she covered the Watergate hearings and reported live the night President Nixon resigned.

In 1976, Chung had to choose between becoming an anchor at KNXT-TV, Los Angeles, and co-hosting the CBS morning news. She decided to take the $300,000 a year to be in local television, and over the next seven years became a crucial part of the station's success, eventually doubling her salary. For a brief time in 1979, Chung and Marcia Brandwynne became the first major market all-female anchor team on KNXT-TV's 11 o'clock weeknight news. In 1983, she moved to NBC, starting up the network's new early morning "Sunrise" broadcast and then adding the Saturday "NBC Nightly News" anchor duties.

Nearing forty, Chung married long-time companion Maury Povich, a Washington broadcaster. In late 1985, Chung joined in another of NBC's periodic efforts to launch a successful weekly news magazine and, when she signed a new contract in April 1986, she earned equal billing with Roger Mudd as co-anchor of the network's latest attempt, "1986." NBC also agreed in the contract to make Chung one of a small group of correspondents, including Mudd and Garrick Utley, who would fill in for "NBC Nightly News" anchor Tom Brokaw when he was away. The first week in August 1986, Chung made history as the first woman to substitute on a regular weekday basis for the weeknight news at NBC.

### Lesley Stahl: No Gossip

Lesley Rene Stahl had more television experience than Chase, Clark, or Chung when she was hired by CBS. She had worked for NBC News from 1967 to 1969 and had been a producer and reporter at WHDH-TV, Boston, from 1970 to 1972. Stahl was born in Lynn, Massachusetts, nine days after Pearl Harbor was bombed. She had grown up in comfort as an only daughter and graduated cum laude from Wheaton College. She married a medical student but soon they were divorced. She started graduate school in zoology but dropped out. Stahl worked for the Rockefeller Foundation and then as a researcher and speechwriter for New York City Mayor John Lindsay before starting her broadcasting career.

Like Chung, Stahl worked the Watergate story, often holding the fort on stakeouts and in hearings, obtaining material that would be used in the pieces the more experienced male correspondents filed. She also scored her share of scoops and was rewarded by being included in the roundtable discussions that were often part of the network's Watergate hearings coverage. Moderator John Hart in New York would ask a question and then the Washington reporters were supposed to kick it around. White House correspondents Dan Rather and Daniel Schorr were often on with Stahl, and they tended to dominate the discussions to the point that CBS producers finally ordered them to let Stahl answer a question. It happened that the first question Hart asked after the dictum came down was about Washington gossip, and Stahl was reluctant to respond to the topic, didn't know the answer anyway, and said she'd pass on it. There was silence as Rather and Schorr followed orders. Finally, Schorr piped up: "Well, John, if it's gossip you want, that's why we have a woman here."[4] Stahl and Schorr, who reportedly gave her a terrible hazing when she first joined the CBS Washington bureau, have had a frosty relationship since.

Stahl stayed with politics until she replaced Sally Quinn in 1977 on the morning news with Hughes Rudd. Later that year Richard Threlkeld succeeded Rudd, but the broadcast remained in third place and Stahl moved on to cover the White House in January 1979. By then she had married writer Aaron Latham and was the mother of a little girl. She added "Face the Nation" to her duties in 1983 and has played a major part in the revitalization of that longtime CBS Sunday staple.

Stahl feels that the women who were hired in 1971 and 1972 were in many cases placed in jobs for which they weren't ready. "Right off, we started above our marks. A lot of us weren't allowed to grow, block by block, one step at a time. Many of us failed, and we failed to establish a solid foundation."[5] But Chase, Chung, and Stahl seemed not only to have survived, but to have flourished.

## WOMEN'S GROUPS

### Working within the System

While CBS had made visible progress in hiring women, many women at the network felt more changes needed to be made. Early in 1973, a group of women joined forces at CBS to put pressure on corporate management for change. There had been meetings since the late sixties about the situation for women at CBS, but this effort had a goal: a confrontation with the president of the corporation, Arthur Taylor. The initial organizing session involved about a half-dozen women in a conference room at the network studios on West 57th Street. Their concerns ranged from the image of women on all network programming to who had to get coffee in offices. Chase attended; so did producer Irina Posner, and Judy Hole, a deputy archivist who had co-authored a book on the women's movement based on research she had done for network coverage of "Women's Strike Day" in August 1970. There was also a representative from the women at the corporate headquarters, who worked in a high rise on West 52nd Street known as "Black Rock."

The women were reacting, in part, to a policy statement Taylor had distributed about women and CBS in February 1973. Taylor also had appointed counselors for women in each of the network divisions. Kay Wight, one of those women who had been working for the last five years for change, was named counselor for the broadcast division.

The newswomen had a sympathetic supervisor in news division president Richard Salant. He had written a lengthy memo ripping the style and substance of a corporate secretarial manual, *A Good Right Arm*. Salant noted that the boss always was referred to as "he" in the manual, and he found the tone of the guide condescending. Freelance researcher Ellen Levine, who had co-authored a book on the women's movement with Hole, recalls that Salant's support was important to the entire women's effort, for as chief of the news division, Salant was not only powerful, but highly visible.

Hole recalls that while the women in the news division may have been the most vocal about the need to improve things for women at the network— perhaps because they were professional communicators—the group members wanted to make it clear that this was a company-wide effort, not just a news division movement.[6]

Some women agreed with the goals of the group but chose not to become active in achieving them. Others participated in the meetings but did not want to sign their names to letters or other documents. Chase was one who wondered how active she could be in the effort.

> It wasn't a difficult decision, but I knew it was a critical decision for me. I felt it could ruin me. I thought it through for a couple of days, and I felt, well, the men are going to resent and won't like me for it, but I can't live with myself unless I do this. If women don't get some equal footing in the broadcast industry, I might as well not be here anyway. My life will be miserable.[7]

Chase had been exasperated by the lack of support of the other reporters. "With the exception of Connie Chung, who was very supportive, I got no response from the other on-air women. Thank God for the Cronkite producers. We had Linda Mason and Janet Roach. I needed some women who were in equally powerful positions to be alongside me.''

Hole, now a news producer at CBS, had been with the network since she started as a secretary in the news division in 1962, her first job after college. She believes that most of the women who participated in the effort to bring their concerns to CBS president Arthur Taylor were, like her, ones who wanted to work within the system for change. However, she also allows that ''there was a lot of anger, and the feeling that if things didn't change the threat of a suit was always there.''

Setting the agenda for the Taylor meeting proved to be difficult, for the women at the corporate headquarters had somewhat different concerns from those at the broadcast center across town. The ''Black Rock'' women tended to focus on wages and working conditions, while the broadcasters additionally were interested in the broad issue of the impact of television and radio on the image of women. Chase and others in the news division were adamant that how women were portrayed on the network be on the list of issues the women wanted addressed. Twenty women, elected from every CBS division in New York, attended the meeting, which was held in Taylor's office in July 1973. Mary Gay Taylor and Jane Tillman Irving of the WCBS-AM news staff, Hole, and Chase were among those present. Chase recalls that the meeting itself was somewhat of a letdown for her. But most of the women left the session with a sense of accomplishment. Feeling that in Taylor they had someone who would listen and react favorably to their concerns, they had laid them out for all to see.

*Changes Are Made.*   Within a month, Taylor had a formal response that augmented the changes of six months earlier. The women who had met with Taylor, called the Taylor Committee, evolved into the Women's Advisory Council, also an elected group. Two different consultants were hired to help the network bring women into the corporate mainstream. By the middle of 1974, there had been a general redesign of salaries for women, a new maternity/paternity benefits program had been established, and the secretary's guide had been redone to eliminate a condescending and often sexist tone. By 1975, some sixty training programs were in place. A study of the changes at CBS found that there continued to be problems in promotions to upper management and in the news and radio divisions, where union restrictions limited upward mobility for low-level employees.

There were additions to network programming, too. Several broadcasts were established on the network. CBS canceled all of its regular weekend features in late July 1973 to present a series called ''The American Woman.'' Pieces were done on the feminist movement, women as sex symbols, and even one with Bette Davis talking about being a woman. In March 1974, as part of the CBS bicentennial series, an hour-long special called ''We, the Women'' was broadcast. Sylvia Chase worked on a program called "Magazine," which was designed for women watching in the traditional "housewives' time," the middle of the day. It preempted a game show six or eight times a year with a magazine format of features. After Chase left CBS in 1977, Sharron Lovejoy anchored the broadcast and then Betsy Aaron. Chase, Marya McLaughlin, Connie Chung, and Stephanie Shelton voiced a weekday version of "The American Woman" on the CBS Radio Network starting in 1975. Perhaps symbolically, the new broadcast replaced "Dear Abby," which had been a mainstay on the network for a dozen years.

*Why Change Happened at CBS.*   One other factor may explain why ABC and NBC faced lawsuits and CBS did not. Arthur Taylor made it clear shortly after he arrived in 1972 that improving things for women was a priority. "In the production areas, and in the business areas, you had innumerable talented women who were frustrated beyond belief. They had seen generations of male managers move beyond them."[8] While he might not have moved as quickly as some women there would have liked or made the sweeping changes some felt were needed to address the inequities, he did change policy, and he made sure his subordinates understood he was serious about it. It was a standing agenda item at every division meeting, to be addressed by each division head. The greatest resistance to change came from male middle managers, who thought the advancement of women and minorities would come at their expense, though Taylor assured them there were enough opportunities for everyone. Some of the rank and file claimed the changes had not affected their work situations at all. Although some business experts thought Taylor's move was a gamble, he did not. "Everyone talks about the big risk. But when this was done, it unleashed such an incredible burst of productivity at CBS that the damn thing went right through the roof." When Taylor left CBS in 1976, the pressure lessened and so did the rate of gains for women at the network.

*"A People's Revolution."*   By the end of 1973, all three commercial networks had committees working to improve the situation for women. CBS had the Women's Advisory Council. At ABC, it was the Women's Action Committee and the Women's Equal Employment Opportunity Committee at NBC. The CBS group met monthly with Sheldon Wool, a vice president for development, and consisted of two secretaries, a deputy archivist, a placement manager, and an editor at Holt, Rinehart and Winston. One of the alternates was correspondent Lynn Sherr. There was also a continuing dialogue with management at ABC in New York that resulted in changes similar to those at CBS. But at NBC, progress was slow. An organizer of the women's group there, Kathy Kish, felt the issue involved the whole organization of the networks.

We're after a people's revolution. Some of the inequities we've discovered affect men as well as women. We're hoping to make some honest-to-goodness changes in the whole bureaucratic mechanism of the broadcast industry. If you do a job too well and stay in a certain slot for a while, you can stay there forever. This not only happens to women, it happens to men, too.[9]

The women activists at the networks kept each other up to date on developments for women through the Tri-Network Women's Committee. Kay Wight says it was an effective way to measure what was being done at one of the networks and see if the other two had comparable programs or benefits. The committee members helped formulate strategy and told each other which approaches had been successful. The lack of information that had delayed advances only a few years before had been replaced by open groups, operating with the blessing of the corporation chiefs.

## MORE COMPLAINTS

### NBC Faces More Charges

Coincidentally, Taylor's policy statement was released the week after another complaint was filed against NBC. The action came in February 1973, when the Women's Committee for Equal Employment Opportunity filed charges of discrimination against the network; its parent, RCA; its New York radio and television stations; and the unions affiliated with the stations. The complaint went to the New York City Commission on Human Rights, the EEOC, and the U.S. Department of Labor. The complaint was signed by fifty women who worked at the network, and the suit was handled by an all-woman law firm. Two years after the filing, the city commission found that there had been discrimination, by which time NBC was able to point out that since 1971, the number of women in executive and managerial positions had nearly doubled. While the network was able to claim that the commission had not found any intentional discrimination or individual cases of discrimination, the commission had shown that a substantial number of men at NBC earned more than $18,000 a year, while half of the women were in the $5,896 to $11,271 range. A class-action suit followed in December 1975 on behalf of the 2,600 women who worked for NBC. Joining in the suit was the EEOC. The case was settled out of court just before trial was to begin in 1977, with NBC not admitting the charges but paying up to $2 million. The settlement included more than $500,000 for back wages to women employees and $860,000 for increased salaries for management jobs to be held by women, so those who would be promoted or who were already in management positions would earn the average salary of a man in a similar post who had five years' experience with the network. Among the other specific solutions were a pledge by the network to fill a third of the news-writing jobs with women through 1981 and a push to bring women in significant numbers into the technical side. And $175,000 of the settlement would go to monitor the proposed improvements.

### The EEOC Sues

In July 1973, a station owned by the *New York Times* became the first to be sued by the EEOC. WREC-TV in Memphis, Tennessee, ranked one hundred eleventh of 144 network-affiliated stations in major markets in terms of employing women. The suit claimed WREC's managers had refused to take any affirmative action to remedy the situation. The suit also made similar charges regarding racial minorities. The article in the *Times* carried the careful headline "Memphis TV Station Is Sued on Bias," and one had to read the article before finding out that the station in question was owned by the *Times*.

## THE ABSENCE OF WOMEN DOCUMENTED

The focus shifted west in late 1974, when the Los Angeles Women's Coalition for Better Broadcasting asked for denials on the renewal applications of four southern California TV stations. The complaint alleged that KNXT-TV had only men as news directors and assignment editors. In monitoring a week of KNXT newscasts during the summer, the coalition members found that 93 percent of the air time had been consumed by male reporters and anchors, 90 percent of the newsmakers were men, and 92 percent of the total air time consisted of male faces and voices. None of the petitions to deny was successful, but the U.S. Court of Appeals did order the FCC to reconsider the cases of three of the stations. The coalition believed there were especially grounds to look again at KNXT, after former writer and producer Melinda Cotton brought a class-action federal suit in 1976 alleging discrimination.

In Sacramento, California, in 1974, the American Association of University Women monitored television newscasts and found that 90 percent of 5,353 hard news stories they watched were about men, as were 84 percent of 1,668 news features. A similar analysis of network news programs by the staff of the U.S. Commission on Civil Rights found that in 1974-1975, only 14 percent of the newsmakers on the networks were women. A follow-up study in 1977 showed a drop off to 7 percent. Still, a United Church of Christ report showed gains for women and minorities from 1973 to 1974. Most of the advances came in major markets. And of the new employees entering commercial television between 1971 and 1974, 58 percent were women.

The first comprehensive study of women in public broadcasting, done by the Corporation for Public Broadcasting in 1975, found that women were underrepresented on the air at both the network and affiliated public stations. The lack of women was also evident in decision-making roles. Women held fewer than 30 percent of all the jobs in public broadcasting and tended to be in lower positions than men. While 25 percent of the men in public broadcasting earned less than $9,000 a year, 65 percent of the women earned less than that.

The leading light for National Public Radio was Susan Stamberg, who was the co-host of "All Things Considered" from 1971 to September 1986. She left "ATC" to host a new NPR program, the Sunday version of "Weekend Edition," which debuted in early 1987. She had been program director and then station manager of WAMU-FM, Washington, in the mid-1960s. Also with NPR since 1971 was political correspondent Linda Wertheimer.

## TAMPA TEST

On Women's Strike Day, November 29, 1975, a nationwide event organized by NOW, a thirty-year-old reporter for Tampa TV station WTVT was fired for taking the day off. Sara Golinveaux had told her news director the week before that she would be taking the day off without pay, explaining that she felt it was an important event. A mother of two, she did not belong to NOW or any other feminist group, but felt the strike day gave her an opportunity to stand up for her beliefs.

> I didn't even think the strike was a very good idea, but I saw it as the only way I could make a statement about my position. We should treat people like individual people, with individual equality. I feel like I didn't get that at the station.[10]

Golinveaux had been at the station for two years and already had filed an EEOC complaint against the station on sex discrimination grounds. She felt that less experienced men were being promoted ahead of her and that a sexist atmosphere pervaded the station's newsroom. Two other similar complaints had been filed by female reporters against WTVT, and one of those women, Lesley Friedsam, warned Golinveaux that if she took the strike day off, management would fire her. The grounds for termination were gross insubordination. After losing her job, Golinveaux filed a second complaint. She lost both cases and never again worked in broadcast news.

In her complaint, Friedsam charged that an important step to advancement at the station was training on the assignment desk, and only men had received that training. Following the filing of her complaint, a woman was given the desired training. After initially winning in an administrative hearing, Friedsam lost her case, and although she continued working for the station as bureau chief in the state capital, she says her broadcasting career was effectively over when she filed the first complaint. Friedsam filed a second complaint when she found out the previous bureau chief had been paid considerably more than she was. The station settled that case, but its terms prohibit Friedsam from discussing how much she received. She studied law at Florida State University and Yale and now practices in Tampa.

## IMPROVING NUMBERS

Despite the hard road to newsroom equality, a 1976 study of television news departments revealed a significant improvement in the number of newswomen on the air. While half the stations had women on their news staff in 1972, 86 percent of the stations had them in 1976, and 20 percent of the anchors and 20 percent of the reporters were women. Although 35 percent of the stations still had no female anchors, 48 percent had one, 14 percent had two, and 3 percent had three or more. In radio, the percentage of stations with women newscasters had gone from 15 percent in 1972 to 49 percent in 1976.

### The Look of Local versus Network TV News

An interesting pattern was detected by Mary Lane Otte, a graduate student at Georgia State University, when she compared the roles of men and women on network and local television newscasts in 1977. Watching in Atlanta, Otte compared the time men and women were on the air. She found that on Atlanta's three network affiliates, males dominated 69 percent of the airtime. On the network newscasts, men dominated 87 percent of the time. At the local stations, the assignments tended to be softer. Twenty-eight percent of the hard news was presented by women, while they did 48 percent of the soft stories. At the networks, women did 16 percent of the hard stories and 14 percent of the soft ones. While the harder nature of the network news may account for some of the results, it would appear that the women were fewer in number at the networks but getting a greater share of hard news stories.

## A NEW SYMBOL OF HOPE

### Jessica Savitch: The Price of Ambition

One of those women determined to break through to equality in assignments was Jessica Savitch. Although her network career lasted only a little more than five years, in the late 1970s she was the hottest prospect in network news and, at the time of her death in 1983, had become the prototype for a female anchor in America.

Jessica Beth Savitch was born in 1947 in Kennett Square, Pennsylvania. Her father followed current events closely, and she remembered starting to read about world events and watching television news so she could participate in family discussions. But David Savitch died when Jessica was twelve, and her mother Florence moved her three daughters to Margate, New Jersey, to be closer to her parents and resumed a nursing career. The death of her father and moving from a rural area to a city were difficult for Savitch, but she found a refuge in radio. While visiting a schoolmate who did a Saturday afternoon show on WOND-AM, Pleasantville, Savitch got on the air for a few seconds. Soon, she was doing "Teensville" herself and continued working at WOND part time until she graduated from high school.

Savitch wanted to study communications in college, but her mother questioned whether there were many opportunities for women in broadcasting. However, her goal was crystalized when she wrangled a press pass to see President Lyndon Johnson land at the Atlantic City airport to accept the Democratic nomination. There waiting to greet the president was Nancy Dickerson, the only woman among the reporters gathered at Bader Field. As he had so many times before, the president disembarked, walked over to Dickerson and said, "Hello, Nancy." What impressed Savitch was not what Dickerson asked during the live interview, but that by waving her hand in the mass of reporters, Dickerson could get the president of the United States to walk over and speak to her.

*"No Broads in Broadcasting."* Because her family was strapped for money, Savitch chose Ithaca College, which offered a communications program at a modest tuition. She had three scholarships but still had to work part time and summers to get through school. Savitch was one of a handful of women in the communications department, and when she went to find out if she could work at the college's two radio stations, she was told no. A protest to one of the station's faculty advisors brought the assessment that "there is no place for broads in broadcasting." Savitch took her case to a college administrator who told the station manager to find a place for Savitch. She finally was given the last shift on Saturday night. She neglected to turn off the transmitter, however, a task that had not been included in her instructions, and was dismissed from the station for the rest of the year.

Through a boyfriend who lived in Rochester, Savitch made contacts in the advertising business and began doing commercials on radio and television, even making some appearances for car dealers. She got a job as a weekend disc jockey at WBBF-AM, Rochester, which called itself "The Bee" after the two B's in its call letters. Savitch became something of a celebrity as the "Honeybee," doing live remotes in the station's van, the "Beemobile."

Savitch graduated in 1968, and after several months of looking for a break while working part time at WBBF, Savitch moved to New York City and started pounding the pavement. She continued to do some commercials, which paid the bills, and attracted the attention of Joan Showalter, head of personnel for CBS. Showalter noted Savitch's determination, and though she couldn't find the young woman a job in news, Showalter hired her as a "floater"—a minion who filled in where needed. Savitch could not type or take shorthand so she wasn't exactly a secretary, but she did a variety of "go-fer" duties. While working at WCBS-AM, she received help with her writing from reporter Ed Bradley, morning anchor Charles Osgood, and station manager Joe Dembo. Showalter advised Savitch to look for a broadcast news job in a smaller city and helped her get a TV audition tape shot. Few news directors were impressed, but Dick John at KHOU-TV, Houston, was, and he hired Savitch in 1970 for $135 a week.

*A Real Reporter.*    Savitch got a taste of Texan attitudes toward women reporters when she answered the phone during her first week at the station.

"May I speak to a reporter?" a male voice asked.

"You're speaking to a reporter."

"No, I mean a *real* reporter."

"I *am* a reporter."

"Honey, put one of the fellows on please."[11]

The station was expanding its evening newscast and needed all the material its reporters could generate. Savitch got a lot of experience in a hurry. Three months after she arrived, open auditions were held for a weekend anchor slot. Savitch didn't think she had a chance at the job and was not going to try out until her boss called her at home and talked her into it. She put on a very serious dress, pulled her hair back and "did her best male imitation."[12] She got the job, but that audition also was the beginning of a severe, mannered style that Savitch developed and, while managing to soften it, she never really abandoned it. It made her seem cold, but when she was the hottest anchor in network television a decade later, dozens of Savitch copycats adopted it.

*Camera Magic.*    Savitch generated a good deal of viewer interest in Houston, and it wasn't long before she generated a lot of interest from news directors in major markets. In November 1972, Savitch signed a five-year contract with KYW-TV in Philadelphia. She started as a general assignment reporter, but by early 1973 had become a weekend anchor. She could not break into the weekday ranks, however, and with an offer from CBS in the wings, tried to break her contract. KYW's management went to court to hold her to it, but her maneuver did get attention. She began anchoring the 6 P.M. news in the summer of 1974, added the noon a year later, and then got both the 6 P.M. and 11 P.M. in February 1976. Savitch generated incredible viewer response in Philadelphia; her relationship with the camera was magical, and she developed an almost emotional bond with viewers.

Savitch also worked with a speech therapist in Philadelphia to reduce a lateral lisp. She wanted her work to be perfect, and saw the lisp as a sign of imperfection. It was a trait that would sometimes cause co-workers to refer to her as "Jessica Savage"; her ideas of how things should be did not always match those of her co-workers, and she sometimes was blunt when diplomacy would have worked better. But the drive for an excellent product also resulted in some very good broadcasts. At KYW, she did a series on women in police work that won a duPont award for best feature, and "Rape . . . the Ultimate Violation" won a Clarion Award from Women in Communications, Inc., and helped bring about legislative changes in several states.

When her contract with KYW expired in 1977, the bidding war for Savitch's services was on, with the three commercial networks joining a few local stations with deep pockets. NBC won by offering her more money than any of its newswomen and a good number of newsmen were making and by promising the anchor chair on the Sunday version of "NBC Nightly News," the Senate beat, and updates during prime time on weeknights. Two months after she joined NBC, Savitch filled in as a weeknight anchor. While John Chancellor covered the Sadat-Begin meeting in Jerusalem and David Brinkley was on from Washington, Savitch anchored the rest of the news.

Savitch was seen by news management as a talented anchor with limited reporting and writing skills. She was taken off the Senate beat in 1978 and put on general assignment. Later, she was assigned to the nightly news in-depth "Segment Three" unit, and in 1979 and 1980 was lead reporter for a magazine in prime time on weekends. She also was seen on "Meet the Press" and "Today."

*No Honeymoon.*    In 1980, Savitch married Melvin Korn, a Philadelphia advertising executive seventeen years her senior. There was no honeymoon; Savitch went on the road to cover a story. They lived in separate cities during the week, and the marriage didn't work out. Within fourteen months, they were divorced. In a matter of months, in March 1981, she married a gynecologist, Donald Rollie Payne, who was eleven years older than she. Four months later, she suffered a miscarriage, an emotional blow to both of them. At about the same time, Payne had a recurrance of serious kidney disease. In August, Savitch returned home to find her husband had hanged himself in the basement. She was devastated. The only consolation seemed to be work; she poured herself into TV news. In her off hours, she worked on her autobiography. And, like newswomen from the times of Dorothy Thompson, she wondered about professional success and personal failure.

> People look at my business and see it as all gloss and glamour, but the glamour is the tip of the iceberg. One of the things that newcomers often don't understand is that, yes, it may be very difficult to have both. In some instances it may be impossible. I never thought about any of this when I was younger and breaking into the business. I didn't say "My career comes first and I don't care about having a husband and children." In fact, I very much wanted a husband; I love children and want them.[13]

Savitch's career seemed to have leveled off. There were other rising stars, most notably Connie Chung, who were given some plum assignments. In 1982, Savitch took a partial leave of absence from NBC to work on the new PBS series, "Frontline." It was a serious broadcast, and Savitch felt it would add to her credibility, while PBS welcomed the attention she would bring.

With her contract about to expire, Savitch was hoping her book and "Front-line" would give her career momentum.

The strategy seemed to work. By fall, she had agreed to a new contract with NBC for about a half-million dollars and was looking forward to some new assignments. Savitch also had a new romance with Martin Fischbein, an executive at the *New York Post*. After attending church in New York City on Sunday, October 23, 1983, the couple went antique shopping in rural Bucks County, Pennsylvania. They had dinner at a French restaurant near New Hope. Departing in a driving rainstorm, Fischbein mistook a canal towpath for the exit from the restaurant parking lot. He drove the car into the canal, where it landed upside down in five feet of water. Both Savitch and Fischbein were killed.

*"Stay Tuned."*   A few weeks before she died, Savitch spoke about her career at a women's conference in Los Angeles. She said women had been through an initial phase of open doors in the sixties and a second phase in which they pondered the problems of dual career families but did not have true equality. She felt women were on the verge of a new era in broadcast news, when they would be judged on their abilities.

> A decade ago I was told women couldn't have jobs in this industry. How will I know there will be a third phase where women will be evaluated on ability in this industry, where women will reach the upper stages of management and keep and hold jobs, despite euphemistic laugh lines, or fully etched crow's feet? I'm offering the logic of social trends, of economic and industry growth. But there are no guarantees. Whether or not I am correct in believing that we are only a few years away from the third phase of equality in this country can only be answered by that old broadcast cliche, "Stay tuned."[14]

## CONCLUSION

The pressure to hire women exploded in the early 1970s. While the civil rights advances of the sixties had focused America's attention on women in the workplace, now the federal agency charged with overseeing radio and television stepped in to make sure the broadcasting media were giving women a fair shot at jobs and promotion.

The new FCC rule in late 1971 mandated affirmative action to remedy past employment discrimination. Now women who believed they had been victims of sex discrimination on the job had more ammunition, and they used it. The new mandate prompted station executives to hire and promote more women, and increase coverage of women; as in most workplaces, affirmative action for women in broadcast news was not instituted until stations were forced to by law. Rather than initiating change, though, the broadcast media were relatively passive, reacting to the women's movement that was sweeping society.

Within two years after the FCC rule was adopted, ABC, CBS, and NBC had committees designed to improve the status of women. Progress varied at each of the networks, but at least management acknowledged women faced problems in the workplace.

In spite of the progress, equality for women had not been achieved. The issues that faced the pioneer broadcast newswomen continued to concern the women of the seventies. Men still dominated the airwaves. Men generally were paid more than women. And men remained in the top decision-making positions.

More change came for women in the 1970s than in any decade since World War II. But true equality remained an elusive goal.

## NOTES

1. "Frontal Assault on Male Chauvinism," *Broadcasting* 80, 3 (18 January 1971): 34.

2. Federal Communications Commission, "Report and Order," Docket Number 19269 RM-1722, "Title 47-Telecommunication," *Federal Register* (Washington, D.C.: U.S. Government Printing Office, 28 December 1971): 25012.

3. Desmond Smith, "Beginning the Day with Connie Chung," *San Francisco Chronicle* (30 August 1983): 11.

4. Joan Hanauer, "Lesley Stahl on Her Job: A 'Glorified Stakeout,' " *Los Angeles Times* (11 November 1984): VI, 21.

5. "Leaner Economy Means Harder Times for Career Women, AWRT Told," *Broadcasting* 100, 19 (11 May 1981): 26.

6. Unless otherwise stated, all quotations from Judith Hole are from a telephone interview with David H. Hosley, 19 September 1986.

7. Unless otherwise stated, all quotations from Sylvia Chase are from an interview with David H. Hosley, San Francisco, 12 September 1986.

8. Unless otherwise stated, all quotations from Arthur Taylor are from a telephone interview with Gayle K. Yamada, 24 September 1986.

9. Maurine Christopher, "Women at Three Major Networks Press for Employment Equality," *Advertising Age* (12 November 1973): 4.

10. "Woman TV Reporter Dismissed for Day Off on Women's Strike," *New York Times* (9 November 1975): 48.

11. Jessica Savitch, *Anchorwoman* (New York: G. P. Putnam's Sons, 1982), p. 62.

12. *Current Biography* (January 1983): 37.

13. Claudia Dreifus, "Talking with Jessica Savitch," *Redbook* (January 1983): 14.

14. Janie Watts Spataro, "Savitch Unlocked Doors for Women," *Los Angeles Times* (31 October 1983): V, 3.

# 6  An Early Start

In most cases of societal change, the evolution seems to accelerate rapidly at one point to a breakthrough, often embodied in an individual. That person becomes a symbol of the change. Upon closer examination, these people often have spent years getting in position to take advantage of the moment of transition. Barbara Walters is the symbol for American women in broadcast news.

## BARBARA WALTERS

Walters's ascent to the top was a slow one, capped electrically by a $1 million a year contract with ABC in 1976. Equally significant is her staying power, for Barbara Walters, now in her mid-fifties, is the standard-bearer for those who see aging on the air as a primary issue today for women in broadcast news.

Walters has achieved success while striving for the personal satisfactions often sacrificed by the most successful women in many fields, including electronic journalism. While becoming a millionaire, she was also a single parent who supported a handicapped sister and an ailing mother. And surveys have found her to be one of the most admired women in America for more than a decade.

Barbara Jill Walters was born September 25, 1931, in Boston to Lou and Dena Walters. Her father was in the entertainment business, and she spent most of the first decade of her life in Boston, where he had started a nightclub called the "Latin Quarter." He launched another successful club in Miami and then a second "Latin Quarter" in New York. Walters went to high school in Miami Beach and New York City, where the family lived in a penthouse on Fifth Avenue, and graduated with an English degree from Sarah Lawrence College. She had hopes of a career as an actress, but a series of disappointing auditions led her to try other avenues. She went to NBC's personnel department but was turned away and told to go to secretarial school, which she did.

> So I got a job as a terrible secretary in a small advertising agency. And then there was an opening on the local station here as the Assistant Director of Publicity. And I knew all the columnists at that time, which meant that my boss went out and had lunches and went to Toots Shorr's and I sat and did all of the work.[1]

## The Only Woman

Walters moved from WRCA's publicity department to a training program for television producers. She soon began working on "Ask the Camera," the youngest and only female producer on the station's staff. Walters then switched to WPIX-TV, where she produced mostly women's programs. When the show she helped produce was canceled, Walters was out of a job. A pattern developed in Walters's early years in television: she would be the only woman working on the production of a show, it would get canceled, and she would lose her job.

Walters next worked at CBS on a series of broadcasts opposite NBC's "Today" show. None of them overtook the ratings for NBC's morning show. Walters also was married briefly to Robert Katz, whose family owned a prominent manufacturing firm. The marriage was annulled after a year. Shortly after that, her father went bankrupt when a new nightclub failed.

## A Trial

Walters had to find a job to support herself. She worked as a theater publicist for Tex McCrary for several years while looking for another opportunity in television. That chance came at NBC's "Today." She was hired as a writer, again concentrating on women's features, and also produced a number of people profiles. As her stock rose, she was allowed to report some of them. Another strong performance was Walters's work in Washington after the assassination of President Kennedy.

In the middle of the 1964 Democratic National Convention in Atlantic City, "Today's" most recent female personality, Maureen O'Sullivan, was fired, and Walters was given a thirteen-week trial at union scale. There had been more than thirty " 'Today' girls" in the thirteen years of the broadcast, most of them singers, actresses, or former beauty queens. They handled the lighter areas of the broadcasts, such as segments on food or fashion.

Walters's first assignments did not do much to change the image of the woman's role on the show. She did features with a "feminine angle," such as what it was like to be a *Playboy* bunny. Her work impressed her superiors, and she became a regular. Host Hugh Downs enthused that, in her new role, Walters was the best thing that had happened to the "Today" show in a long time. But she was still only an adjunct to the male host; it would be years before she could change that situation.

Walters was able to expand the scope of her segments, however. She began to establish her trademark of obtaining hard-to-get interviews that made headlines. Walters felt that in the beginning of her dozen years on "Today," those interviews provided her greatest opportunity for equal footing on the broadcast.

> If I just came into the studio every morning, I would never be chosen as the interviewer instead of another man. I have to get my own interviews. I'm not whining or bitter, I feel no competition with the other man—that would ruin the show. But there are certain things I have to do to maintain my position. . . . Also, I'm here to provide some femininity.[2]

## A Different Category

Walters was careful to mold an image that was not threatening to NBC's viewers or the male hosts. She felt that women identified with her because she was neither beautiful nor remote. "I'm a kind of well-informed friend, they don't want me to be a glamour puss and that's fine. It means I won't have to quit or have face lifts after forty: I'm in a different category."[3] She also tried to defer to the men on "Today" to avoid a perception of aggressiveness. "I was always a little reticent, even a little subservient, because I felt that was the best way to be, that it was the most comfortable for the men, and I guess the most comfortable for the audience."[4]

Walters had married for a second time in December 1963 to Lee Guber, a theater owner and theatrical producer. They wanted to have children, but it was not to be. After Walters had a miscarriage, they adopted a little girl, named Jacqueline Dena after Walters's sister and mother. Guber and Walters were divorced in 1976.

## Early Morning Reign

For a dozen years, Walters got up at 4 A.M. on weekday mornings, a record for longevity on a morning show that no one has matched. Walters also did commentaries for the NBC radio network for many of those years, and starting in 1971, she hosted a local broadcast primarily aimed at women. Aline Saarinen had been the hostess of "For Women Only," and when she was sent to Paris as the network's first female bureau chief, Walters took over. The name of the program was changed to "Not for Women Only." It was broadcast in New York from 9 to 9:30 A.M. weekdays on WNBC-TV and syndicated nationally. Guests included leaders of the women's movement, and the broadcast explored such topics as sexual dysfunction and the use of marijuana as well as more traditional women's fare.

By the early 1970s, Walters was a national figure of such repute that she regularly made lists of the top women in the country: *Harper's Bazaar*'s 100 Women of Accomplishment, *Time*'s 200 Leaders of the Future, and the *Ladies' Home Journal*'s 75 Most Important Women. When she signed a new contract for nearly a half million dollars in 1973, NBC finally guaranteed Walters she'd be named co-host of the program if host Frank McGee left the show. She did not know that McGee was ill and soon would die.

### In Second Place

Walters's increased standing brought even more recognition, including a cover story in *Newsweek*. Still, she sometimes found herself frustrated on "Today."

> At least once a week with assignments over the air, I find here I am again doing just the sort of silly female assignment, the whole feeling of a woman being second place on this program. I think if you sit around and become bitter about it you lose your sense of humor and your ability on the air. And I know that I'm hired on the "Today" program because I'm a woman, and they want to have a kind of softness and femininity, and hope that you look nice.[5]

Walters's role as the most prominent woman in broadcast news was underlined by a 1974 poll sponsored by King Features Syndicate. She was the only female of the eleven electronic news people rated, and was ninth in recognition, with seven out of ten Americans knowing who she was. That put her well behind Walter Cronkite and David Brinkley, with 98 percent recognition, but just behind Dan Rather and well ahead of Garrick Utley and Hughes Rudd. Walters was perceived to be liberal, scored relatively low in objectivity and trust, but ranked fifth as someone who was "often watched." For an anchor on a morning show, it was an impressive showing. And for executives at ABC, whose nightly news ratings had been slipping, a female anchor, particularly one of Barbara Walters's stature, presented some interesting possibilities.

Among those also under consideration were Lesley Stahl of CBS, Hilary Brown from ABC's London bureau, and former network reporter Liz Trotta, then at WNBC-TV in New York. ABC was hoping to expand its half-hour nightly newscast to forty-five minutes or an hour. That would provide extra time for the kind of newsmaking interviews Walters did. It also would give the network more time for commercials, which appealed to those interested in the bottom line. And by breaking ground with the first woman to regularly anchor a network weeknight newscast, ABC would attract the kind of publicity money couldn't buy.

### A Million Dollars a Year

When negotiations heated up early in 1976, NBC executives were determined to keep Walters. They were willing to match the money ABC was offering.

They were ready to promise Walters first shot at a nightly anchoring post should NBC decide to go to double anchors. But ABC would put her in the anchor seat immediately, and the proposed longer newscast was attractive; so was the package of prime time specials ABC put together. In order to boost its offer to the million dollar range, ABC had come up with a half-million from the news division and another half-million from the entertainment division for four specials each year that would be produced by Walters's own production company, with financial backing from ABC. In her spare time, Walters could host some broadcasts of "Issues and Answers" and participate in ABC News documentaries and other special programs.

As the terms of the contract became known, ABC got more publicity than its executives had counted on, much of it unfavorable. NBC officials commented that her agent's demands had become "larger than the journalism profession" and scoffed at requests for a hairdresser and other "things you would associate with a movie queen, not a journalist."[6]

## A Fine Line

ABC's anchorman, Harry Reasoner, had a reputation as a sexist, and there was talk that he had threatened to quit if Walters was hired. In a moment of humor the week before her five-year deal was made final, Reasoner allowed that "if women have lived with unequal pay for equal work for this many years, I guess I can live with it for five."[7] That Walters would become the first woman to anchor a network weeknight newscast paled beside the million dollar figure. Former CBS News president Fred Friendly, who had become a kind of media watchdog, observed:

> We make all kinds of statements about the right of the public to be informed. Those things can't get mixed up with million-dollar-a-year personalities. It's sort of a throwback to the days of Walter Winchell when news was done by name people who got a lot of money—but there wasn't much journalism in it.[8]

Other observers felt the distinction between journalism and entertainment had been blurred. Commented *Washington Post* ombudsman Charles B. Seib, "The line between the news business and show business has been erased forever. It was a mighty thin line at best, so not much has been lost."[9] Actually, several prominent men in broadcasting had preceded Walters in crossing the line and making a fortune. Lowell Thomas's salary of more than a half-million dollars in 1949 and Edward R. Murrow's $315,00 in 1955 were both ahead of Walters's deal in real dollars. And Thomas's newscasts had a strong storytelling element in them. Murrow had, with some misgivings, crossed over into entertainment television in the late 1950s with his "See It Now" broadcasts, which often featured celebrity interviews.

What seemed to really anger some people was that a woman was making that kind of money. John Pastore, the Rhode Island senator who chaired the communications subcommittee complained, "The networks come before my committee and shed crocodile tears and complain about their profits. Then they pay this little girl a million dollars. That's five times better than the President of the United States makes. It's ridiculous."[10] Walters defended the salary with a reminder of reality.

> We know that news makes money. If we didn't care for ratings or sell to advertisers, news would be quite a different thing. Nobody questions it when Johnny Carson makes three million dollars a year. But there is a theory that if you're a news person you should be too pure to think about things like that.[11]

Interestingly, in announcing the agreement between his network and Walters and trying to put his reported attitude toward it behind them, Harry Reasoner chose to compare the recent deluge of publicity of a star Yankee pitcher.

> Some of you may have seen some speculation about this in the newspapers; it's had more attention than Catfish Hunter, and Barbara can't even throw left-handed. Many of the stories said that I had some reservations when the idea came up; if I did they have been taken care of, and I welcome Barbara with no reservations.[12]

ABC went to great lengths to make the pairing a success. Executives arranged a meeting between Walters and Reasoner, hoping to ease the tension by letting them talk about their concerns rather than read about what each other was saying. To assure nervous affiliates and the public, they mounted a public relations campaign that included an appearance at the affiliates meeting where Walters and Reasoner answered questions from local station managers. ABC was spending a considerable amount of time and money to improve its news product. That had been a part of its pitch to Walters. Reasoner urged the managers to make a similar commitment, arguing that both the local stations and his news broadcast would benefit. He admitted that their chances for success depended on how well Walters did.

For someone who had just made broadcasting history, Walters was miserable. "I felt for a while as if I had committed a crime." Off the air since the signing, Walters had the opportunity for a nice long vacation since "ABC News with Harry Reasoner and Barbara Walters" would not debut until fall. She did not enjoy the inactivity, however, worrying that "If the show doesn't make it, I'm finished. But if it does make it . . . my God, how fantastic."[13]

The first night's ratings were twice the norm, more than CBS and NBC combined. But the next night they were back to normal. For the week, the broadcast's Nielsen rating rose from an 8.2 to an 11.3. The ABC share of those watching television was also up, from an 18 to a 23. The interest caused by Walters's move to the anchor chair resulted in more people watching news on all three networks. After two months, ABC had 700,000 more viewers for the broadcast than at the same time a year before. But CBS had increased its overall lead since Walters joined Reasoner, and ABC was still in third place.

In addition to the new anchor, ABC was trying a number of other new things on the nightly news: making the writing more informal and mixing new features with the news maker interviews. This cut down on the number of hard news stories, because the network had been unable to convince the affiliates to give up more time; the nightly news was still a half-hour broadcast and would remain so.

## Not a News Reader

The new anchor combo never clicked. The frostiness that was often evident in the newsroom seemed to distance the two on the air. The nightly news ratings for ABC never overtook those of the two older networks. Walters's delivery—a little bit of Boston, a little bit of a lisp—was the subject of parody. Consultant Frank Magid presented ABC executives with a study that found a sample audience had an almost uniformly negative reaction to her as an anchor. News chief Roone Arledge realized Walters was too different from the norm of news anchors. "Barbara is not essentially a news reader and never has been. She's an interviewer. When we get some other things going, whether it's specials or a magazine show or an enlargement of the Sunday interview shows, I think Barbara's talents will become very apparent to people."[14]

Even Walters's interviewing came under attack. She ended an interview with president-elect Jimmy Carter by saying, "Be wise with us, be good to us." A number of observers, including Morley Safer of CBS, thought it a bit much. In a radio commentary, he said that with those closing comments, Walters had effectively removed herself from the profession of journalism and compared her to a talk show host.

## All Over Again

A year and a half after her debut, Walters was removed from her anchor chair. She was wounded by the failure, and particularly by the harsh criticism of the media, which she felt was, at times, vicious. She would later look back at 1977 as the worst year of her life. Her beloved father died that year, and Walters felt that while she had led the way for other women, the personal cost was high.

Walters felt she had to prove her abilities all over again, and in order to do so she relied on what she did best—interviews that made headlines. She scored a series of scoops by reaching world leaders before the competition, and getting them to say things they hadn't said in public before. Some of the exclusives came on the nightly news, others on "20/20" or "Issues and Answers."

Walters's prominence won her a place on a *World Almanac* list of the twenty-five most influential women in the United States in 1979. She was ranked fifth, behind Katherine Graham, Jane Fonda, Rosalynn Carter, and Ann Landers. A study of teenage girls to determine which female television stars appealed to them during their important adolescent development found Walters was the only non-entertainment woman on the girls' "most notable female characters" list of twenty-one women. Walters was at the top of the list when rated for being most in control of her life and over situations. Next were the character portrayed by Mary Tyler Moore, and "Maude," played by Bea Arthur.

### A Home

As Walters turned fifty, she vowed to limit the demands of work on her personal life. She had tried to do that many times before, but now, with her daughter becoming a teenager, Walters felt the need to spend more time with her and more time on herself. With her contract expiring at ABC, there was thought about jumping networks. Some at CBS thought Walters would complement the men on "60 Minutes." NBC also was interested. But Arledge was able to offer her what she wanted—some security and what Walters called "a home." That home is "20/20." After signing a second five-year contract that gave her a raise and still called for the periodic specials, Walters said she was extremely happy.

While publicly pointing to the commercial value of her prime time specials to the network, Walters privately has enjoyed her involvement in them. A producer who has worked on a number of the specials says that the celebrity shows give Walters power over what goes on the air to an extent not possible in her other work. At this point in her career, that feeling of control is important to Walters.

With the ease brought by a sense of security, Walters is also enjoying new personal happiness. In May 1986, she married Merv Adelson, the chairman of Lorimar, Inc. She also has a new feeling of self-confidence. "When I was young, I didn't feel that there was anything really that I could do well. Maybe that's why I worked. In the last few years I've realized that it isn't all luck, that I am good at what I do."[15]

### THE MORNING SHOWS

Walters's move from a network morning show to the evening news demonstrated a pattern of mobility in network news. It is not uncommon for newspeople to work on morning shows before taking on assignments more geared to hard news, for those programs offer the greatest opportunity for developing young talent and testing innovative news formats. NBC "Nightly News" anchor Tom Brokaw once anchored "Today," and CBS's Diane Sawyer and Lesley Stahl each held down CBS's morning news program before moving on to "60 Minutes" and the White House.

The network morning programs are also the arena in which the blurring of journalism and entertainment is greatest. They have given morning viewers former Miss America Phyllis George and former model Joan Lunden, and a succession of actresses and beauty queens have been NBC's " 'Today' girl."

### Jane Pauley: "Praise Be to the FCC"

Walters's replacement on "Today" was a twenty-five year old with limited journalistic credentials. Jane Pauley had three years in local television at WISH-TV, Indianapolis, and less than one at WMAQ-TV, Chicago. A graduate of Indiana University in political science, Pauley had been part of the explosion of women anchors and reporters in the early 1970s. When she interviewed at WISH-TV, the station had no women reporters and its license was up for renewal. Her only work experience was a few months as a campaign aide for the state Democratic central committee, but Pauley heard WISH news director Lee Giles was looking for a "female-type person." Pauley acknowledges her first TV job with, "Praise be to the FCC."[16]

Pauley received $140 a week as a cub reporter in her hometown and gradually worked her way up to weekend anchor, and then co-anchor of the 6 and 10 P.M. broadcasts. Then she moved to the number three market in the country. As Floyd Kalber's co-anchor at WMAQ-TV, Pauley was Chicago's first regular woman anchor on the evening news and made more than a thousand dollars a week. She was introduced to viewers in an ad campaign that claimed, "This woman's place in is your home."[17] But Pauley with Kalber did not set the market on fire, and she was cut back to anchoring one broadcast a night and street reporting. That did not stop NBC's executives from picking her over more than 2,000 other applicants, including the more experienced Catherine Mackin and Betty Furness, for Walters's job. As in Pauley's first job in television, she believes that timing had a lot to do with her ascent to "Today"; it was the opportunity of a lifetime that will never happen again.

> Today, the reservoir of women who have made a career in broadcast journalism is deep enough that to choose an inexperienced co-ed with any new degree in broadcast journalism is no longer legitimate. It would only telegraph your low regard for women or for the job. Or both. Obviously, our credibility as news professionals, from local to network, has suffered for the perception that we recruit on-air talent from the field of runners-up in the Miss America pageant.[18]

When Pauley was selected for "Today," she did not receive the co-host title that Walters had held. Given the decade it took for the network's executives to grant equal billing to Walters, it is not surprising that the young woman from Indiana did not assume the title. But she did receive a gracious telegram from Walters, who advised Pauley to get a good alarm clock and enjoy her new life on "Today."

*Stability a Key.*    Walters's last co-host on "Today" had been Tom Brokaw, and he and Pauley were teamed for more than five years. The stability on "Today" seemed to provide a competitive advantage over the morning broadcasts on CBS and ABC, and when Brokaw left, Bryant Gumbel took over in a remarkably smooth transition. Pauley added weekend anchoring to her duties in 1980, first replacing Jessica Savitch on Saturday's "NBC Nightly News" and then switching to Sundays for two years. At the time, she felt it was unlikely she would be considered for a weekday anchor position because she was only in her early thirties and had not served a tour of duty as a correspondent. She saw that the heirs apparent at the networks were men and felt that Walters's not working out at ABC would delay ascension of a woman to the weeknight anchor chair.

Pauley, whose role models included Nancy Dickerson, was happy after five years with the network to see so many women in broadcast news, for she had felt pressure as the woman with the most air time in network news. Along with that recognition had come indications that sexism was still very much a fact of life. Pauley was honored as a native son by the leaders of Indianapolis and received a plaque that read, in part: "In recognition of his outstanding contribution."[19]

In the time Pauley has been with "Today," the balance of duties with her male host has evolved to something resembling equality. And Pauley has come to terms with the show business aspects of the job. "I'm a journalist, but my performance is a very important aspect of how I communicate. I'm now co-anchoring and co-writing four newscasts, and that part of my work is straight journalism. But once I get on the air, I had better be something of a performer."[20]

*Not Short-changed.*    The financial compensation for anchoring the morning show had improved as well. When she joined "Today," Pauley was earning just over $100,000. By 1984, her salary topped half a million dollars a year. She also was a mother, having married cartoonist Garry Trudeau in 1980, and become the mother of twins December 30, 1983. They had another child in the summer of 1986. Unlike the pregnancy of Florence Henderson in the early days of "Today," Pauley's changing figure was not hidden by desks, tables, and flower arrangements.

Pauley finds room for both roles. She declares that she does not love her job a fraction as much as she loves her children but feels that, as long as she works for NBC and is paid a full salary, the network has a right to expect a full-time employee and that her career generally doesn't get short-changed.

### Joan Lunden: Morning Mom

Pauley was preceded in television pregnancy by Joan Lunden of ABC's "Good Morning America" ("GMA"). In fact, Pauley joked that Lunden's widely reported pregnancy had benefited "GMA"; as Lunden's stomach grew, so did the show's ratings.

In addition to national coverage in the leading weekly magazines, daily newspapers, and on her own broadcast, Lunden's pregnancy also was a focal point for women in broadcasting and other fields who were pressing for improved maternity policies. Lunden still was working for WABC-TV in New York, and moonlighting on "GMA" when she became pregnant in 1979. She listed for her news directors the kinds of stories she did not want to cover during her pregnancy. They included assignments that would require rides in helicopters—which often are not pressurized and might have caused a miscarriage—and those that might expose her to hazardous chemicals. She also did not want to be near microwave equipment, an important concern at a time when "live" trucks were being introduced in the country's major markets.

Lunden was a sort of permanent fill-in on "GMA," and it was important to her to stay on the air. After the birth of her daughter, Lunden was named to the job officially and had her contract altered to allow for child care at work and facilities for her baby near her office and dressing room. How far network attitudes toward anchor maternity had come was illustrated shortly after Lunden returned to work. As she was putting her baby down for a nap, Lunden looked up to see an amazed Barbara Walters peering into the makeshift nursery. Lunden remembers Walters saying, "How wonderful it is that you're able to do this. When my daughter was a baby they would have laughed me out of the studios if I'd asked to bring her to work with me. It would have been like asking to bring my puppy to the office."[21]

*California Girl.* Lunden's role on ABC's morning program represents the show business side of the journalism-entertainment mix. One writer commented that "Miss Lunden is a leading figure in the ranks of those who know next to nothing about news but can expect to make a quarter of a million dollars annually for dispensing it."[22]

She was born Joan Elise Blunden on September 19, 1950, in northern California, the daughter of a surgeon, who was killed in a private plane crash when she was a teenager, and a housewife. Motivated and smart enough to skip a year of high school, Lunden had a college experience with an international flavor and didn't graduate from Sacramento State University until she was in her mid-twenties. She had been a beauty contestant, modeled while going to school in Mexico City, and was a sorority girl at Sacramento State. Her entry into television came after she started her own modeling school in Sacramento and had far more to do with her looks and poise than any journalism training, for she had none. But she did have the kind of on-camera presence that causes people to watch, and that made for a fast climb from a $30-a-week weather trainee to weather girl to consumer reporter to a $240-a-week weekend anchor. It also landed her a job earning more than $50,000 a year as a street reporter in New York when she had covered exactly one outside story in her life. The first thing her new boss did was ask her to change her name because he feared "Blunden" might come out "Blunder."

Lunden received an icy reception at WABC-TV, which had pioneered a news program whose staff represented every significant ethnic group in New York. The blonde Californian did not look like part of the family and wasn't adopted either. Despite that obstacle, she was able to get an exclusive interview with Henry Kissinger during her first week at WABC and, before a year was out, had started doing consumer pieces for "A.M. America," the forerunner of "Good Morning America." Debuting in January 1975, it was produced by ABC's entertainment division and targeted at a younger, primarily female, audience. It lasted less than a year. When David Hartman and Nancy Dussault pioneered "GMA," the program was designed with Hartman as the lead and Dussault in a secondary role. That relationship extended to Hartman's contract, and Dussault was increasingly unhappy with her assignments and treatment on the broadcast. ABC's executives weren't entirely pleased with Dussault, either, and started looking for a replacement. Lunden was a prime candidate, but the job went to Sandy Hill, who had eight years of experience in TV news, including stints at KIRO in Seattle and KNXT and KABC in Los Angeles. She was a former Miss Washington who had majored in Spanish at the University of Washington, maintaining an A-minus average; she also belonged to a sorority. Like Lunden, Hill had received a cold reception in her first major market job, where some of the KNXT staff members felt she had been hired for her looks rather than her reporting skills.

*Sub-host.*    Hill had dreamt of having Walters's job on "Today"; instead, she got Dussault's on "GMA." That meant Hill got most of the lighter stories, the secondary interviews, and the definite feeling that she didn't have much say about the program or her role on it. After covering the Winter Olympics for ABC in 1980, Hill didn't return as "sub-host" of the broadcast, arranging instead to complete her contract as a special correspondent.

Lunden was now with "GMA" full time as a reporter and backup anchor, and became the primary fill-in while Hill was away. She also had married Michael Krauss, a producer at ABC who went on to become a producer for

"Today" before starting his own production company. That company now features Lunden in syndicated programs about parenting.

It was a great time to become a bigger part of "GMA." ABC's fortunes had been improving, and "GMA" was part of that success story. It was overtaking "Today," and Lunden seemed to contribute to that gain. Today, though she considers her job one of the best in television, she has admitted frustration that her role has been secondary to her male anchor's.

> In my job, one of the most glamorous in television, I quite often feel like the window dressing the critics sometimes accuse me of being. I don't think it's been a conscious decision on the part of management; it's just part of a prevailing attitude in the business. . . . The inequalities are there, and the feeling of being a second-class citizen is always there as well. And let's face it, that feels really bad.[23]

*Growing with Society.*    When Lunden originally was considered for the seat alongside David Hartman, she had a curious meeting with his agent. Among the questions asked was what she thought her role on the broadcast should be. Lunden carefully replied that she would be happy with the role the way it was, but would expect to grow in the role in proportion to the way women's roles grew in broadcasting and in society. She has stuck by that expectation, turning down such completely entertainment-oriented opportunities as acting in film and TV game shows in order to preserve her news image. Now a mother of three, Lunden has recently become more assertive about a woman's place in electronic journalism and seems to have traveled a good distance philosophically in just over a decade in broadcasting. In her most recent contract, she was named co-host of "Good Morning America."

## Sally Quinn: Promises, Promises

To prepare her for New York and network television, some friends had given Lunden a copy of Sally Quinn's book, *We're Going to Make You a Star.* It was a scathing account of Quinn's treatment by CBS during a brief stint in 1973 as co-anchor of the "CBS Morning News." Quinn's short time as a broadcaster was a painful experience for nearly everyone involved.

CBS had been looking for a winning combination in the early morning hours for years, never able to overcome "Today." The network's executives were also under pressure to make the morning program's next anchor a woman. Ironically, an appearance on Barbara Walters's "Not for Women Only" broadcast by Quinn, who had been with the *Washington Post* for four years, got the attention of the CBS brass. The "next anchor" turned out to be Quinn. It was not what the newswomen at CBS had wanted, for Quinn did not come from within their ranks; she was not even a broadcaster. Quinn had worked for CBS before, however, as an assistant to an assistant for the network at the 1968 Democratic convention. It was one of many interesting jobs Quinn had held since her graduation from Smith College as a drama major. She had been a librarian, a public relations assistant, a social secretary, a German translator, and even a go-go girl at a trade fair. In 1969, she successfully interviewed with Ben Bradlee at the *Post*; he was looking for a society reporter who could go to parties and report on who was there and what gossip was passed along. Despite having no journalism experience, she had made a name for herself at the *Post*.

When Hughes Rudd and Quinn replaced John Hart and Nelson Benton on the "CBS Morning News," Rudd was selected for his gruff wit and journalistic skills while Quinn was competition for Walters. She was younger and blonder and soon sadder but wiser. CBS put together a promotional campaign that gained national attention for the new morning duo before the two ever went on the air. When the network should have been training Quinn and putting the program through dry runs, she and Rudd were entertaining television writers around the country. To one public relations expert it was a classic case of over-sell.

> The publicity promised a glamorous sex bomb who had set Washington on fire, but what the viewer got was an inexperienced television personality who didn't project much excitement. The reaction to Sally Quinn was severe because the product wasn't as promised.[24]

Appalled by the way the new morning team was being promoted, news chief Richard Salant issued a memo that said, in part,

> CBS News does not hire people because they are sex bombs, male or female, or because they are blonde or brunette or bald. We hire them for their journalistic competence. That is precisely why Sally was hired, and we will exploit, publicize and promote that and nothing else.[25]

*The Red Light.*   Quinn was so inexperienced that she didn't even know that when a studio camera was "hot," a little red light over the lens would go on. That meant she didn't know where to look to make eye contact with her viewers until someone clued her in several days after her debut. Quinn's first show was even more of a trial because she was sick. Working with a fever, she passed out before the program, was revived, and went on the air. The next day, Rudd's mother died. It was a difficult start from which to recover.

Since she had had little coaching, Quinn tried to be what she thought a broadcaster should look and sound like. She forced her voice lower and adopted a strained delivery. Only after several weeks did she learn to be more herself. She never did adjust to the hours. And she displayed the values of a woman who had lived all over the world while growing up and who had mixed with the high society of Washington and New York. Her writing was aimed at that audience and not middle America, and it didn't wash west of the Hudson. It took six months for Quinn to quit the $70,000 a year job, by which time CBS was looking at a 1.6 rating and for a graceful way to get her off the air. After initially accepting an offer from the *New York Times*, Quinn went back to the *Post*, where she resumed a successful career in print journalism.

### Diane Sawyer: "60 Minutes"

Although Quinn's experience on CBS's morning program was a disaster, the mornings provided career boosts to several other women as the network tried many solutions to its third-place ranking. CBS's best showing in the ratings came when Diane Sawyer co-anchored the broadcast. Even her presence could not bring the "CBS Morning News" out of the basement at a time when everything else looked good for the network's news line-up. Few other challenges in broadcasting have gotten the better of the woman from Kentucky. As a member of television's most highly rated news broadcast, "60 Minutes," Sawyer now rivals Barbara Walters for making an impact on electronic journalism today. Many insiders believe she may follow Walters's lead and become the second woman to win a permanent seat in a weeknight network anchor chair.

Diane Sawyer has been able to make things that left stigmas on others in broadcast news seem like assets, most notably a reign as 1963 America's Junior Miss and eight years in the employ of former president Richard Nixon. She is also the only network correspondent to be offered a million dollars to pose in *Hustler* or to be the love fantasy of a character in a popular political cartoon strip.

Raised in Louisville, Kentucky, Sawyer was taught in the third grade by her schoolteacher mother, who gave Diane and her older sister Linda a background in the arts and music. Diane looked up to Linda, who was America's Junior Miss runner-up before Diane competed for the title. Her father was a judge who died in a car accident in 1969. In school, Sawyer was active in everything from basketball to cheerleading and was also editor of the yearbook. After graduating from Wellesley College in 1967, Sawyer returned to Louisville and lived at home while becoming a weather girl at WLKY and a reporter.

*Nixon's "Smart Girl."*   Sawyer went looking for a job in 1970 on the East Coast. Among the people she talked with were Don Hewitt and Bill Small of CBS, and Ron Ziegler at the White House. Hewitt rejected her request to join "60 Minutes." Small was interested, but a hiring freeze prevented him from putting her on staff. Sawyer's father had been active in Republican politics in Kentucky, and those connections resulted in an interview with the president's press secretary. Ziegler offered her a job writing releases and speeches in the White House press office. A statement Sawyer wrote for the president about his mother got Nixon's attention, and he praised "the smart girl" to her boss. Within a year, Sawyer had an administrative position in the press office.[26]

For someone who would later rely a great deal on information from political contacts in Washington, Sawyer wasn't a very good source for White House correspondents. Dan Rather remembers that when he covered the president, "She was a total non-source, close to the cuff. But if you needed a statistic or a spelling at the last minute, she was always the one you went to."[27]

Before he resigned, Nixon asked Sawyer to help write his memoirs, and when he left Washington, she was on the plane to California with him. She assisted him with the manuscript for four years. She did it out of loyalty; she had been with Nixon, she says, during the good times and would be there for the bad. "We were beyond a point of moralizing. It was a human consideration. Here was a man whose dreams were shattered. If I didn't come through for him at a time when he needed me, I couldn't have lived with myself."[28]

When the manuscript was completed, Sawyer auditioned at ABC and CBS, and both offered her a job. She chose to return to Washington as a general assignment reporter with CBS at the age of thirty-two. She lacked the kind of experience the others on the Washington staff had, and most of them, including Rather, opposed her joining the bureau. "I advised against hiring her. I felt she had no credibility, that she'd been discredited. But she was hired anyway and she proved me wrong. She was a team player, taking the bad assignment, working weekends without complaining. And she was clearly a good reporter."[29]

Sawyer soon was teamed with Robert Pierpoint on the State Department beat. Pierpoint was a veteran Washington correspondent but new to the State Department, and both of them had to scramble to keep up with network rivals who had better inside information. During the Iranian hostage crisis, it was clear that the gap had been closed. Sawyer impressed network executives with her live reports on the morning news. Anchor Charles Kuralt's interviews with her sparkled, and the idea was born that the two might make a good team.

*Morning News.*    In 1981, when plans for expanding the morning news from an hour to ninety minutes were under way, the co-anchor position was offered to Sawyer. That fall, she and Kuralt became the latest hope for ratings respectability. In the spring of 1982, more revisions were made. The broadcast was expanded again, to two hours, and Bill Kurtis of WBBM-TV, Chicago, replaced Kuralt. Sawyer was given equal responsibility with Kurtis and for a while it looked promising. The ratings grew, but never enough to get the broadcast out of third place.

*"One of the Boys."*    The producer of "60 Minutes," Don Hewitt, was one of the CBS executives impressed with Sawyer's reporting at the State Department. In 1983, rumors began that Hewitt thought Sawyer would be a worthy addition to the program. Women had been on the broadcast before, and several had come close to joining it full time. Hewitt had considered adding Michele Clark before her death in a plane crash in 1972. When Barbara Walters was contemplating her options before going to ABC in 1976, there had been talk of her joining "60 Minutes." Margaret Osmer, Lucy Salenger, and Sylvia Chase all had done pieces on the program in the seventies. But the on-air staff remained male.

In 1984 Sawyer broke the mold. Hewitt cracked that he would have hired her if her name had been *Tom* Sawyer. He later added, "She is one of the girls who is one of the boys."[30]

The first piece Sawyer did was an attention grabber. It was about a North Carolina grandmother who was about to become the first woman to be executed in the United States in twenty-two years. Sawyer did not have the editing time usually available for pieces on the broadcast. Still, it was riveting, and got Sawyer off to a flying start.

### Phyllis George: Miss America

That was not the case for Sawyer's replacement, who was grounded by a history as a television showpiece. Phyllis George, the former Miss America who had been a frivolous addition to CBS's pro football coverage in the mid-1970s, was called "a celebrity without journalistic background."[31] The network was accused of being "less interested in finding a serious journalist than an attractive young clotheshorse, preferably with a child or two to counterprogram Jane Pauley and Joan Lunden."[32] George did qualify as an attractive thirty-five-year-old mother of two, the wife of former Kentucky governor, John Y. Brown, Jr.

When George joined Bill Kurtis in January 1985 at the "CBS Morning News," she was prepared for criticism. Many at CBS had believed the network had a greater commitment to news than NBC and ABC, and George's hiring disillusioned them. Former CBS news chief Richard Salant felt it demeaned the network news business. "If they want to do that, put the show in the entertainment division or the record division or the toy division. But get it out of news. Once we start playing those games, we lose all our credibility."[33] Cohost Kurtis was not happy about the appointment either, and it was a key part of his decision later to leave the broadcast to return to Chicago as an anchor at WBBM-TV.

George commanded a salary believed to be close to three-quarters of a million dollars a year. The ratings generated in less than a year on "CBS Morning News" did little to justify it. The celebrity status and good looks had not changed the network's fortunes in the morning hours.

### The Last of a Line

Maria Shriver, one of the Kennedys, replaced George. But the results were no better, and in the summer of 1986, the network gave up on head-to-head competition with the more successful morning shows on ABC and NBC. CBS decided instead for a ninety-minute straight news presentation with more "windows" for local news, followed by a ninety-minute entertainment program.

CBS's impatience had prevented any of the promising morning anchor teams from the slow growth "Today" and "GMA" had shown with Pauley and Lunden. In the end, CBS's ratings were not better than when it began the musical anchor chair exercise, and the network's image had suffered a good deal in the eyes of its affiliates as well as those of the public.

## CONCLUSION

The morning news programs have been seen by many as less significant than other segments of network news. But for women, they've been tremendously important. They have been the launching pad for several of the central TV newswomen today. Moreover, they're the first broadcasts where some women anchors have had true parity with their male co-hosts. The nightly newscasts have not come as far and neither have most local stations.

## NOTES

1. Judith S. Gelfman, *Women in Television News* (New York: Columbia University Press, 1976), p. 26.

2. James Conaway, "How to Talk with Barbara Walters about Practically Anything," *New York Times* (10 September 1972): VI, 40.

3. Gloria Steinem, "Nylons in the Newsroom," *New York Times* (7 November 1965): II, 23.

4. Barbara Matusow, *The Evening Stars* (Boston: Houghton Mifflin, 1983), p. 172.

5. Gelfman, *Women in Television News*, pp. 72-73.

6. "Walters Deal the Opener for Longer Network News?" *Broadcasting* 90, 17 (26 April 1976): 19-20.

7. Ibid., p. 20.

8. "The $5 Million Woman," *Newsweek* (3 May 1976): 80.

9. "The Supersalaried Superstar: Eyebrows Are Up Everywhere over Walters's High Price Tag," *Broadcasting* 90, 18 (3 May 1976): 30.

10. Ibid.

11. "Together, for the First Time on any Stage . . . ," *Broadcasting* 90, 22 (31 May 1976): 58.

12. "Walters Deal," p. 20.

13. H. F. Waters et al., "The New Look of TV News," *Newsweek* (11 October 1976): 68-70.

14. H. F. Waters, ed., "Roone at the Top," *Newsweek* (16 May 1977): 103-4.

15. Eliot Wald, "Barbara Walters in Command," *Los Angeles Times* (2 January 1978): IV, 18.

16. Jennifer Allen, "The Women Who Make the News," *Life* (June 1982): 104.

17. Mary Kerner, " 'Female Type' Makes Good," *Los Angeles Times* (21 April 1980): VI, 7.

18. Jane Pauley, "Ten Years," *RTNDA Communicator* (October 1985): 14.

19. Kerner, " 'Female Type' Makes Good," p. 7.

20. Didi Moore, "Talking with Jane Pauley," *Redbook* (April 1982): 12.

21. Joan Lunden with Andy Friedberg, *Good Morning, I'm Joan Lunden* (New York: G. P. Putnam's Sons, 1986), p. 215.

22. Robert Scheer, "The Rise of Joan Lunden: News Sense Unimportant," *Los Angeles Times* (29 May 1977): I, 1.

23. Lunden with Friedberg, *Good Morning*, pp. 172-74.

24. Les Brown, "Sally Quinn May Be Out of TV Anchor Role," *New York Times* (9 January 1974): 70.

25. Sally Quinn, *We're Going to Make You a Star* (New York: Simon and Schuster, 1975), p. 93.

26. Tony Schwartz, "From Nixon's Aide to Kuralt's Co-anchor," *New York Times* (30 September 1981): III, 23.

27. Ibid.

28. "CBS Morning News's Getting-Ready-for-Prime-Time Player: The Class Act of Diane Sawyer," *Broadcasting* 103, 21 (22 November 1982): 39-40.

29. Schwartz, "From Nixon's Aide," p. 23.

30. Edwin Diamond, "The Girl Who Is One of the Boys," *New York* (25 February 1985): 16.

31. "CBS Morning News to Get Softer Look," *Broadcasting* 107, 24 (10 December 1984): 97.

32. Judy Flander, "Women in Network News," *Washington Journalism Review* (March 1985): 42.

33. "CBS Morning News to Get Softer Look," p. 99.

# 7 A Symbolic Case

Many of the hurdles women in broadcast news face today were framed by the Christine Craft case. It began with a lawsuit in 1983 against Metromedia, a media conglomerate that owned KMBC-TV in Kansas City, Missouri. During the years Craft's case wound through America's legal system it took on a life of its own and, regardless of the legal outcome, had a tremendous impact on women in broadcast news, both from the public's perception and within the industry.

## CHRISTINE CRAFT'S LAWSUIT

### A Search for Ratings

Christine Craft was thirty-six years old when she was hired at KMBC in December 1980. The station's management had been looking for a personable woman anchor to join Scott Feldman on the 6 and 10 P.M. weeknight local news. KMBC's ratings had been slipping, and research showed one reason might have been that solo anchor Feldman was thought to lack warmth by some viewers.

Craft had started her broadcasting career late, had worked for CBS briefly in sports, and most recently had been an anchor at a very small station in California, KEYT-TV in Santa Barbara. She had gone through a cosmetic "makeover" while working for CBS, and made it clear before accepting the job in Kansas City that she didn't want to go through the experience again.

Yet general manager Kent Replogle and news director Ridge Shannon had almost immediate concerns about her on-camera appearance and performance and called in the station's consultant to work with Craft. In addition to make-up advice, Craft eventually had to follow a clothing schedule to guarantee she'd wear what management felt was appropriate.

After her lawyer negotiated a two-year contract for $35,000 and then $38,500, Craft signed a standard staff announcer's contract in late January

1981, three weeks after she had started anchoring. She apparently didn't read it closely. Among other things, it allowed management to assign Craft to a reporting position if she didn't work out as an anchor.

That's what happened seven months after Craft started at KMBC. The change came on the advice of the station's consultants, who had used accepted industry methods in doing research on Craft and other aspects of the station's news presentation. The change was made despite improved ratings that showed KMBC in first place in one service's July results and second in the other's.

Craft refused the demotion and, after several meetings with management failed to resolve things, returned to her old job in Santa Barbara.

### Taking Her Case to Court

Craft filed a complaint with the Equal Employment Opportunity Commission, but it was not until January 1983 that she was able to file her lawsuit against Metromedia. By that time, KMBC-TV had been sold to the Hearst Corporation, which was not a party to the lawsuit.

There were four counts in the complaint: sex discrimination, unequal pay, fraud, and intent to injure. The sex discrimination charge was based on Title VII of the Civil Rights Act of 1964. The unequal pay claim was based on the Equal Pay Act of 1963 and charged that Craft was paid less than men who did the same job. The fraud charge alleged that station executives intentionally misrepresented their intentions when they offered Craft the job, saying she was being hired for journalistic abilities when on-camera appearance was foremost, and that, among other things, they intended to make Craft over. The last count—that even if the station's management had been legally right, what it did was designed to hurt her reputation and perhaps make things so unpleasant that Craft would quit—was dropped during the trial. Craft's lawyers asked $200,000 in actual damages and $1 million in punitive damages, in addition to reinstatement, lost wages, and benefits.

By the time the case went to trial in federal court in Kansas City in July 1983, news director Shannon was no longer with the station. He had left KMBC by "mutual agreement," which is usually a nice way of saying that someone has been let go by management and has received a certain amount of money to accept that fate. One aspect of the decision may have been that the new owners of KMBC wanted to distance the station from the case, which by that time had gained national prominence. The Craft case was embraced by a number of special interest groups, most significantly elements of the women's movement.

The case became two separate trials. One of them was in the courtroom. But the more significant was the public debate that grew out of the lawsuit, the trials, and the ensuing rulings. The Craft case brought the values and practices of local television news managers into the open, and many people, both inside and outside the industry, cringed at what was revealed. The debate focused on a phrase that Craft used to describe what Shannon had told her were the reasons for removing her from the anchor chair, that she was "too old, too unattractive, and not deferential enough to men." Shannon vehemently denies he ever used the phrase, but it was quoted frequently in articles about the trials and came to represent the situation, as some saw it, for women anchors in general.

The aging issue was the coming concern for women in broadcast news. A decade after the first significant gains in the newsroom, many of the 1970s' wave of women television newscasters were approaching middle age and wondering what their futures held. Americans were aware of the country's aging population, and the idea that someone not yet forty could be considered too old to anchor a television newscast seemed irrational. It also seemed an unlikely reason for dumping Craft, because KMBC's managers had known exactly how old Craft was when she was hired, and she wasn't significantly older eight months later when she was demoted.

Attractiveness as a requirement for a broadcast journalist had been unspoken but was a given in television news. Attractiveness can be perceived in many ways, and there were those who felt that balding, portly Charles Kuralt of CBS was attractive. Craft seemed to equate attractiveness with beauty queens, and local television news certainly had its share of former title winners. She believed that the standard of attractiveness was applied differently to women and men. The idea that television newscasters had to be good looking seemed to replace in her mind the concept that they had to be attractive—that they literally had to attract viewers to the station to be successful. That broadcasters employed consultants to aid them in creating programs that would attract viewers, that they would hire and fire people based on the recommendations of these consultants, and that they would order employees to wear certain clothes on certain days, cut their hair, and change the way they looked, was a shock to many who thought their newscasters were primarily journalists and not performers.

But not being deferential enough to men was the clincher. Everyone who objected to chauvinism in American society empathized with someone who claimed she would have to feign deference to be successful.

## A Symbol

By the time the case went to trial, Craft had become a symbol. While the courtroom proceedings were still under way, the *New York Times* featured a front-page article that discussed the emphasis on appearance in the television news industry and the impact of the Craft suit. Nationally, the case received similar coverage.

On August 8, 1983, the four-woman, two-man jury awarded Craft $375,000 in actual damages and $125,000 in punitive damages on the fraud charges. The jury also issued an advisory verdict of guilty to Judge Joseph E. Stevens, Jr., on the sex discrimination charge. But it found Metromedia not guilty of the equal pay charge.

Craft was careful about the implications of the verdict. "I have no illusions that this is going to make a huge difference in television news. But if it keeps one news director at one station someplace, somewhere, from doing the same thing, I hope it does that." She cited one instance where it apparently did make a difference.

> I know of one woman reporter, in her fifties, whose contract was up a week after the decision in my court case. She thought the station would can her, but she was given another contract. She told me she had a sneaking suspicion it was because of me. If it makes a difference for even one person, that's enough.[1]

Some, like Texas Christian University communications professor William Jurma, hailed the Craft verdict while observing that the industry was a long way from equality.

> But disturbing factors that affect women as media mannequins remain. Women with intelligence, education, talent, and experience are still likely to be judged on their attractiveness first, and their reporting ability second. Since women are not represented in top levels of news management, this trend seems likely to remain for some time.[2]

### Overturned

Judge Stevens did not take the jury's advice. Rather, he ruled that Craft was not a victim of sex discrimination. He also threw out the jury's half-million-dollar award, saying that the award of much more than Craft was asking for may have been partially the result of erroneous instructions to the jury, and that the jury had been affected by "pervasive and relentless publicity and could not have been immune from its effect."[3] Stevens set a new trial on the fraud charge alone for January 1984 in Joplin, Missouri, with a twelve-person jury that would be sequestered to hear the case. This time, Craft asked for $3.5 million in damages.

At the end of the eight-day trial in Joplin, the jury awarded Craft $225,000 in actual damages and $100,000 in punitive damages. After the verdict Craft told reporters, "Two juries, eighteen people I've convinced. How many more do we have to go? How much more justice can I afford?"[4]

### The Appeals

Metromedia's attorneys appealed to the U.S. Court of Appeals for the Eighth Circuit, which threw out the award. The court ruled that Craft had not proved that Replogle and Shannon had intended to make her over all along. Craft's attorneys had appealed the equal pay and discrimination verdicts from the first trial, and those appeals were denied.

Craft took her case to the U.S. Supreme Court, but the justices declined to hear it. Only Justice Sandra Day O'Connor indicated she would have accepted the case for review.

By then, Craft had made more than seventy lectures across the country for fees of up to $4,200. Much of the money went to pay bills that stemmed from the lawsuits. She had received other support from groups such as the American Federation of Television and Radio Artists, Women in Communications, Inc., the National Women's Political Caucus, the Federation of Republican Women, and the Grey Panthers. And she had begun a new anchoring job at KRBK in Sacramento, California, doing the thirty-minute newscast at 10 P.M. on an independent station, whose main fare was reruns and old movies. She had left KEYT-TV several months after the first trial ended because she felt she was too absorbed in the case, had been getting many requests for lectures, and wanted to write about the issues she felt she had raised.

### The Legacy

Craft was eager to get back to anchoring. She didn't want to be seen as a martyr but as someone who had challenged the worst parts of local television news, convinced two juries that she was right, and gone on to a fulfilling life in her profession. But in the five years since she had started anchoring on KMBC-TV, Craft had become the focus of debate about broadcast journalism and women's place in it. The legal battle was lost, but the questions raised by her lawsuits continued. The Craft case forced the television news industry to examine its practices, especially how it woos anchors and reporters, and caused public illumination of its methods for generating ratings. In a larger sense, the Craft case spurred the examination of sexism and ageism in America. As veteran broadcast correspondent Marlene Sanders said at the start of Craft's first trial, "she is raising issues that it is good for everyone to talk about."[5]

## FACE VALUE: WHO IS ON THE AIR?

The aging issue seems to be one that women on the air are winning every day. That probably reflects a change in societal attitudes more than enlightened broadcast news management.

"They can't get rid of us now," says ABC's Lynn Sherr. "We are going to have some female wrinkles on television news. And guess what? The public's going to like that because the public can handle female wrinkles."[6]

Sherr is one of several network newswomen in her forties who see an optimistic future for older women on the air. The graying of female newscasters is closely tied to the number of women on the air. Their progress has been visible over the years. They made significant gains in the decade between 1972—the year after the FCC included women in equal employment opportunity guidelines—and 1982. A survey of television news directors in 1972 found half the stations had anchorwomen, while ten years later 92 percent had women anchoring the news. Although that number dropped slightly in 1985, to 89 percent, it still represents a big change. The female share of anchor positions also has grown since the FCC order. Eleven percent of all anchors were women in 1972, 20 percent in 1976, and by 1982 the figure was 36 percent, a figure that has remained the same through the mid-1980s.[7]

One of the most extensive studies to document the progress of women on the air was undertaken by the U.S. Commission on Civil Rights. Analyzing five videotapes each of ABC, CBS, and NBC news broadcasts randomly selected from March 1974 to February 1975, researchers concluded women and minority correspondents were outnumbered nearly nine to one by white men, who also tended to cover more important stories. When the report was updated in 1977, the conclusions weren't much different: television network news continued to be dominated by men. A 1979 study of female correspondents on TV network news corroborated those findings, suggesting that though women were getting more important assignments, there was still a difference in the kinds of stories men and women reported. When a group of ABC News employees monitored that network's on-air reporting between May and December 1985, it found just under 12 percent of the reports on "World News Tonight" were done by women. The figure for "Nightline" was even lower, slightly more than 7 percent. For "This Week with David Brinkley," the group counted thirty-four news reports, none done by women. Only the program traditionally aimed at women, "Good Morning America," showed a higher tally of news reports by women, at about 20 percent. The group also cited a behind-the-scenes example of inequity in assignments: six of the seven women sent to the Geneva superpower summit in 1985 were desk assistants, one of the lowest level jobs in a TV newsroom.[8]

Not all recent reports have been discouraging, though. The updated Commission report in 1979 also concluded more women were anchoring newscasts. The programs were usually "throw-away times"—weekends and early mornings—but they did represent progress. On radio, women were newscasters at 53 percent of stations in 1985, up from 15 percent in 1972. Lynn Sherr finds progress for women expressed in another way. Instead of questions about what it's like to be a woman on television, people ask her to

talk about being an older woman on television. . . . I don't remember any stories asking [ABC correspondent] Sam Donaldson how he felt about men aging on television. . . . I'm not sure what the next question is going to be that on the surface is sort of insulting but that in fact illustrates progress.

## The Aging Anchors

A study by Audience Research and Development Corporation found a dramatic difference in the numbers of male and female television anchors over the age of forty: nearly half the men were, compared to only 3 percent of the women. Marlene Sanders, who was born in 1931, believes that "in broadcasting, authority ought to go with age," but doesn't know whether women will have on-air careers as long as their male counterparts. "We all hope that our credentials, our work and our abilities will be the deciding factors." Her sentiments are echoed by NBC correspondent and anchor Connie Chung. "If I fall by the wayside, I don't want it to be because I've gotten old." "You can argue, if you want to be charitable," says CBS's Diane Sawyer, "that the networks haven't had the talent they have now. We'll see if there continues to be a double standard on age."[9]

Sheer believes "we will be allowed to grow old in a way that most of our predecessors were not, because there are too many of us." CNN vice president/New York, Mary Alice Williams, who also anchors a nightly newscast, sees strength in numbers. "We are going to be allowed to age on the air . . . because the bulk of the population—and we are post-war baby boom kids—is going to be our age." Beyond that, "MacNeil/Lehrer NewsHour" correspondent Judy Woodruff says, management is finding "it is not efficient economically to invest all that time and money training and promoting women just to lose our services in our most productive years."[10]

*The Local Litmus Test.*   The aging question for women will be tested more thoroughly on the local level. While few women become network news anchors, hundreds of women anchor local news programs. People identify more closely with the men and women who report and present the concerns of their particular communities. Local news broadcasts are different from network ones in another major way: they tend to be more "show biz," with more bells and whistles; often that means greater attention to cosmetic appeal. Testifying at the Craft trial, KMBC-TV general manager Kent Replogle said, "I would put appearance at the top of the list" of an anchor's credentials." But there is a double standard. "Men get more distinguished with age," says KPIX-TV, San Francisco anchor Wendy Tokuda, "but women just get older. I hope that will change. I hope we are appreciated as we get older for our journalistic values."[11]

A 1985 survey of television news directors in the top fifteen markets found more than 20 percent of the female anchors over the age of forty. When discussing the appealing qualities of their anchorwomen, the news executives who did the hiring generally ranked ability higher than attractiveness, and most of them said they didn't think age was a major factor in whether their audiences liked the female newscaster. Bruno Cohen, while news director of KPIX-TV, San Francisco, said,

> the biggest point I would like to make is my sense of how quickly the audience's acceptance of mature women on the air is changing. I am certain that women as skilled as Wendy [Tokuda, KPIX's lead female anchor] and [reporter] Linda Schacht will begin having the same career longevity as men.[12]

Jerry Nachman, while at WNBC-TV, New York, said his two primary anchorwomen, both older than forty, were equally, if not more, appealing than younger women because "maturity counts in a wisdom-hungry world." Steve Wasserman, then news director of WPLG-TV, Miami, thought other factors were more crucial. "Variety is the spice of life. What's important is not the relative age—it's the age and style mix of the anchor teams." In fact, Sherlee Barish, who heads Broadcast Personnel, Inc., and has handled anchors since 1960, finds in the mid-1980s "the trend has been to mature female co-anchors."[13]

There is no paucity of older anchorwomen in major markets: Ann Bishop, WPLG, Miami; Maureen Bunyan, WUSA, Washington, D.C.; Sylvia Chase, KRON-TV, San Francisco; Jean Enersen, KING-TV, Seattle/Tacoma; Pat Harper, WNBC-TV, New York City; Natalie Jacobson, WCVB, Boston; Kelly Lange, KNBC-TV, Los Angeles; Renee Poussaint, WJLA, Washington, D.C.; and Sue Simmons, WNBC-TV, New York City.

Time is the only test for women like these, who earned their credentials through years of reporting before they got to their anchor chairs. "I think it's premature to decide whether they're going to let women in their forties stay on the air or not," said Ann Bishop. "People say we don't have older women broadcasters. That's because we just got into it. We haven't been here long enough to age." As TV is changing, noted Rita Channon, a San Francisco reporter and anchorwoman, "Looks aren't going to be that important. The Charles Kuralt look is just as salable as the high-cheekbone look."[14]

## EQUAL PAY

While some see aging on the air as the biggest hurdle women in TV news face today, CBS correspondent Diane Sawyer calls equal pay for equal work the most serious issue. The problem is not new. Back in the mid-1940s CBS's Paul White recalled a notice he saw for news writers at a large Kentucky station. It offered $50 a week for a good rewrite woman, or $60 for a man. An industry study in 1960 found 84 percent of the women in broadcasting earned less than $96 a week, while only 17 percent of the men did. And a survey of University of Maryland journalism graduates from 1951 to

1981 found that most female journalists earned less than their male colleagues, with women comprising 77 percent of those earning less than $15,000 annually. In many newsrooms, union contracts regulate salaries, which prevent pay discrimination. But many newspeople have personal services contracts that compensate them above scale, and many other positions, particularly in small markets, are not governed by unions.

In 1986 some women who worked for ABC News thought they were being discriminated against when it came to salaries, alleging that across the board women were paid 30 percent less than men in the division. According to correspondent Lynn Sherr, who has been involved in women's rights throughout her career,

> the company said, "Oh, pooh-pooh. Not true." They undertook a [producer] salary study, and lo and behold, they found all the women were bunched at the bottom. All the men were bunched at the top. Guess what? Women, and some men, have now gotten pay increases to make up for that. Increases of up to $11,000 a year!

Sherr goes on to say that the company did not believe it was discriminating but that the salary differences were the result of how people had gotten their jobs.

> There were two different pay systems going on. Most of the women were being promoted from within and most of the men were brought in from outside, which means that they started out at higher salaries. And inside you only got to increase 10 percent as opposed to a big increase if you had an agent or a contract. But they're starting to fix it now.

A related problem is likely to occur because the majority of broadcast journalism students today are women. As they enter the work force, they will also be at the low end of the salary scale. A decade from now, we may find two main groups of employees in the industry: over forty and mostly male and under forty and mostly female. This pattern already exists today in some places, and managers are going to have to be very careful in deciding whether pay differentials constitute sex discrimination. In the Craft case, it was judged that her male anchor received a higher salary because of his experience and qualifications. But when the duties are exactly the same, can that account for the inequalities existing in many cases? Women who find themselves at the low end of the pay scale may test that concept again in the courts.

The greatest pay discrimination will be found in local radio and television. Unions are more prevalent at the networks and in major markets. The largest companies, including the networks, tend to make the greatest effort to avoid the problems unequal pay can cause. But attitudes are likely to be entrenched in smaller markets, and differential pay patterns will change more slowly. Of the challenges facing women in broadcast news today, equal pay may be the most difficult to meet. The number of women on a news staff and their ages can be easily established but salaries tend to be confidential, and the dollar value of experience and other qualifications are hard to determine.

## CONCLUSION

While it is possible that aging may not be a major issue for women broadcasters in a decade, equal pay for equal work seems likely to linger on. Women will continue to take a larger percentage of the entry level positions in broadcast news. Experience is likely to be used as a reason for lower pay for women doing the same job as a man, especially in support positions. Where there are direct measures, such as ratings provide, and women can show themselves to be the dominant factor in a station's success, parity is more likely. Ironically, Christine Craft now has entered the arena where progress for women is very slow and the future does not look bright—management. Not only is she KRBK's anchorwoman, but she also has taken on news management duties.

## NOTES

1. "Not Just a Pretty Face," *Macleans* (22 August 1983): 46; Ruthe Stein, "From Sex-Bias Suit to Lecture Circuit Star," *San Francisco Chronicle* (30 September 1983): 35.

2. William E. Jurma, "Media Mannequins," a speech delivered in Fort Worth, Texas, 9 September 1983. See *Vital Speeches of the Day* 50, 4 (November 1983): 64.

3. Christine Craft vs. Metromedia, Inc., U.S. District Court No. 83-0007-CV-W-8, Memorandum Opinion and Order, 31 October 1983.

4. Peter Kerr, "Jury Awards Christine Craft $325,000," *New York Times* (14 January 1984): I, 43.

5. Sally Bedell Smith, "TV Newswoman's Suit Stirs a Debate on Values in Hiring," *New York Times* (6 August 1983): I, 44.

6. Unless otherwise stated, all quotations from Lynn Sherr are from an interview with Gayle K. Yamada, New York City, 20 August 1986.

7. See Vernon A. Stone, "Women Gain but Minorities Barely Hold Their Own in Broadcast News Jobs," *RTNDA Communicator* (Washington, D.C.: Radio-Television News Directors Association, April 1983): 20; idem, "Survey Shows Little Change for Minorities or Women," *RTNDA Communicator* (Washington, D.C.: Radio-Television News Directors Association, June 1985): 37; and idem, "Women Hold Almost a Third of News Jobs," *RTNDA Communicator* (Washington, D.C.: Radio-Television News Directors Association, April 1986): 29.

8. See two reports prepared by the U.S. Commission on Civil Rights, *Window Dressing on the Set: Women and Minorities in Television* (Washington, D.C.: U.S. Government Printing Office, August 1977), pp. 50-51, and *Window Dressing on the Set: An Update* (Washington, D.C.: U.S. Government Printing Office, January 1979), p. 32; Loy A. Singleton and Stephanie L. Cook, "Television Network News

Reporting by Female Correspondents: An Update," *Journal of Broadcasting* 26, 1 (Winter 1982): 487-91; and Kevin Goldman, "ABC News Women on Warpath: Present Arledge with Complaints During Powwow in Washington," *Variety* (22 January 1986): 39.

9. Both Sanders quotations are from Jean Gaddy Wilson, "What It Takes to Be a Pro," *Working Woman* (October 1985): 133; Marian Christy, "Connie Chung's Passions: Success and Shopping," *The Miami Herald TV* (30 September-6 October 1984): 4; and Joan Barthel, "Power to the Women!" *TV Guide* (13 August 1983): 11.

10. Philip Nobile, "TV News and the Older Woman," *New York* (10 August 1981): 15; Mary Alice Williams, interview with Gayle K. Yamada, New York City, 21 August 1986; and "AWRT '84 Tackles Opportunities and Problems for Women," *Broadcasting* 23, 106 (4 June 1984): 43.

11. Smith, "TV Newswoman's Suit," p. 44; and Paul Liberatore, "New Hope for the Anchorwomen," *San Francisco Chronicle* (10 August 1983): 5, 1P.

12. See Gayle K. Yamada, "Older Local Television Anchorwomen in Major Markets," Master's thesis, University of Florida, 1985, pp. 28-33; and Bruno Cohen, letter to Yamada, 24 April 1985.

13. Jerry Nachman, letter to Gayle K. Yamada, 22 April 1985; Steve Wasserman, letter to Yamada, 22 April 1985; and Sherlee Barish, interview with Yamada, New York City, 20 August 1986.

14. Ann Bishop, interview with Gayle K. Yamada, 5 June 1985, Miami; and Sylvia Rubin, "Anchorwoman: Is There Life After 40?" *San Francisco Chronicle* (20 October 1981): 38.

# 8 The Challenges of the 1980s

Women in broadcast journalism have come a long way since the days when they were relegated to "women's news." Today not only is it common for us to hear and see women reporting news, we do not hear many stories like the one CBS's Lesley Stahl tells about election night 1974. Finally included in the roundtable discussion on a political program, she walked onto a set and found the male correspondents had their names in front of their chairs— "Cronkite," "Mudd," and "Wallace." Hers said, "female."

But there is still a distance to travel to equality in broadcast news. Perhaps the broadest issue facing women in broadcast news today is power. It is only now that significant numbers of women have a decade or two or three of experience—the kind of experience that prepares them for top decision-making positions. With more qualified women in the talent pool, are they being promoted fairly? When will they break the barrier of the highest levels of news management and hold positions of power at the pinnacle of the newsroom pyramid? There are a few network vice presidents today and some female news directors, but their numbers do not remotely reflect the proportion of women in the work force.

## WOMEN IN NEWS MANAGEMENT

The network weeknight news anchors are all men. In the top on-air positions in the country, they symbolize what's happening behind the cameras and microphones. Men hold most of the very top news positions on both the local and national levels, and the last bastions of male dominance in broadcast news are the board rooms and presidencies. Even a notch below, at the vice presidential level, there are few women. Female news executives still are not common in the 1980s; large numbers of women are not in policy-setting positions at either the local or national level. While it is true that a few women were station managers in the early days of radio, such as Judith Waller, who was hired to run WMAQ, Chicago, they are the exceptions; women news executives have been even rarer.[1] It was not until 1973 that Stephanie Jo Rank was named news director of KHJ-TV, Los Angeles, becoming the first female television news director in a major market.

The U.S. Commission on Civil Rights documented the dearth of high-level women in news in the 1970s. But the figures are getting better. A 1985 survey of radio and television news directors found women in 10 percent of the commercial TV news directors' posts, up from just 1 percent in 1972. The radio results were just as encouraging: 21 percent were women, five times more than in 1972. Although the figures show women are making progress, "those gains, to date, have been less than the raw numbers suggest because a disproportionate number of women and minorities are heading news operations at low-staffed, low-budget independent stations."[2]

### A Reflection of Society

The status of women in news reflects a pattern in American society on the whole. A 1986 study concluded the top jobs in most U.S. companies are not being filled by women, that "women simply are not making it out of the middle ranks of management." In 1987, another study found virtually no change in the number of women in top management jobs in the past decade. "Until women are in top management positions in numbers," says CBS's Marlene Sanders—who was once a network news vice president—"we will never have our fair share of the jobs. That may take years. How long will probably depend on the progress women make in our overall society." Ed Joyce does not put a timetable on women in upper management. When he headed CBS News in 1984, he believed, "the scarcity of women at the top levels of CBS News is a reflection of the past, not of the present. . . . I don't see any reason why we shouldn't expect more women senior executives at CBS News in the future." At that time, he said 47 percent of the middle-management positions—the talent pool from which high executives are chosen—were held by women. But the very top jobs still are going to men.[3]

### "A Raffish Pursuit"

The attitudes toward women in broadcast news will change as women attain the power that reflects their numbers in society. When, in early 1986, a group of ABC News women discussed frustrations about women's status there— and lack of it—with boss Roone Arledge, correspondent Carole Simpson said, "He expressed interest. He pointed out that he really hadn't thought about it, and I think that's true. I don't think that they had thought about it and it's because no women were up there making them think about it." And Ed Joyce has conceded that broadcast news had always found a place for a few women who were stars. But below that level, our profession from the beginning has had a masculine frame of mind, occasioned perhaps by male dominance of the technical aspects of our work and also by the old belief that journalism is a swashbuckling and raffish pursuit that should be reserved to men alone. It has been particularly galling to women, I am sure, that they have not been readily granted equal access in a profession which is supposed to be more rational than most, more objective than most, and more vigilant than most concerning the principles of a democratic society.[4]

That there is progress is evident. That it is slow in coming can be argued. That more will come is yet to be seen, for like the issue of whether women will be allowed to age on the air, the waters are uncharted. That there is hope can be summed up by Natalea Brown, news director of WJZ-TV, Baltimore, who said at a women's resource panel at the 1986 Radio-Television News Directors Association meeting in Salt Lake City, "A few years ago someone asked me what the advantage of being a female news director was. I said there was never a line at the ladies' room when they had the breaks between the meetings. You know what? Yesterday, there was a line."[5]

### Different Paths

Those who are setting the standards for women in positions of power have gotten there in a variety of ways. So few women are in upper middle management that no career pattern has been established yet. Perhaps by examining the careers of some of the most successful we can better understand what it takes to succeed at the highest levels of management women have reached.

### Pamela Hill: From Researcher to Network Vice President

Pamela Hill is one of the most powerful women at ABC News. Vice president and executive producer of the "ABC News Closeup" documentary unit, she was handpicked by ABC News president Roone Arledge to head the division in 1979; she is the only female vice president at ABC-TV news and only the second woman in her position.

Born to a Buick dealer who "used to tell us girls we could be anything we wanted" and a woman who "taught us that the world of opportunity was in the East, where the arts were," Pamela Abel was born in Winchester, Indiana, on August 18, 1938. She grew up dreaming of adventure; "I didn't know any woman who had a career, but my fantasies were to *go* somewhere. Whenever I played with paper dolls, I had mine go to the Waldorf-Astoria."[6]

Hill's dream took the form of art, and she went to Bennington College in Vermont to study to be a painter. Soon her interests turned to contemporary

European history, and she spent her junior year abroad at the University of Glasgow in Scotland before getting her degree in 1960. After graduate work at the Universidad Autonoma de Mexico, she landed a job as a foreign affairs analyst with Nelson Rockefeller's presidential campaign, working for Henry Kissinger. She lived in New York with the man she had married, advertising executive David Hill. By 1965 the marriage was over, and Pam had custody of their three-year-old son, Christopher. And she was looking for another job, something that would combine her creative and intellectual abilities.

*Getting a Start.*    A television program provided the spark that launched Hill's documentary career. "I was one of those people who knew at a certain point instantly what I wanted to do. . . . I had seen Fred Freed's 'Decision to Drop the Bomb' [on Hiroshima] in 1964 on TV, and I thought I wanted to make documentary films."[7] So she got a job as a freelance researcher at NBC, working with Freed. Hill researched a documentary on which she later based a book, "United States Foreign Policy: 1945-1965." She moved up to associate producer in 1966 and three years later was the director of NBC's "White Paper" documentary unit. Hill wound up her career at NBC in 1972 as producer of Edwin Newman's weekly program, "Comment."

The eight years at NBC provided Hill with a strong base in documentaries. She learned a lot from Freed, who she considered a mentor. A personal relationship developed as well as the professional one and the two married in 1971; the following year they divorced. Freed died two years later.

Another figure who had a great influence on Hill was Aline Saarinen, a writer who had become a "Today" reporter and later, NBC's first female bureau chief. "She was an intellectual woman, and when I knew her, her husband was dead. And she had her own career and she was really an authority on the arts. And she lived alone, and she managed. And she basically instilled in me that I could do that, too."[8]

*Joins ABC.*    Hill switched networks in 1973, joining ABC News as the investigative documentary unit was formed. Her first program set a pattern for the type of work she would do there: "Fire" earned two Emmys, and the Peabody, duPont, and National Press Club awards. Nearly five years later, in January 1978, she was named executive producer of the network's documentary unit and the following January assumed the additional role of vice president.

> There was a female vice president before me [Marlene Sanders], and that was a factor in my being chosen, I think. It was not *the* factor, but it was a factor. I mean, it made it easier as Roone was building his own team to keep a woman in this job. The major factor was that Av Westin, who's always been like a mentor to me, was recommending me so strongly.

Hill has tackled a wide variety of issues in her documentaries at ABC, from youth gangs to homosexuality to Palestinian terrorists. She has won praise for her work, turning out what *Newsweek* magazine called, "some of the most provocative news programs since the golden age of Murrow."[9] Her programs also have sparked controversy. The Anti-defamation League of B'nai B'rith charged that "Terror in the Promised Land" was pro-Arab, and a former ABC News crew member alleged that gang scenes were staged in "Youth Terror." In the latter case, two separate investigations, by the FCC and an independent law firm ABC hired, found no merit to the charges.

*A Different Approach.*   On July 30, 1986, "Closeup" presented a documentary on how the women's movement has changed American society. Hill found she related to some of the findings; "I felt that first act was just almost mine, because [of] some of the issues we raised in that first act about women competing with men." One of those issues was

> male discomfort with women . . . at many different levels. And the most obvious level is what do you talk about when you go to lunch, you know, or how do you sort of pal around together—I mean, you're all working together and you're traveling together. How do you get into kind of an easy camaraderie?

Hill does not believe she has ever been discriminated against in broadcasting, and as a woman has never had problems with men in terms of "the sheer professional sense," of getting the work done. But at a deeper level, she says there are unacknowledged rivalries between the sexes that involve very different ways of doing things.

> I really do believe that women tend to operate more and have a team spirit. It comes out of a nurturing and the business of being mothers and raising families and holding families together. . . . The male ethic is much more a sort of an authoritative, singular . . . "Do it my way" approach, where the woman's approach is more sort of team-oriented, "Let's all get together and solve this problem. You know, we don't have to have winners and losers in all of this."

*A Middle Ground.*   The problems Hill encounters in her position stem from stylistic differences such as these and are often subtle.

> I feel problems of communication, differences in communication sometimes, with the men that I work with. I feel that there is, you know, from time to time, that double standard. . . . If you're tough you're a bitch and if you're not tough you're too soft. . . . And it's so hard to find that middle ground that's acceptable, you know, in terms of a management style.

The women who Hill believes are most likely to succeed in the competitive business of broadcast news are those who are professionally detached and bring the least amount of traditional psychological baggage to their jobs.

> And by that I really mean inhibitions about competing and inhibitions about beating men. . . . It took me a long time to understand that. Once I had some successes I somehow thought that they would be etched in stone. . . . But of course that's not true, you know. Things are crumbling and being rebuilt every day, and in an organization, it's just a giant group of squeaky wheels all the time and everybody's in some sort of pull and tug relationship with regard to everyone else . . . and you have to be very competitive.

That Pam Hill seeks competition and challenge is apparent in her manner. She is an intense, energetic woman, who gives the impression that her mind is moving faster than she can speak. At the same time there is a vulnerability about her and a sense of honesty about her fears and her need to succeed. "I think a lot of what I've achieved has come out of a fierce insecurity," she once said, and she used to wear a gold bracelet inscribed, "Damn I'm Good."[11] But she shed it as her confidence grew and, though she still runs somewhat on insecurity, it's "not so much. . . . I have a better sense now of if I like a program and the critics don't like it, it's all right. I still like it. . . . I think I work a lot more out of just the passion for doing it." But in the competitive world of network news, "one would be wrong to ever totally give up fear as a motivation."

Fear is a motivator for women, says Hill, because "they're not used to success." When she first headed up the documentary unit at ABC, she was "obsessive" about her job. "I was so eager to do well in this job that I just said to my family, 'You'll excuse me, but I'm taking a vacation for three years. I'm going to make this job work.' "

*A Dual Media Marriage.*   Hill's present family consists of novelist and *New York Times* columnist Tom Wicker—they married March 9, 1974—her son Chris, stepdaughters Kaycee and Lisa Freed, and Tom's daughter Cameron and son Grey. Hill and Wicker have had to balance two successful careers, and the adjustment has not always been easy. It was hardest, says Hill, the first couple of years, because Wicker's first wife had stayed at home, while Hill was often away on assignment.

> I was just getting going on documentaries at that moment, and I wasn't thinking about anything but those shows and whether or not they were going to be good. There was a period of his being quite angry and my not even wanting to deal with that because my view was that I couldn't take the energy away from my shows to be angry. I eventually decided that my marriage was important enough that I didn't want to work twenty-four hours a day.[10]

Now that Hill is in charge of documentaries, Wicker says there is less of an around-the-clock pattern. He also has come to understand those kinds of hours are part of the industry. In fact, their work has drawn them together.

> I think it's fair to say she relies on me a lot for the really broad questions of her work: Do I think it's a good idea to do a film on this subject? Is it fair to make

a statement about something? And she takes considerable interest in my books. She's a very tough editor and doesn't spare my feelings.[11]

*A Better Balance.*    Looking back on the sacrifices her career has meant for her family and herself personally, Hill says she would have tried to seek a better balance of home and work. It is one of the qualities traditionally associated with women in the family that gives Hill one of her greatest pleasures in her work—a very "female view of the work force." Aside from the programs themselves, Hill enjoys "nurturing talent. . . . It's a pleasure to see people you've hired develop and grow themselves"; she also enjoys mixing and matching talents, "putting together teams that work."

The notion of helping others, of networking, is more interesting to Hill these days. As she has moved up the corporate ladder she has found that women need each other morally and professionally to progress. She believes networking will lead to more advances for women in broadcast news.

> As much as there have been numerous successes in terms of women coming into broadcasting and in journalism in general, at the very top you've still got that very male society. It's going to be the really remarkable woman who breaks through and becomes the president of a news division . . . and I don't see that happening very soon. I see it happening after there are more women at the vice presidential level and there's more networking involved among women.

### Barbara Cohen: From Newspapers to Broadcast Management

The executive producer of "Meet the Press," Barbara Cohen was with the *Washington Star* for ten years and then news director of National Public Radio before taking her present position. Born June 16, 1945, in Akron, Ohio, Barbara Stubbs was editor of the Swarthmore College paper. She graduated with an English degree in 1967, and went on to get her M.A. in journalism from Columbia University. There she fell in love with fellow student Richard Cohen. When he got a job on the *Washington Post*, she looked for one in the nation's capital, too, and landed one on the rival *Star*'s copy desk. They got married, and she moved up the ladder quickly at the *Star*, taking time out to have a baby in 1972.

Cohen was named national editor in 1974, and managing editor in 1978. But with the paper facing financial difficulties, Cohen listened when NPR chief Frank Mankiewicz sought her to head the expanding news operation.

> Frank was holding out an organization where I really would be in charge. I would get to make the decisions and to do things as I wanted to do them. It seemed to be an organization that could use the experience I had, even though I didn't know anything about broadcasting. And it was growing. They were about to start a new morning news program and expand the staff. And so instead of dealing with an atmosphere where we were shrinking and scrimping and saving, I could go into a situation that was growing and thriving and seemed to be on its way up.[12]

After joining NPR in 1979, Cohen doubled the size of the news staff to a hundred and launched "Morning Edition" to complement NPR's highly acclaimed afternoon news program, "All Things Considered." The freedom to create appealed to her.

> The reason I love National Public Radio is because it is a superb arena in which to practice professional journalism. You have the luxury of time; you have the luxury of not having to fight someone about having to bump commercials, and as long as you have the resources, you can do as much as you want to do.[13]

In 1982, Cohen was named NPR's vice president of news. But the public broadcasting network was in serious financial trouble, and the resources were drying up; in fact, NPR faced a huge deficit. During the difficult budget-cutting sessions, it seemed being a woman made a difference. "I felt I was subjected to a much tougher standard because there was an assumption that I was just a feather-headed woman who really didn't understand the budget or do what had to be done to get the budget in line."

Cohen had been approached by NBC before the bad budget news arrived. When a second wave of cuts was ordered, Cohen decided to accept NBC's offer to become manager of the network's political unit in Washington. Coming from the pro-female atmosphere of NPR, Cohen noted the difference in the more traditional male-clubbiness environment at NBC.

Cohen hesitates to make generalizations about the differences between male and female managers.

> I will say one thing. You don't find unqualified women managers. For women to get into management positions, they generally have to be not only good, but better than the men with whom they compete for those positions. Sometimes you do find a man in a management position who is not very well suited for the position he has.

In May 1985, Cohen was named executive producer of "Meet the Press," the longest-running program on network television. One thing has been constant during her dual media marriage: she believes that her husband's career as a columnist for the *Post* complements her own. Like Pam Hill and Tom Wicker, Barbara and Richard Cohen benefit from bouncing story ideas off one another. "And if there is a late breaking something or other you don't have to explain to your spouse why you can't be home to cook dinner."

### Mary Alice Williams: From Rookie Reporter to Vice President

She works for "the kingpin of good old boys," heading up the New York bureau of Ted Turner's Cable News Network and co-anchoring a nightly newscast.[14] Mary Alice Williams, one of two female vice presidents at CNN, knew she wanted to be in news when she was a teenager and got into the business right out of high school.

Mary Alice Williams spends most of her day as an executive with Cable News Network, then anchors from New York on the twenty-four-hour news service. Williams is one of a handful of women at the vice-presidential level in network broadcasting. Courtesy CNN.

Williams grew up in Minneapolis, where she was born in 1949. At the age
of eighteen, she landed a reporting job at KSTP-TV, Minneapolis-St. Paul.

> I suspect that a number of things came into play. First of all, that I was a woman
> who actually was applying for a job, a breathing person with a pumping heart of
> the female persuasion who they could put on the air. That was one. But also
> maybe it was I was certainly non-threatening . . . because I was young and
> had a lot to learn. . . . My air presence was utterly non-threatening because I
> was 165 pounds and had a high soprano voice.[15]

Williams spent the next four years commuting from Creighton University
in Omaha, Nebraska—student fares were only $12.50 round-trip—to work
at KSTP during weekends, school breaks, and summer vacations. She found
the newsroom veterans—they were all men—went out of their way to help
her.

> I was the age of some of their daughters, so maybe that was an advantage, you
> know. A lot of them were really very paternal toward me and really took the
> time after their normal working hours to sit me down and say, "Do it this way.
> Let's learn how to write that way. Perhaps this is a better way to do this."

Many of the stories Williams covered in those early days were on the "woman's beat," from azalea festivals to turkey gobbling contests. Then she
found herself in a unique position,

> when young people were *the* story, when everything that was happening with
> the youth movement, whether it was rock festivals or marches against Vietnam
> or the front line of the women's movement, it was all happening in '68. And it
> was wise for a station to take a basically enthusiastic young woman with a modi-
> cum of intelligence who could report on her own species, which is what I was
> doing. . . . So while they may have hired me just because of my plumbing, or
> perhaps because I was non-threatening, and let me cut my teeth on dumb-o
> stories that didn't matter one way or the other whether they had to blow them
> off because they simply weren't good enough to put on the air, suddenly I be-
> came an enormous asset to them because I understood what those kids were
> doing out there.

*First Management Position.*    After her graduation in 1971 with a degree
in English and political science and a minor in journalism, Williams was
hired full time to produce the early evening newscast at KSTP. Eventually
she was promoted to executive director, in charge of all the newscasts. Her
top salary: $4,700 a year, while her writers and producers—all men—made
$15,000 and $16,000. Although she might have not been earning what men
in lesser positions were, she didn't see her gender as a stumbling block.
*Everyone Wins or Loses.*    Perhaps the most memorable experience for
Williams at KSTP was the team effort that went into the newscasts. When
she began, there were only six people in the newsroom, and "with that small a

group, everyone has an investment in everyone else's success. If the producer falls down and screws up on the air, the reporters whose pieces go into
that program, the anchors whose faces are on that program, don't look
good.'' As a result, Williams says she didn't have any trouble as a young
woman supervising older men—she just asked them to help her. "It was a
very small family. We all knew each other and each others' wives and children and sisters and brothers and parents."

*New York Beckons.*    Williams left the Midwest for the bright lights of
New York. She became executive producer at WPIX-TV at the age of twenty-
three and the following year got a call from WNBC-TV across town, which
was getting ready to debut its two-hour newscast. After interviewing with
several people there, she told them she never wanted to produce another
newscast, and the station hired her as a reporter instead, at an annual salary
of $20,000. Six months later, she says, WNBC tore up her contract and paid
her what the top male reporter was making.

The next five years Williams spent covering all sorts of stories, from political conventions to the aftermath of flooding in Pennsylvania; she also anchored the morning news. Then, in 1979, Ted Turner's upstart network tapped
her to set up its second largest bureau, New York.

*No Bad Habits.*    The advent of cable news opened opportunities, not
just for women but for everyone in broadcast journalism.

> Early on, when we had no money and an idea that we were going to do this in-
> credibly outlandish thing, I mean, producing twenty-four hours of news
> . . . we needed a lot of people who were going to work very hard who were
> willing to make it by dint of their own will, and who could do it for very little
> money. The people who fit that description, as it happens, were women, just
> because women at that time were willing to take less money.

Williams saw 400 women's resumes every week to 50 men's. Pay wasn't
the only factor though; she believes CNN attracted more women because it
was an unknown,

> and I think women are more willing to go into something unknown, something
> that doesn't have an absolute guarantee along with it, than men. Men in our
> generation, baby boom, post-baby boom generation, were brought up to think
> that they carried the burden of being the breadwinner and had to start a career
> path and a corporate pattern and study learning curves and stuff like that.
> Women tend to be more entrepreneurial.

The net effect was that when CNN debuted June 1, 1980, it "didn't have to
break any bad habits''—half its staff was women. Although that staff is not
the small one Williams knew at KSTP, she tries to create the same atmosphere in the New York operation that she had known in Minneapolis.

In addition to her responsibilities as bureau chief, Williams co-anchors "Newswatch" every night, from 5 to 6:30 P.M. Eastern time. It is dual duty she chose. She sees a very optimistic future for women in both of her roles.

> Women were not in the business in numbers until twenty years after men were. So just in terms of earning your stripes, being a veteran . . . we are just now getting to the age where we have the veteranhood, if you will, and clout to get into management positions or very, very top air positions. Men have been at it a lot longer. . . . I see it happening. It's going to happen slowly.

The way it will happen, says Williams, is for the women paving the way to show it can be done, and done well.

> What I did at the very beginning—I mean, poor Ted [Turner, founder of CNN] didn't even know I was a girl! Nobody told him. And so we faced off. And ever since, you know, I learned immediately that when I go into board meetings with the division budget, it is wham, wham, this is what we've done, this is what we need, this is what I can deliver to you, period. I never had another problem with anyone there. Sometimes you just have to face it off. But the way you do it—do the best you can, do your homework before the meeting begins, and they can't question you on it.[16]

Williams has had to adjust some of the ideas about women's roles with which she was raised and sometimes mulls over the decisions she makes. She feels an enormous amount of pressure to succeed—she was named a CNN vice president in 1982, when she was only in her early thirties. Part of that pressure comes from herself, but she also feels "those of us in management are under a terrible weight of others' expectations of us."

## Anna Mae Sokusky: From Secretary to Executive

A woman who followed the secretarial route to the newsroom and eventually to the executive suite is Anna Mae Sokusky. As a graduate from D'Youville College in Buffalo, New York, Sokusky headed west to San Francisco, where she worked several temporary jobs before joining KCBS-AM as a secretary/publicist in the all-news station's two-person promotions department.

Sokusky was born in May 1947 in Philadelphia and received her education at all-girl Catholic schools. In college she majored in speech and drama and was editor of her campus paper. A significant qualification for her first job at KCBS was that she could spell, for the station's press releases had been going out with errors in them. Soon she moved to a secretarial position in the sales department where she helped write sales proposals and learned how to read a ratings book. Then it was on to assist the editorial director and the chief engineer before becoming secretary to the general manager. By that time, she had a pretty good working knowledge of the station and was fortunate to have as general manager Neil Derrough. He was an open administrator who welcomed questions, and Sokusky was not shy about asking them. When Derrough left to continue a climb up the corporate ladder at CBS, Sokusky started eyeing the newsroom. She took a pay cut in late 1971 to become a desk assistant—someone who made beat checks, answered phones, ripped wire copy, and made coffee.

*"A Person and a Half."*   The news department had an unusual number of women on staff then, largely due to hires made in the previous two years by news director Jim Simon, who had been known to say that hiring a woman meant he'd have a person and a half because women worked so hard. Heidi Schulman, Sharron Lovejoy, and Nancy Herr were beginning on-air careers that would take them on to network jobs. A half-dozen other women worked behind the scenes. In general, all-news stations provided great opportunities for women because there were so many jobs to be filled. The experimental formats of some of the first all-news stations included segments on women's sports and the women's movement.

Sokusky remembers some ill will about pressure to hire ethnic minorities in the early seventies at KCBS but does not recall any resentment about the increased number of women on the news staff. As she rose from desk assistant to editor and then managing editor, she did get a sense that women might not be paid equally with men. When she became part of management and had access to salary information, it turned out to be true in some cases.

As an editor, Sokusky also got some on-air experience. She became a substitute traffic reporter and was honored with an "Anna Mae Sokusky Fan Club." She also started a report on women in 1974, preparing two brief segments weekly, mostly on her own time. In 1975, Sokusky left KCBS to become executive producer of the network's news service for its AM stations. She supervised a small Washington staff and was responsible for coordinating a group of features sent out weekly to the owned stations.

About six months after Sokusky took the position, the news directors of the CBS-owned stations met to discuss new ideas for features. She presented them with demonstration tapes similar to her KCBS reports on women. The news directors thought it was a broadcast they could use, and she began a decade of producing five segments a week, heard on up to twenty major stations around the country. In the last year or two of the reports, their title was changed to "Lifestyle Reports," because Sokusky felt that many of the issues women had initiated were now the concerns of both men and women.

*Joining the Club.*   Sokusky stopped doing the reports when she was promoted to executive director of news, CBS-owned AM radio stations. Now she concentrates on aiding the management of the local stations, most of which are still all-news or news-talk operations. Her duties include in-house consulting and recruiting. Sokusky's boss is now a woman, vice president for AM stations Nancy Widman. And as she travels around the country, Sokusky finds that others consider her to be a role model. While at KNX in Los Angeles, a female anchor told Sokusky that she had never had a conversation with a network executive in the ladies room before.

Why did Sokusky become an executive? She isn't afraid to lead. That, she feels, goes all the way back to her childhood.

> I had a lot of things going for me that made me independent growing up. I was the oldest daughter, and for eight years, an only child. I went to Catholic schools and my high school and college experiences were in all-female environments. If I went to a mixed school, would I have been more reticent about being on the debate team, would I have been more reticent about taking a leadership post on the college newspaper? Perhaps I would have been. I think when you're in those environments, you don't need permission to be different because you're not different. . . . I was acclimatized not to fear leadership positions.[17]

As for hurdles for women, Sokusky finds that the old boy network still exists but feels that she's been allowed to join the club.

> We are reaching that point where the generations are beginning to change. I'm now at the midpoint in my career. I see now that the old guard, and perhaps the more conservative men of the business, they're moving out. So the older way of thinking is moving out. And the old boy network is changing. I'm in the old boy network.

When asked if a woman can become president of CBS News, Sokusky points to Joan Richman, senior vice president for special events in the news division, as a candidate. Still, she believes that a woman seeking a top network job will not be judged solely on accomplishments as a man would be, but will have to offer other proof because she is a woman. Another factor is competition. "Now there are more managerial women, more talent women, who have come from the basement and are now on the third floor. As the pinnacle narrows, the competition is going to get tighter for all of us, men and women."

### Bonnie Chastain: From Board Operator to News Director

While a woman going from a secretarial position to news management is not all that rare, an engineering route to news director is almost unheard of. Engineering seemed to be the last male bastion to fall, and whatever inroads had been made during World War II had long since eroded by the time women started being seen in numbers in news and other professional areas of broadcasting.

Bonnie Chastain is an example of a housewife who entered the work force in broadcasting, as well as of a woman who started on the technical side and is now a news director. She had been married right out of high school in Ohio and twelve years later moved to California with her husband and three children.

In 1968, against her husband's wishes, Chastain went to the College of San Mateo. An outstanding student in elementary and high school, she got into radio and television courses because of her interest in music. She thought being a disc jockey on campus radio station KCSM might be interesting and took a third-class radio telephone instruction course to get the license required to be a board operator. KCSM had a strong broadcasting program headed up by Dan Odom. The courses offered included a much more difficult first-class radio telephone license sequence, which Chastain also took.

*"The He's a She."*   When her marriage faltered, Chastain asked Odom for some academic and career advice. She had planned to transfer to San Jose State and was hoping to become a lawyer. But with a divorce on the way, a job was more important, and Odom was able to recommend Chastain to KCBS chief engineer Howard Immekus. Several former College of San Mateo students had worked out well as technicians at the station, and when Odom added that he had a minority for KCBS to consider, Immekus was interested. There might be a job for the candidate, but Immekus said he had to be able to handle the duties right away for there was no time for training. Odom expressed confidence the candidate could step right in, but added, "The he's a she."

KCBS had never had a female technician, but Chastain was hired. She never felt any sexism from the eighteen men on the technical staff. The older engineers especially went out of their way to train her, for Chastain had a lot to learn. She caught on so quickly that within a year she was handling drive time shifts and was considered a magician at editing tape.

Chastain says she did feel pressure, most of it self-imposed. For one thing, she didn't want to disappoint Odom, who had put his reputation on the line in helping her land the job. And, says Chastain, there was a greater motivation. "Financially, I had to have that job. It meant the difference in keeping custody of the children or having them live with their father."[18]

Chastain was named a back-up traffic reporter for the station in 1975 and left in 1977 to take a vacation relief news position at KSFO-AM. That became a permanent appointment, and Chastain moved up to morning drive newscasts and then, in 1982, to co-host of the morning show at $75,000 a year. When the station was sold, Chastain was out of a job. But she did vacation relief as a talk show host on KGO radio in San Francisco and KEEN and KBAY in San Jose. When Bonneville Broadcasting established an experimental "yuppie" format on KXLR-AM in San Francisco in 1985, Chastain became a news anchor. After the format failed to attract ratings, the call letters were changed, but Chastain stayed on as the news director and morning drive anchor of KOIT-AM-FM. Her morning schedule makes it somewhat difficult to spend time with her husband, Dave McElhatton. The co-anchor for KPIX-TV's 6 and 11 P.M. weeknight newscasts, he gets home from work about three and a half hours before she gets up to be at work by 4:30 A.M.

### Carolyn Wean: From Producer to General Manager

All McElhatton has to do to see the next rung of the ladder for women news directors is look to his general manager's office. Carolyn Wean is the vice president and general manager at KPIX, her second general manager post for Westinghouse. Wean has been with the corporation for seventeen years, starting out as a talk show producer at WBZ-TV in Boston in 1970. Born in Baltimore, Wean studied history and foreign languages at Washington College in Maryland. She did graduate work at Northeastern University in Boston.

From WBZ she moved to WJZ-TV, Baltimore, where she was a news producer and then executive news producer. In 1977, she became news director of KDKA-TV, Pittsburgh, and two years later joined KYW-TV, Philadelphia, in the same capacity. As a news director, she was able to gain valuable experience with budgets, promotion, and engineering. That helped when, at the age of thirty-six, she became a station manager at KDKA, adding the vice president's title two years later. Wean joined KPIX in February 1986.

Wean finds being a woman in the manager's office "affords a great deal of visibility that can help you, but where your failures are also more visible.[19] She notes that upper management in large broadcasting corporations is sparsely populated by women and is concerned that the number of women becoming eligible for top management jobs is still very small.

### THE FUTURE

The issues facing the broadcast industry are problems American society must confront as a whole. As Barbara Cohen observes, "Men are coping with the integration of family life and working life as much now as women are." While broadcasting is becoming more responsive to business concerns, it continues to fulfill its role of illuminating our society. The gains for women in broadcast journalism will more closely conform to women's progress in general, and the importance of reporting those changes will be more crucial than ever.

Aside from moving into news management, equal pay and aging on the air seem to be the key arenas for advancement by women in broadcast news as we move toward the year 2000. Equal pay in this field may differ from other parts of corporate America when considered in light of the operating philosophies most managers have about women in newsrooms and especially on the air. The aging of women on the air will be the most visible battle in the next decade; all you have to do is turn on your radio or TV to learn how it goes.

## NOTES

1. For more on Waller, see Catharine Heinz, "The Voice of Authority, or, Hurrah for Christine Craft," *Feedback* 25, 4 (Spring 1984): 3-6; for a list of other early women radio managers, see "The First Fifty Years: And They Call Broadcasting a Man's Game!" *Broadcasting* 99, 20 (17 November 1980): 74.

2. See two reports prepared by the U.S. Commission on Civil Rights, *Window Dressing on the Set: Women and Minorities in Television* (Washington, D.C.: U.S. Government Printing Office, August 1977), and *Window Dressing on the Set: An Update* (Washington, D.C.: U.S. Government Printing Office, January 1979); and Vernon A. Stone, "Women Hold Almost a Third of News Jobs," *RTNDA Communicator* (Washington, D.C.: Radio-Television News Directors Association, April 1986): 30.

3. "Top Jobs Still Eluding Women," *San Jose Mercury News* (19 September 1986): 5E; Mary Ann Von Glinow, "Why American Women Still Aren't Making It to the Top," *San Francisco Chronicle* (9 March 1987): 27; Marlene Sanders, "Women in TV News—Where We've Been and Where We're Going," *Television Quarterly* 18 (Spring 1981): 56; and Edward M. Joyce, remarks presented to the Annual Convention of the American Women in Radio and Television, Chicago, 30 May 1984.

4. "The Phil Donahue Show," transcript #12115, Multimedia Entertainment, Inc., Cincinnati, 1984, p. 2; Joyce remarks.

5. "Women's Resource Center: Managing Success," Seminar at the forty-first annual Radio-Television News Directors Association convention, Salt Lake City, 28 August 1986.

6. Kristin McMurran, "Pamela Hill," *People* (26 July 1982): 49-50.

7. "ABC's Pam Hill: Making News with Her Documentaries," *Broadcasting* 97, 17 (22 October 1979): 97.

8. Unless otherwise stated, all quotations from Pamela Hill are from an interview with Gayle K. Yamada, New York City, 22 August 1986.

9. Harry F. Waters, "Documentary Woman," *Newsweek* (17 December 1979): 87.

10. Christine Doudna, "How a Marriage Has Survived Two Hectic Lives," *San Francisco Chronicle* (14 September 1981): 13.

11. Ibid.

12. Unless otherwise stated, all quotations from Barbara Cohen are from a telephone interview with Gayle K. Yamada, 24 September 1986.

13. "NPR's Barbara Cohen: From Printer's Ink to Radio with Elan," *Broadcasting* 100, 19 (11 May 1981): 103.

14. Mary Alice Williams at RTNDA Seminar.

15. Unless otherwise stated, all quotations from Mary Alice Williams are from an interview with Gayle K. Yamada, New York City, 21 August 1986.

16. Williams, RTNDA Seminar.

17. Unless otherwise stated, all quotations from Anna Mae Sokusky are from an interview with authors, Salt Lake City, 27 August 1986.

18. Bonnie Chastain, telephone interview with David H. Hosley, 10 September 1986.

19. Edmund M. Rosenthal, "At Least Thirteen Women Now in Top Jobs at Television Stations," *Television/Radio Age* (28 April 1986): 90.

# Selected Bibliography

## BOOKS

Barnouw, Erik. *The Golden Web: A History of Broadcasting in the United States, 1933-1953*. New York: Oxford University Press, 1968.

———. *The Image Empire: A History of Broadcasting in the United States from 1953*. New York: Oxford University Press, 1970.

———. *A Tower in Babel: A History of Broadcasting in the United States to 1933*. New York: Oxford University Press, 1966.

Barrett, Marvin, ed. *A State of Siege: Survey of Broadcast Journalism, 1970-71*. New York: Columbia University Graduate School of Journalism, 1971.

Beasley, Maurine, and Sheila Gibbons. *Women in Media: A Documentary Sourcebook*. Washington, D.C.: Women's Institute for the Freedom of the Press, 1977.

Brown, Donald E., and John Paul Jones. *Radio and Television News*. New York: Rinehart & Company, 1954.

Butler, Matilda, and William Paisley. *Women and the Mass Media*. New York: Human Sciences Press, 1980.

Cantril, Hadley, and Gordon W. Allport. *The Psychology of Radio*. New York: Harper, 1935.

Ceulemans, Mieke, and Guido Faucounier. *Mass Media: The Image, Role and Social Conditions of Women*. Paris: UNESCO, 1979.

*Contemporary Authors*. Vol. 49. Detroit: Gale Research, 1975.

Dunning, John. *Tune in Yesterday: The Ultimate Encyclopedia of Oldtime Radio, 1925-1976*. Englewood Cliffs, N.J.: Prentice-Hall, 1976.

Fang, Irving E. *Television News*. New York: Hastings House, 1972.

———. *Those Radio Commentators*. Ames, Iowa: Iowa State University, 1977.

Gallagher, Margaret. *Unequal Opportunities*. Paris: UNESCO, 1981.

Harrington, Ruth Lee. *Your Opportunities in Television*. New York: Medill McBride, 1949.

Hewitt, Don. *Minute By Minute. . . .* New York: Random House, 1985.

Hiett, Helen. *No Matter Where*. New York: Dutton, 1944.

Hosley, David H. *As Good as Any: Foreign Correspondence on American Radio, 1930-1940*. Westport, Conn.: Greenwood Press, 1984.

Jordan, Max. *Beyond All Fronts: A Bystander's Notes on This Thirty Years War.* Milwaukee: Bruce, 1944.

Knight, Ruth. *Stand by for the Ladies.* New York: Coward-McCann, 1939.

Love, Barbara J., ed. *Foremost Women in Communication.* New York: Foremost Americans Publishing, 1970.

McBride, Mary Margaret. *A Long Way from Missouri.* New York: G. P. Putnam's Sons, 1959.

————. *Out of the Air.* Garden City, N.Y.: Doubleday, 1960.

Marzolf, Marion Tuttle. *Up from the Footnote: A History of Women Journalists.* New York: Hastings House, 1977.

Matney, William C., ed. *Who's Who among Black Americans.* 4th ed. Lake Forest, Ill.: Illinois Educational Communications, 1985.

*The National Cyclopaedia of American Biography.* Vol. E. New York: James T. White, 1938.

Powers, Ron. *The Newscasters.* New York: St. Martin's Press, 1977.

Quinlan, Sterling. *Inside ABC: American Broadcasting Company's Rise to Power.* New York: Hastings House, 1979.

Schlipp, Madelon Golden, and Sharon M. Murphy. *Great Women of the Press.* Carbondale: Southern Illinois University Press, 1983.

Stein, M. L. *Blacks in Communications.* New York: Julian Messner, 1972.

White, Paul W. *News on the Air.* New York: Harcourt, Brace, 1947.

*Who's Who in the Midwest.* Chicago: Marquis, 1986.

*Who's Who of American Women.* 3d ed. Chicago: Marquis, 1964.

*Who's Who of American Women.* 8th ed. Chicago: Marquis, 1974.

*Who's Who of American Women.* Vol. 13. Chicago: Marquis, 1984.

*Who's Who in America, 1984-1985.* 43d ed. Chicago: Marquis, 1984.

*Who's Who Overseas Press Club of America, 1962-63.* New York: Overseas Press Club, 1962.

## NEWSPAPERS

*Bangor* (Me.) *Daily News.* 5 July 1985.

*Chicago Tribune.* 13 December 1972.

*Detroit News.* 8 November 1982.

*Grand Haven* (Mich.) *Tribune.* 18-20 May 1983.

*Los Angeles Times.* 7 August 1974; 18 June 1976; 12 May 1977; 12 November 1978; 16 January 1979; 9 May 1979; 20 June 1981; 1 December 1981; 26 December 1982; 14 January 1983; 24 September 1983; 20 March 1985; 11 July 1985; 21 October 1985; 14 December 1985; 5 March 1986.

*Miami Herald.* 30 August 1986.

*New York Times.* 21 June 1941; 8 June 1949; 23 August 1961; 8 October 1961; 7 May 1965; 5 July 1965; 7 January 1967; 19 June 1968; 6 January 1969; 9 February 1970; 1 March 1970; 13 August 1970; 19 May 1971; 14 July 1971; 13 June 1972; 15 July 1972; 8 February 1973; 16 February 1973; 28 June 1973; 20 July 1973; 17 March 1974; 2 December 1974; 24 January 1975; 22 September 1976; 17 October 1976; 24 November 1976; 21 December 1976; 3 January 1977; 13 February 1977; 17 February 1977; 24 February 1977; 16 July 1977;

12 November 1979; 17 January 1980; 4 February 1980; 3 August 1981; 9 September 1981; 27 July 1983; 28 July 1983; 29 July 1983; 30 July 1983; 2 August 1983; 5 August 1983; 9 August 1983; 11 August 1983; 1 September 1983; 7 September 1983; 21 October 1983; 25 October 1983; 1 November 1983; 12 May 1984; 11 September 1984; 21 September 1984; 29 June 1985; 3 July 1985; 4 March 1986.

*San Francisco Chronicle.* 31 January 1977; 3 December 1978; 16 April 1979; 29 January 1981; 30 January 1981; 7 February 1981; 11 February 1981; 14 May 1984; 11 July 1984; 15 May 1985; 12 June 1985; 22 December 1985; 26 June 1986; 4 March 1987.

*San Francisco Examiner.* 7 August 1986.

*San Jose Mercury News.* 11 September 1986.

*Washington Post.* 5 October 1972; 7 June 1985.

*Washington Star.* 14 June 1977.

## PERIODICALS

"Anchorwoman Charges Metromedia with Bias." *Jet,* 11 June 1984, 26.

"Apologia pro Sally Quinn." *Broadcasting,* 28 July 1975, 34.

"AWRT Reviews Broad Spectrum of Issues in Toronto." *Broadcasting,* 9 May 1983, 31-33.

Bachrach, Judy. "Gorgeous George." *New Republic,* 10 June 1985, 28-29.

"Bah-bar-ah's Bow." *Time,* 18 October 1976, 61.

Ball, Aimee Lee. "Jane Pauley and Sandy Hill: This Is Your Life." *Redbook,* November 1977, 94 + .

"Barbara Jill Walters: Not for Women Only." *Broadcasting,* 28 July 1975, 57.

"Barbara Walters in First Week: 3.1 Rating Gain for ABC-TV News." *Broadcasting,* 18 October 1976, 54-55.

"Barbara Walters to AWRT 23rd Annual Convention, New York." *Advertising Age,* 20 May 1974, 6.

"Barbara's Heir." *Forbes,* 1 October 1977, 102.

Barrett, Mary Ellin. "Keeping Up with Barbara Walters." *Cosmopolitan,* June 1982, 21.

Barthel, Joan. "He Gets Richard Burton, She Gets an Expert on Lice." *TV Guide,* 11 June 1983, 35 + .

_____. "Network Newswomen Explain Why There Are Still No Female Dan Rathers." *TV Guide,* 6 August 1983.

Battiata, Mary. "Lesley Stahl." *Washington Journalism Review,* October 1982, 43-46.

"Behind the Mike." *Broadcasting,* 15 September 1941, 32.

"Behind the Mike." *Broadcasting,* 21 September 1942, 42.

"Behind the Mike." *Broadcasting,* 22 March 1943, 30.

"Behind the Mike." *Broadcasting,* 26 April 1943, 78.

"Behind the Mike." *Broadcasting,* 7 June 1943, 34.

"Behind the Mike." *Broadcasting,* 5 June 1944, 48.

"Behind the Mike." *Broadcasting,* 26 July 1944, 44.

Berman, Claire. "TV's Female Brain Trust." *Good Housekeeping,* July 1965, 42.

"Bias Against Women Charged to NBC." *Broadcasting,* 15 November 1971, 41.

"Brief Encounter: Diane Sawyer." *Esquire,* July 1982, 68-70.

Brinley, Maryann Bucknum. "Jane Pauley: The Frustrations of a Working Mother." *McCall's,* November 1984, 68.

*Broadcasting,* 15 July 1939, 11.

*Broadcasting,* 1 June 1940, 45.

*Broadcasting,* 23 June 1941, 14.

*Broadcasting,* 3 August 1942, 16.

*Broadcasting,* 1 February 1943, 22.

*Broadcasting,* 15 March 1943, 51.

*Broadcasting,* 22 November 1943, 58.

*Broadcasting,* 5 June 1944, 48.

*Broadcasting,* 24 July 1944, 48.

*Broadcasting,* 16 July 1945, 79.

*Broadcasting,* 3 March 1947, 53.

*Broadcasting,* 3 December 1973, 46.

*Broadcasting,* 8 December 1980, 33.

"By George, She's Gorgeous." *Woman's Day,* 15 October 1985, 83 +.

Carter, Betsy, and Lucy Howard. "NBC's Golden Girl: J. Savitch." *Newsweek,* 15 January 1979, 86.

"Catching Up: Negro Reporters." *Newsweek,* 4 December 1967, 96 +.

Cathcart, William L. "Viewer Needs and Desires in Television Newscasters." *Journal of Broadcasting* 26, no. 1, Winter 1969-1970: 487-91.

"Catherine Mackin (Obituary)." *Time,* 29 November 1982, 97.

"Catherine Mackin (Obituary)." *Variety,* 24 November 1982, 108.

"CBS Morning Blues." *Newsweek,* 20 August 1973, 65.

"CBS Rebuilding Morning News Show." *Broadcasting,* 4 December 1978, 49 +.

"CBS Taps Stahl, 'Super Woman,' as 'Nation' Host." *Variety,* 3 August 1983, 45, 57.

"CCR Remains Down on EEO at Stations." *Broadcasting,* 21 May 1979, 74-75.

Christopher, Maurine. "AWRT to Keep Pressure for Equality." *Advertising Age,* 20 May 1974, 6.

"Closed Circuit: Everybody Wins." *Broadcasting,* 11 October 1976, 5.

"Closed Circuit: Hometown Girl." *Broadcasting,* 10 December 1973, 5.

Conant, Jennet. "Waking Up with Maria Shriver." *Rolling Stone,* 30 January 1986, 23-24.

"Connie Chung, Reporter." *Jade* 2, no. 2, Winter 1974, 12-13.

"Court Orders Another FCC Look at L.A. Discrimination Cases." *Broadcasting,* 25 September 1978, 54.

"CPB Study Finds Women Underused and Underserved." *Broadcasting,* 24 November 1975, 31-32.

Craft, Christine. "How I Found the Courage to Make Waves." *Glamour,* November 1983, 92.

———. "The Marketing of TV News." *Ms.,* November 1983, 134.

"Craft Decision Leaves Questions." *Broadcasting,* 15 August 1983, 28-30.

"Craft Goes on Stump to Raise Funds for Suit Against Metromedia." *Broadcasting,* 30 April 1984, 136.

"Critiquing the Craft Case." *Broadcasting,* 26 September 1983, 32-33.

*Current Biography,* 1971, 432-34.

*Current Biography,* 1981, 352-54.

Eisenberg, Lawrence. "Diane Sawyer: What Mike Wallace, Andy Rooney, All the Men on '60 Minutes' Really Think of Her." *Good Housekeeping,* September 1985, 159.

"EEOC Contends FCC Erred in Rejecting Two Station Challenges." *Broadcasting,* 13 October 1975, 36-37.

"EEO Reckoning." *Broadcasting,* 17 August 1981, 105-6.

"Engineering Looks to Wartime Demands." *Broadcasting,* 9 March 1942.

Fang, I. E., and F. W. Gerval. "Survey of Salaries and Hiring Preferences in Television News." *Journal of Broadcasting* 15, no. 4, 1971, 421-33.

"Fates and Fortunes." *Broadcasting,* 6 August 1962, 78.

"Fates and Fortunes." *Broadcasting,* 6 December 1971, 51.

"Fates and Fortunes." *Broadcasting,* 28 May 1973, 70.

"Fay Wells: Whether in the Air or on It, She's Been at Her Best on the New Frontiers." *Broadcasting,* 22 August 1977, 105.

"FCC Is Wrong Agency to Impose Hiring Policies, NRBA Survey Concludes." *Broadcasting,* 23 February 1981, 71.

"FCC Targets Network for EEO Scrutiny, Tightens Up on Stations, Too." *Broadcasting,* 18 February 1980, 43-44.

"FCC Turns Back NAB Objections to EEO Guidelines." *Broadcasting,* 7 July 1980, 30.

"First Fifty Years of Broadcasting: 1976." *Broadcasting,* 31 August 1981, 45-49.

"The Fortune Survey." *Fortune,* January 1940, 92.

Goodman, Mark. "Morning Glories." *Gainesville Sun Family Weekly,* 18 July 1982, 4 + .

Haller, Scott. "The Two Faces of a Newswoman: Everything People Thought Jessica Savitch Was, She Wasn't." *People,* 7 November 1983, 47-56.

Hamburger, P. "Mary Margaret McBride." *Life,* 14 December 1944, 48.

Harriman, Margaret Case. "The 'It' Girl, Part Two." *New Yorker,* 27 April 1940, 23-29.

Harrison, Barbara Grizzuti. "Barbara Walters: Survivor," *McCall's,* January 1985, 28 + .

Harwood, Kenneth, and Don C. Smith. "Women in Broadcasting." *Journal of Broadcasting* 10, Fall 1966, 339-55.

Heinz, Catharine. "Women Radio Pioneers." *Journal of Popular Culture* 12, Fall 1978, 305-14.

"Helen Hiett, NBC Woman Commentator, First of Sex to Win Headliners Award." *Broadcasting,* 23 June 1941, 14.

Hennessee, Judith. "Some News Is Good News." *Ms.,* July 1974, 25-29.

_____. "What It Takes to Anchor the News." *Ms.,* August 1979, 84 + .

_____. "What Progress Women at CBS?" *Personnel,* July/August 1975, 33-44.

"High Price of NBC's Deal with Its Women." *Broadcasting,* 21 February 1977, 63-64.

Hosley, David H. "As Good as Any of Us: American Female Radio Correspondents in Europe, 1938-1941." *Historical Journal of Film, Radio and Television* 2, no. 2, 1982, 141-56.

Howard, Margo. "Diane Sawyer." *People,* 5 November 1984, 79-80 + .

"How's Barbara Doing?" *Time,* 6 December 1976, 83.

"The Huge Radio-TV News Staff: Nationwide Survey Shows That over One-third of Station Personnel Have Duties in Presentation of News." *Broadcasting,* 9 November 1964, 50.

"Images on the Airwaves, Or, Who Would Believe a Woman, Anyway?" *National Business Woman,* February/March 1983, 8-9.

Kasindorf, Jeanie. "Reporter Fights CBS News Ax." *New York,* 4 November 1985, 16.

Krupp, Charla. "The Hiring of Phyllis George as Morning News Anchor: Is There a Message Here for Serious Women Journalists?" *Glamour,* April 1985, 242+.

———. "Update: Women in TV News—Just How Far Have We Come?" *Glamour,* September 1981, 249+.

"Ladies Next." *Broadcasting,* 19 January 1942, 34.

"Lady Newscaster: Elizabeth Bemis." *Broadcasting,* 1 June 1940, 24.

"Leonard Dangles Bunch of CBS News Goodies in L.A." *Broadcasting,* 18 May 1981, 69.

*Library Journal* 76, 1 October 1951, 1554.

"Long Row to Hoe for Quinn and Rudd." *Broadcasting,* 13 August 1973, 34-35.

Lull, James. "Girls' Favorite TV Females." *Journalism Quarterly* 57, Spring 1980, 146-50.

MacDougall, W. L. "Ahead: Rising Role for Women in TV News." *U.S. News and World Report,* 22 August 1983, 56.

Machado, Mario. "News Anchorperson." *Jade* 2, no. 4, July 1978, 6+.

Madrigal, Alex. "Fallout from Sexual Liberation." *Miami Herald TV Week,* 27 July-2 August 1986, 3.

Mallowe, Michael. "Jessica Savitch Reconsidered." *Savvy,* September 1984, 58-63.

"Marlene Sanders: The Other Woman in Network News." *Broadcasting,* 8 November 1976, 105.

Marshall, M. "Black Anchorwomen: Making It in the Tough World of TV News." *Ebony,* November 1981, 52-54+.

Maxa, Cathleen. "Look, It's Mom: How Three Top TV Newswomen Juggle Careers and Families." *Washingtonian,* December 1982, 130.

"Meet the Ladies: Carol Gay." *Broadcasting,* 15 October 1940, 66.

"Meet the Ladies: Frankie Basch." *Broadcasting,* 4 May 1942, 44.

Meyer, Karl E. "Arledge Leads the Way: News Program on ABC." *Saturday Review,* August 1978, 39.

———. "Money Game." *Saturday Review,* 12 June 1976, 53.

"Milestones: Died, Lisa Howard." *Time,* 16 July 1965, 93.

Mills, Kay. "Fighting Sexism on the Airwaves." *Journal of Communication* 24, Spring 1974, 150-53.

"More Distaff Leadership." *Broadcasting,* 8 May 1961, 80+.

"Morning News Becalmed: CBS Drops an Anchor." *Broadcasting,* 14 January 1974, 39.

"Most Popular Radio Stars Picked in Fan Poll." *Broadcasting,* 1 July 1939, 46.

"NBC Defends Policies in Female Rights." *Broadcasting,* 4 December 1972, 38+.

"NBC Denies Sex Bias Claim, Points to Female Promotion." *Advertising Age,* 3 February 1975, 24.

"NBC Re-signs Jessica Savitch." *Variety,* 31 August 1983, 88.

"NBC's Jessica Savitch Killed: *NY Post* Exec also Dies in Auto Mishap as Car Plunges into Delaware Canal." *Variety,* 26 October 1983, 380.

"Newsroom Issue Goes to Court." *Broadcasting,* 1 August 1983, 24-25.

"OMB's EEO Proposal Makes Rounds at FCC." *Broadcasting,* 30 November 1981, 82.

"Opening Gun in Latest Battle for Television News Ratings." *U.S. News and World Report,* 11 October 1976, 42-44.

Oppenheim, Beatrice. "Tune in on Radio Jobs." *Independent Woman,* April 1943, 104-6 + .

"The Other Woman on '60 Minutes' Is Sylvia Chase." *Broadcasting,* 3 May 1976, 31.

"A Potent Push Behind the Cause of Co-educational Broadcasting." *Broadcasting,* 26 December 1960, 75.

"Pretty Poison: S. Quinn." *Newsweek,* 2 July 1973, 50.

"Prime Time for TV Newswomen." *Time,* 21 March 1977, 85-86.

"Programs." *Broadcasting,* 8 October 1945, 60.

Rohrer, Stuart. "Connie Chung: NBC's Voice at 'Sunrise.' " *Washington Journalism Review,* September 1983, 33-37.

Rose, Brian. " 'Good Evening, Here's What's Happening . . .': The Roots of Local Television News." *Journal of Popular Film and Television* 7, no. 2, 1979, 168-80.

Rosenblatt, R. "One More Piece on Barbara Walters." *New Republic,* 23 October 1976, 31-33.

Ryan, Michael. "When a Rookie Breaks into Sportscasting . . . Being a Former Miss America Helps." *TV Guide,* 20 December 1975, 12-13.

"Sarnoff, McCosker Receive Citations as Press Women Make Annual Awards." *Broadcasting,* 1 July 1939, 46 and 185.

Scharffenberger, Ann. "Success Style: TV Newswomen." *Mademoiselle,* November 1979, 196-203.

Schultz-Brooks, Terri. "Is the News Business Fair to Women?" *Working Women,* December 1984, 119-22 + .

Seligman, Daniel. "Ugly Words." *Fortune,* 5 August 1985, 95 + .

Simpson, Carmen McCormack. "Foreign Correspondent." *Independent Woman,* January 1941, 6-8.

"Sixty Minutes Team to Host New CBS Afternoon News." *Broadcasting,* 29 June 1981, 62.

Smith, Desmond. "Waking Up with Connie Chung." *New York,* 8 August 1983, 30-33.

Smith, Don C., and Kenneth Harwood. "Women in Broadcasting." *Journal of Broadcasting* 10, no. 4, 1966, 339-55.

Stone, Vernon A. "Newswomen's Numbers Level Off, More Become News Directors." *RTNDA Communicator,* July 1984, 122-23.

———. "Then and Now." *RTNDA Communicator,* October 1983, 28-29.

"Susan Stamberg: Considering All Things." *Broadcasting,* 16 June 1986, 87.
"Television: Keep Young and Beautiful. . . ." *Economist,* 13 August 1983, 21.
"To EEO or Not to EEO?" *Broadcasting,* 30 June 1980, 64-65.
"Today's Woman." *Newsweek,* 19 May 1969, 73.
"Tops in TV Newscasters." *Ebony,* January 1979, 110-15.
"Tragic Sign-off for a Golden Girl: Jessica Savitch, 1947-1983." *Time,* 7 November 1983, 100.
"Transition—Died: Lisa Howard." *Newsweek,* 19 July 1965, 63.
"TV News Hens: Negro Television Newscasters." *Ebony,* October 1966, 44-46+.
"TV Reporter Lisa Howard Loses Show." *Editor and Publisher,* 23 January 1965, 16.
"UCC and NOW Join Forces in Major EEO Push." *Broadcasting,* 7 July 1980, 29-30.
"UCC Finds TV Slightly Improved as EEO Employer, but Suspects Input for Study Is Off." *Broadcasting,* 24 January 1977, 30+.
"UN-AWRT Conference Examines Problems of Women in Broadcasting." *Broadcasting,* 7 February 1983, 81.
"Upsurge in TV News Girls." *Ebony,* June 1971, 168-76.
"Whom Do You Trust in Network News?" *Broadcasting,* 17 June 1974, 33.
"Will the Morning Star Shine at Night?" *Time,* 3 May 1976, 51+.
Wilson, Jean Gaddy. "The Career Crisis of Christine Craft." *Glamour,* November 1983, 88+.
"WNAX Girl Newscaster." *Broadcasting,* 14 December 1942, 45.
"Women Make Good in Radio Jobs." *Broadcasting,* 26 July 1943, 57.
"Women Militants Charge Exclusion." *Broadcasting,* 2 April 1973, 36.
"Women Seek Denial of WRC-TV Renewal." *Broadcasting,* 4 September 1972, 22.
"Women Take Charge for War Duration of Balaban and Katz Station." *Broadcasting,* 26 October 1942, 66.
"Women vs. ABC." *Newsweek,* 15 May 1972, 57.
Women's Institute for Freedom of the Press. *Media Report to Women,* 29 September 1972, 9.
_____. *Media Report to Women,* 1 November 1973, 7.
_____. *Media Report to Women,* 1 September 1974, 11.
_____. *Media Report to Women,* 1 November 1974, 3.
_____. *Media Report to Women,* 1 December 1974, 1, 13.
"Women's Revolt Hits ABC News." *Broadcasting,* 17 August 1970, 27.
"WRC-AM-FM-TV Charged with Sex Discrimination." *Broadcasting,* 8 March 1971, 34-35.
Wulfmeyer, K. Tim. "Perceptions of Viewer Interest by Local TV Journalists." *Journalism Quarterly* 61, no. 2, Summer 1984, 432-35.

## INTERVIEWS

Beasley, Maurine, associate professor of journalism, University of Maryland. Telephone interview with Gayle K. Yamada, 29 September 1986.
Bliss, Edward W. Jr., former CBS News writer and editor. Interview with Gayle K. Yamada. Salt Lake City, 29 August 1986.

Davis, Paul, news director, WGN-TV, Chicago, and son of Zona B. Davis. Interview with authors. Salt Lake City, 27 August 1986.
Dembo, Joe, vice president, CBS News, Radio. Interview with Gayle K. Yamada. New York City, 20 August 1986.
Dribben, Elizabeth L., CBS Radio News producer/writer. Interview with Gayle K. Yamada. New York City, 19 August 1986.
Edwards, Douglas, CBS News anchor. Interview with Gayle K. Yamada. New York City, 20 August 1986.
Feurey, Benita, former New York City television newswoman. Interview with Gayle K. Yamada. New York City, 21 August 1986.
Friedsam, Leslie, attorney and former Tampa, Florida, reporter. Telephone interview with David H. Hosley, 12 August 1986.
Heinz, Catharine, director, Broadcast Pioneers Library. Interview with Gayle K. Yamada. Washington, D.C., 15 August 1986.
Herr, Nancy, San Francisco television reporter. Telephone interview with David H. Hosley, 11 September 1986.
Levine, Ellen, freelance journalist. Telephone interview with David H. Hosley, 14 October 1986.
Lomax, Almena, writer. Telephone interview with David H. Hosley, 9 September 1986.
Murrow, Janet, wife of Edward R. Murrow. Interview with David H. Hosley. Pullman, Washington, 17 April 1981.
Otis, Lee, former CBS writer and editor. Telephone interview with Gayle K. Yamada, 28 September 1986.
Pittman, Tarea Hall, former Oakland, California, radio broadcaster. Telephone interview with David H. Hosley, 14 September 1986.
Schechter, Abel A., former NBC news director. Telephone interview with David H. Hosley, 4 April 1981.
Vandegrift, Barbara J., National Press Club library director. Interview with Gayle K. Yamada. Washington, D.C., 15 August 1986.
Wight, Kay J., vice president, sales development, CBS Broadcast International. Interview with Gayle K. Yamada. New York City, 21 August 1986.

## OTHER REFERENCE MATERIALS

"Anchorwoman Who Testified at Christine Craft Trial Files Complaint." Associated Press Newswire, 20 September 1986.
Audience Research and Development Corp. *Christine Craft Research: Professional Assessment.* Dallas: Audience Research and Development, 1983.
Hill, Edward. "Connie Chung Moves from Sunrise to Prime Time." Associated Press Newswire, 3 July 1985.
"History in Sound" (Milo Ryan's collection). Seattle: University of Washington Press, 1963.
Horst, Craig. "Christine Craft." Associated Press Newswire, 28 June 1985.
Kerr, Jennifer. "Woman Who Sued Kansas City TV Station Begins New Anchor Job." Associated Press Newswire, 22 January 1986.

Lublin, Joann S. "Discrimination Against Women in the Newsroom." Master's thesis, Stanford University, 1976.

"Martha Deane Program." Tape 12747-10B, Cut B2, Disc 2-1927. Washington, D.C.: Library of Congress, 3 June 1940.

"Meet the Press." Tape 5, LW07332, Cut A-1. Washington, D.C.: Library of Congress, 18 September 1955.

Milford, Barbara. "Women in Journalism." Associated Press Newswire, 15 October 1985.

"News and Commentary with Lisa Sergio." Tape 12736, Cut 3A, Box E4140, Disc 20741. Washington, D.C.: Library of Congress, 20 June 1941.

Otte, Mary Lane. "Sexism in Local and Network Television News." Ph.D. diss., Georgia State University, 1978.

Peterson, Mark. "Christine Craft: Former Anchorwoman's Case Back in Court." Associated Press Newswire, 13 January 1985.

Seppy, Tom. "ABC Suit: Lawyer Says NOW Attorneys Leaked Amount of Settlement." Associated Press Newswire, 10 July 1985.

Sherr, Lynn. Speech to the Radio-Television News Directors Association Convention. Hollywood, Florida, 4 December 1980.

_____. Speech to the Radio-Television News Directors Association Convention. Salt Lake City, 29 August 1986.

Washington newswomen. Papers. National Press Club Library, Washington, D.C.

# Index

# About the Authors

DAVID H. HOSLEY is Station Manager at KQED-FM, San Francisco, and is on the faculty of Stanford University's Mass Media Institute. He is the author of *As Good as Any: The Development of Radio Foreign Correspondence in the United States, 1930-1940* (Greenwood Press, 1984). He has been a radio program and news director and a reporter and anchor.

GAYLE K. YAMADA is Senior Producer of television projects for KQED-TV, San Francisco. She has been a television news producer, assignment editor, radio news director, anchor, and a newspaper columnist.